MARYLAND
Real Estate
PRACTICE & LAW

Donald A. White

ELEVENTH EDITION

Real Estate Education

President: Roy Lipner
Vice-President of Product Development and Publishing: Evan Butterfield
Associate Publisher: Louise Benzer
Senior Development Editor: Anne Huston
Director of Production: Daniel Frey
Quality Assurance Editor: David Shaw
Typesetting: Ellen Gurak
Creative Director: Lucy Jenkins

Published by Dearborn™ Real Estate Education,
a division of Dearborn Financial Publishing, Inc.®
30 South Wacker Drive
Chicago, IL 60606-7481
(312) 836-4400
http://www.dearbornRE.com

CONTENTS

PREFACE

As a student entering a real estate course you face exciting challenges. You must learn a large body of theory and then apply it to practice. You will want to know legal principles and real estate theory so well that when you get your license you will be able to do the right thing almost automatically.

If you fail to understand and appreciate law and theory, you can suffer devastating financial and legal consequences. On the other hand, if you build your educational foundation in real estate well, you should be able to make the money you want and not lose the money you make through costly mistakes.

The purpose of this volume is to present clearly many of the laws and operating requirements for real estate brokerage in the State of Maryland. It builds on basic information presented in Dearborn™ Real Estate Education's real estate principles texts. The author has made a serious effort to avoid duplicating information presented in the principles texts. Therefore, you should study each subject area in *both the basic text and in this book* (see the table on page ix). Online information can be accessed using the Web addresses available throughout the text and in Appendix D in the back of the book.

As you finish each chapter, and before you go on to the next, be certain that you are able to answer *and understand* each question presented. An answer key for all of the tests is included at the end of the book.

You will want to make frequent use of Appendix D, Maryland Real Estate-Related Web Sites. It contains several carefully chosen "hub" sites that give you access to multiple official sources for real estate law and regulation at various levels of government.

While the author has exercised care in providing information pertaining to the laws governing the practice of real estate in Maryland, the reader is urged to consult with legal counsel regarding any statutory enactment and should not rely solely on this publication as legal authority for compliance with any statute.

Throughout your real estate course, you'll be studying and taking tests in preparation for the Maryland Real Estate Licensing Examination. That examination is prepared and administered for the State Real Estate Commission by an independent testing service, PSI Examination Services, Inc., Las Vegas, Nevada. *Maryland Real Estate: Practice & Law* is designed to familiarize you with the subject matter you will find on that examination. The questions at the end of each chapter are prepared in a multiple-choice format similar to the one used in the licensing examination.

■ ABOUT THE AUTHOR

Maryland Real Estate: Practice & Law, Eleventh Edition, is written by Donald A. White, DREI, of Gambrills, Maryland. Mr. White has been a Maryland real estate licensee since 1967, and has held an associate broker license since 1972. He holds degrees in music (BS MusEd), in religious education (MRE), and in business (MA). He is professor emeritus in the Department of Business at Prince George's Community College where he has taught real estate licensing courses continuously since 1972. He served several terms as Chair of the Education Committee of the Prince George's Association of REALTORS®. A past-President of the Maryland Real Estate Educators Association, he is presently a member of the Educational Advisory Committee to the Education Committee of the Maryland Real Estate Commission.

The author holds the DREI (Distinguished Real Estate Instructor) designation from the Real Estate Educators Association, of which he is a charter member. He has taught frequently in REALTOR® continuing education seminars. He also was the principal author of *Questions and Answers on Maryland Real Estate*; coauthor, with Maurice Boren, of the *Study Guide to Maryland Real Estate License Examinations*; and author of *Maryland Exam Prep*, Third Edition.

■ HOW TO USE THIS BOOK

The conversion table on the next page provides a quick and easy reference for using *Maryland Real Estate: Practice & Law* in conjunction with various principles books. For instance, *Maryland Real Estate: Practice & Law's* Chapter 16, "Closing the Real Estate Transaction," may be read in conjunction with Chapter 22 in *Modern Real Estate Practice*; Chapter 17 in *Real Estate Fundamentals*; Chapter 12 in *Mastering Real Estate Principles*; and Lesson 22 in *National Real Estate Principles* Software.

Chapter Conversion Table

Maryland Real Estate: Practice & Law, 11th Edition	Modern Real Estate Practice	Real Estate Fundamentals	Mastering Real Estate Principles	National Real Estate Principles Software
1. Maryland Real Estate License Law and Regulations	—	—	16	—
2. Real Estate Agency	4	9	13	4
3. Real Estate Brokerage	5	9	13	5
4. Listing and Buyer Representation Agreements	6	7, 9	15	6
5. Interests in Real Estate	7	3	7	7
6. How Ownership Is Held	8	5	9	8
7. Legal Descriptions	9	2	6	9
8. Real Estate Taxes and Other Liens	10	3, 10	5, 25	10
9. Real Estate Contracts	11	7	14	11
10. Transfer of Title	12	4	10	12
11. Title Records	13	6	11	13
12. Real Estate Financing	14, 15	12, 13	Unit VII	14, 15
13. Leases	16	8	8	16
14. Environmental Issues and the Real Estate Transaction	21	16	3	21
15. Fair Housing	20	15	17	20
16. Closing the Real Estate Transaction	22	17	12	22

ACKNOWLEDGMENTS

The author appreciates the constructive suggestions on the updating and revision of this text provided by the following reviewers: Richard Garnitz, Professional Development Institute and Carl Kessler REALTORS®; Linda S. Ludford, Long & Foster Institute of Real Estate; Farhad Rozi, Training Director and Instructor, Long & Foster Institute of Real Estate; Jean Ritter, Coldwell Banker Residential Brokerage School of Real Estate; Ed Smith, Ed Smith School, LLC, and the staff of the Office of the Maryland Attorney General. He also extends thanks to Elizabeth Gill White for her sharp eye and encouragement, and to Anne Huston, Senior Development Editor at Dearborn™ Real Estate Education, who diligently shepherded this work to completion.

CHAPTER ONE

1

MARYLAND REAL ESTATE LICENSE LAW AND RELATED REGULATIONS

■ OVERVIEW

In this chapter you will learn some of the history of brokerage regulation in Maryland; learn which Maryland statutes and regulations govern the industry today; come to understand the structure, duties, and powers of the Maryland Real Estate Commission; and begin to appreciate the mechanics of obtaining, maintaining, and upgrading a brokerage license. You will also delve into various requirements and prohibitions that guide the everyday life of a real estate licensee.

■ HISTORY AND SOURCES OF MARYLAND LICENSE LAW

The *Maryland Real Estate Brokers Act*, a law designed to protect the public interest, became effective on June 1, 1939. Since then there have been frequent revisions. All the work of real estate licensees is affected by this important statute. It is therefore the basis of much of this chapter.

The Maryland Real Estate Brokers Act appears as Title (Chapter) 17 in the *Business Occupations and Professions* Article of the Annotated Code of Maryland. In this book, the author refers to this statute as the "Brokers Act" and as "Title 17."

Real estate brokerage is governed both by statutory law, such as the Brokers Act mentioned above, and by administrative law, found in the Code of Maryland Regulations (COMAR). Regulations governing the practice of real estate brokerage are passed and enforced by the Maryland Real Estate Commission—a body within the executive branch of government. The Maryland

Real Estate Brokers Act was enacted by the legislative branch of Maryland government: the General Assembly. Therefore, it is an example of legislative (statutory) law.

In addition to statutes and regulations, **common law** applies to real estate brokerage. Common law, often—and unfortunately—called *the unwritten law*, is in actuality recorded in print. Many, many volumes contain lengthy written decisions by courts of appeal. Such decisions are needed in situations where no relevant statute exists or when an existing statute is challenged as unconstitutional. They also arise in cases of ambiguity where uncertainty of language or intent make a statute difficult to interpret.

On occasion, older laws no longer seem to make sense to the courts called on to give their opinion. Judges who then "modernize" the law are practicing **judicial activism**. This is in contrast to **strict construction**, which takes statutes at their face value and supports the original intention of their writers. The U.S. Supreme Court's decision in 1965 that the Civil Rights Act of 1866 should still be applied literally and was still applicable nearly a century later is an example of strict construction.

Statutes are *voted into law* by legislative bodies but **common law** is *handed down* by judges. Decisions made by courts of appeal become binding on lower courts within their judicial area. The higher the court of appeal making a decision, the more numerous the courts in which that decision becomes the standard—the **precedent**—for decisions made later in those lower courts.

The Maryland Real Estate Commission in the Department of Licensing and Regulation makes and enforces regulations to implement the Brokers Act. These regulations are **administrative law.** Administrative law seeks to apply statutes to particular situations.

The Brokers Act and Regulations from COMAR relating to real estate may be found in many college and public libraries in bound volumes in the Legal Reference Section. They are available for study and downloading from the Web site of the Maryland General Assembly:

www.mlis.state.md.us/

That site also provides information about pending and recently passed legislation. Proposed and adopted changes to the Regulations may be found in Legal Reference Sections of public libraries, updated every two weeks in the Maryland Register. Legislative changes are only available in yearly updates.

The statutes and regulations to which this book refers are those enacted at the time of its publication, including changes taking effect on October 1, 2005.

■ DEFINITIONS OF TERMS [§17-101]

As used in Title 17, certain words have specific definitions that apply either to a section of the law or the entire statute. For example, a **real estate broker** is defined as an individual who provides **real estate brokerage services.** These services are then defined as any of the following activities:

- For consideration, and for another person: selling, buying, exchanging, or leasing any real estate; or collecting rent for the use of any real estate
- For consideration, assisting another person to locate or obtain for purchase or lease any residential real estate
- Engaging in the business of regularly buying, selling, or trading in real estate or leases or options on real estate
- Engaging in a business that promotes the sale of real estate through a listing in a publication issued primarily for that purpose
- Engaging in the business of subdividing land and selling the subdivided lots
- For consideration, serving as a consultant for any of the activities in this list

Although Maryland law generally defines **persons** as "individuals, receivers, trustees, guardians, personal representatives, fiduciaries, or representatives of any kind and any partnership, firm, association, or other entity," only **natural persons** (individuals) may hold licenses. Licenses are also issued that show names under which licensed individuals deliver brokerage services. These are called their *designated names*.

In the statute and in this volume, *Commission* refers to the State Real Estate Commission. When the term *licensed* is used, it refers to the status of an individual licensed by the Commission.

■ LICENSES ISSUED BY THE COMMISSION (TITLE 17, SUBTITLE III)

The Commission issues three levels of license for those delivering real estate brokerage services: broker, associate broker, and salesperson. Currently there are approximately 46,800 active licenses comprising all three categories. These include almost 39,000 salesperson licenses, with the rest being broker and associate broker. The Commission also holds in excess of 45,000 additional licenses that either are inactive or have expired. Expired licenses are held four years from the date of their expiration. Persons named on inactive or on expired licenses may not perform acts of real estate brokerage.

Every licensed salesperson and associate broker must be affiliated with and supervised by a licensed broker. When individuals affiliate with brokers, they enter into either an employee or nonemployee contractual relationship with them. Almost all licensees affiliated with brokers today claim a nonemployee relationship with their brokers. Even though many **affiliates** meet the IRS requirements for "qualified real estate agent" and are self-employed from the point of view of income taxation, they are all still subject to supervision and control by their broker.

Throughout this book, *affiliate* (the noun) refers either to a licensed associate broker or a licensed salesperson. **Associate brokers** are individuals who have met educational, experience, and testing requirements for becoming real estate brokers but who request, rather than broker licenses, licenses that authorize them to provide real estate brokerage services only *under a broker* with whom they are affiliated. Despite their education and experience, their duties and authority are no greater than those of salespersons. **Salespersons** are individuals who aid brokers with whom they are affiliated in providing real estate brokerage services.

Real estate salespersons and associate brokers affiliate with real estate brokers by entering into either employee or nonemployee relationships with them. The vast majority of salespersons and associate brokers are in a nonemployee relationship with their brokers.

Affiliates meet the Internal Revenue Service requirements for nonemployee (self-employed) status when their broker does not withhold federal or state income taxes, Social Security, or Medicare assessments. Also, the broker does not make any contribution to the affiliates' Social Security account. Affiliates' paychecks are "net" to them; they are responsible for all their own taxes. Section 3508 of the IRS Code specifies that such "Qualified Real Estate Agents" may report their income as self-employed persons using Schedule 1040C. To be recognized as a qualified real estate agent, affiliates must

- be licensed real estate agents (hold an active real estate license);
- receive "substantially all" of their brokerage remuneration based on production rather than upon hours worked (no specific percentage is stated); and
- act pursuant to written contracts with their brokers stating that the affiliates will not be treated as employees for federal tax purposes.

Real estate, as used in the Brokers Act, is defined as any interest in real property anywhere. Such interests include, but are not limited to, interests in condominiums, time-share estates, and time-share licenses, as those terms are defined in the *Real Property* Article.

In the Brokers Act, the term *state* refers to any state in the United States, its territories, possessions, or the District of Columbia. In this book when *State* is capitalized, it refers to the State of Maryland. In the statute, *Department* refers to the Department of Labor, Licensing, and Regulation under whose authority the Commission operates. *Secretary* refers to the Secretary of Labor, Licensing, and Regulation, the executive officer of that Department.

Persons Not Governed by the Brokers Act [§17-102]

Certain persons who perform real estate activities are not governed by the Brokers Act. They are

- persons acting under a judgment or order of a court;
- public officers performing the duties of their office;

- owners or lessors of any real estate, unless the primary business of the owner or lessor is providing real estate brokerage services;
- persons engaging in a single transaction that involves the sale or lease of any real estate, if they are acting under a power of attorney executed by the owner of that real estate;
- licensed auctioneers selling any real estate at public auction; and
- persons acting as receivers, trustees, personal representatives, or guardians.

Who Must Conform to the Act [§17-301(b)]

In contrast, other persons, when performing acts of real estate brokerage, are governed by and must conform to the relevant requirements of the Brokers Act, although they need not hold real estate licenses. They are

- financial institutions in the leasing or selling of property they have acquired through foreclosure or by receiving a deed or an assignment in lieu of foreclosure;
- lawyers not regularly engaged in the business of providing real estate services and who do not communicate to the public that they are in such business;
- homebuilders in the rental or initial sale of homes they have constructed;
- agents of a licensed real estate broker or of an owner of real estate, while managing or leasing that real estate for its broker or owner;
- persons who negotiate the sale, lease, or transfer of businesses when the sale does not include any interest in real property other than the lease for the property where the business operates; and
- owners who subdivide and sell not more than six lots of their own unimproved property in a calendar year. If they or their family have owned the property for ten years or more, there is no limit on the number of lots they may sell.

■ THE MARYLAND REAL ESTATE COMMISSION [§§17-201–17-214]

The Maryland Real Estate Commission is one of several commissions within the Department of Labor, Licensing, and Regulation. It consists of nine members, five of whom are licensee members chosen, one each, from the Eastern Shore, Baltimore Metropolitan Area, Baltimore City, Southern Maryland, and Western Maryland. They must have held Maryland real estate licenses at least ten years and have resided in the areas from which they are appointed for at least five years, both immediately prior to their appointment. The other four members are consumer members who may not have had an ownership interest in or received compensation from an entity regulated by the Commission in the year just before their appointment.

Members are appointed by the Governor with the advice of the Secretary and the advice and consent of the Senate. Membership terms, which are staggered to ensure regulatory continuity, begin on June 1 and end four years later, either with reappointment or on the appointment of a qualified replacement. Members may be removed before the end of their terms by the Governor in cases of incompetence or misconduct.

Each year members of the Commission elect from among themselves a chairperson to preside at their meetings. This officer is covered by a surety bond. The Commission holds a public meeting each month with a majority of the members then under appointment constituting a quorum.

The Commission has adopted bylaws for the conduct of its meetings and regulations for the conduct of hearings and for issuance of licensing applications. With ten days' advance written notice, a member of the public may speak before the Commission.

The Commission's Executive Director, who is appointed by and serves at the pleasure of the Secretary, is not one of its members. The Executive Director should not be confused with the Chairperson. The Executive Director, a State employee who is also covered by a surety bond, directs the day-to-day operations of the Commission and supervises its office staff and field inspectors between monthly meetings.

Duties and Powers
[§§17-209, 17-212]

The Commission's primary duties are administration and enforcement of the Brokers Act through the licensing process. To carry out this duty, the Commission is empowered to

- investigate complaints of unlicensed brokerage activity,
- investigate complaints about licensee behavior,
- conduct hearings and administer oaths,
- issue subpoenas for attendance of witnesses or production of evidence,
- take depositions, and
- seek injunctions (in certain circumstances).

The Commission adopts, maintains, and enforces a Code of Ethics and General Regulations that set forth standards of conduct for all individuals who are under the authority of the Brokers Act. The Code of Ethics and the General Regulations are part of **COMAR**—the Code of Maryland Regulations. This code addresses licensees' relations with the client, the public, and with other licensees. It is quite different from the Code of Ethics of the National Association of REALTORS®.

The Commission must investigate any written complaint, made under oath, alleging that an unauthorized person has provided real estate brokerage services. The Commission has statutory authority to hold hearings on such a complaint and to impose a financial penalty not to exceed $5,000 for each proven violation. (An unauthorized person is an individual who neither holds a required license nor is exempt from the requirement to have one.)

Authority over Nonlicensees
[§17-613 (c)]

The Commission is also empowered to hold hearings and assess fines as much as $5,000 per violation not only on licensees but on any persons (individuals or business entities) who violate any part of the Brokers Act.

**Other Powers
and Duties
[§§17-208–17-214]**

The Commission has many other powers and duties. In the course of its operation, it routinely

- issues, renews, suspends, or revokes licenses;
- orders investigations and holds hearings as needed;
- reprimands and/or fines licensees who have violated law or regulation;
- collects license fees and pays them into the General Fund of the State;
- collects fines and pays them into the General Fund of the State;
- submits an annual report of its activities to the Secretary;
- certifies, on request of any person and payment of the required fee, the licensing status and qualifications of any person who is the subject of the request;
- approves the content of educational courses for licensing and for continuing education;
- adopts regulations and a code of ethics to implement Title 17;
- appoints hearing boards (panels) of three members, at least one of whom must be a consumer member and one a professional member (licensee) from among the commissioners; and
- administers a Guaranty Fund to reimburse members of the public as much as $25,000 for actual losses caused by licensees and their employees.

■ REQUIREMENTS FOR LICENSURE [§17-305]

Before providing real estate brokerage services in the State, individuals generally must be licensed by the Commission as real estate brokers, associate brokers, or salespersons affiliated with and working under licensed brokers. Licenses are granted for a two-year term from their date of issuance.

Brokers [§17-305]

To qualify for the real estate broker license, applicants must

- be of good character and reputation, and be at least 18 years of age;
- have completed a 135-hour course in real estate—including three clock hours of real estate ethics—approved by the Commission for real estate brokers;
- have been licensed as real estate salespersons actively and lawfully for at least three years; and
- have passed the broker prelicensing examination.

For applicants who have been admitted to the Maryland Bar, the Commission waives the education and experience requirements, but not the examination requirement. Broker education requirements for all others are in addition to the salesperson requirements they may have previously met. However, an individual who has been engaged in real estate practice as a licensed real estate broker in another state for at least three of the five years immediately preceding submission of application is considered to have satisfied the broker educational requirements.

**Associate Brokers
[§17-304]**

To qualify for the associate real estate broker license, an applicant must meet the education and experience requirements for a broker license. The applicant must also obtain a written commitment from a licensed real estate broker to accept the applicant as an associate broker when all the other associate broker requirements have been satisfied.

Salespersons [§17-305]

To qualify for issuance of the salesperson license, an applicant must

- be of good character and reputation;
- be at least 18 years of age;
- successfully complete a basic 60-hour course in real estate, including three clock hours of real estate ethics, approved by the Commission;
- pass the required examination; and
- obtain a written commitment from a licensed real estate broker to accept the applicant as a salesperson when all other licensing requirements have been satisfied.

General Rules [§17-307]

Applicants must successfully complete prelicensing education requirements before taking salesperson or broker examinations. General Regulation .26 states that after passing both parts (General and State) of the exam, application for licensure must be made within one year or reexamination will be required. The Commission's application forms must be used. The required fees are shown in Figure 1.1.

Requirements for Nonresidents [§17-514]

Salesperson, associate broker, and broker applicants who are not residents of the State must submit to the Commission their **irrevocable consent.** This consent allows a licensee to be served with official documents without the server's having to travel to a foreign (out-of-state) jurisdiction to present them. Applicants are required to submit any additional documentation that the Commission requires in order to determine their professional competence or good character and reputation. Broker applicants must also submit or pay for a credit report.

Nonresident Commercial Brokers [§§17-536–17-540]

In this recently added section, a "nonresident" is a licensee who—regardless of where he (or she) resides—does not hold a real estate license granted by the Maryland Real Estate Commission. The nonresident commercial broker may be either an individual, a partnership, joint venture, limited liability company, limited liability partnership, or corporation licensed in a jurisdiction other than Maryland. The nonresident commercial salesperson must be an individual licensed under a nonresident commercial real estate broker who has complied with detailed requirements that grant that broker a temporary license to do Maryland commercial brokerage. The nonresident broker may qualify for such license only if the broker's own state grants similar privileges to Maryland licensees. The nonresident broker must do business in Maryland only through and under a licensed Maryland real estate broker with whom the nonresident has a written agreement detailing their entire relationship for specific proposed transactions.

Reciprocity [§17-308]

The Commission may waive any requirement for individual licenses for applicants who hold comparable or equivalent licenses granted by another state if those applicants pay the required application fees, meet the relevant require-

FIGURE 1.1

License Fees

	Original License Fee	Guaranty Fund Assessment*	Total Original Fees	Renewal or Exchange of License Fee
Broker	$95	$20	$115	$95
Associate Broker	$65	$20	$85	$65
Salesperson	$45	$20	$65	$45

The proper fees must accompany every request. These fees are established by statute and as such are subject to change by the General Assembly. Applicants are also required to pay the testing service a $60 examination fee to register and to take or retake any real estate examination. Standard examination registration fees, which are neither refundable nor transferable, may be paid by check, money order, company check, or cashier's check. Cash is not accepted.

Fees for other services:

Certificate of License History	$10	Reinstatement of License/Late Fee	$100
Broker Business Address Change	5	Transfer to another broker	10
Broker Business Name Change	5	Time Share Registration	100
Branch Office License	5	Duplicate License/Pocket Card	5
Personal Name Change	5	Dishonored Check	25
Reactivate Inactive License	10		

* The Guaranty Fund initial assessment is paid on issuance of the first license to an applicant. It is not paid on renewals.

ments, and submit certification of license history from the other state. If applicants are seeking broker licenses based on their comparable licenses in another state, they must provide adequate evidence of actively maintaining brokerage offices there.

Pocket Cards and License Certificates [§17-309]

License certificates and pocket cards that the Commission issues show

- the name of the licensee,
- the designated name of the licensed real estate broker with whom a salesperson or associate broker is affiliated,
- the date the license will expire, and
- the registration number of the licensee.

When issued for affiliates, certificates and pocket cards are sent to the broker. The pocket cards are detached and given to affiliates, but the actual license certificates are maintained and conspicuously displayed in the office out of which each licensee operates. Although no such requirement is explicitly stated anywhere in the Broker Act or in any regulation, the Commission has informed the author that licensees are expected to carry their pocket cards whenever they engage in real estate brokerage activity.

Real estate broker's licenses authorize licensees to provide real estate brokerage services to the public. Persons who hold associate brokers' and salespersons' licenses may never provide real estate brokerage services in their own name or in the name of any broker with whom they are not affiliated.

Exchange of Licenses and Additional Licenses and Affiliations [§§17-311–17-313]

A licensed real estate broker may also hold licenses as a real estate salesperson or associate broker, affiliated with another licensed real estate broker. This requires submission of proper application and payment of additional license fees. Each broker who works for another broker must also obtain a commitment for such affiliation from the other broker and inform the other broker of all other licenses and affiliations. Brokers may also operate more than one real estate company, but for each additional real estate brokerage company, they must obtain a separate real estate broker's license.

Licensees who hold salesperson, associate broker, or broker licenses may exchange those licenses for other levels of license by complying with procedures established by the Commission and paying the required additional fees. Affiliates may obtain additional licenses and become affiliated with additional Maryland brokers by obtaining a commitment from each additional broker, paying the required additional licensing fees and giving notice of such multiple relationships to all their brokers.

Reinstatement after Nonrenewal [§17-314]

Reinstatement of an expired license presently requires that applicants show proof of meeting all applicable continuing education requirements for the period since expiration and pay past-due renewal fees as well as a $100 reinstatement fee. They must also meet the requirement of good character and reputation. Neither timely nor late renewal of a license affects the power of the Commission to bring charges for prior acts or conduct.

Transfer of Affiliation [§17-311]

Affiliates may apply to the Commission to transfer their affiliation from one broker to another after obtaining from the new broker a commitment stating that, on termination of the current affiliation and issuance of new license certificates and pocket cards, they will become affiliated with the new broker. They shall also submit, either from their former brokers or from themselves, a statement confirming termination of their prior relationship with their transfer applications. It is advisable in every case, although not clearly required by law or regulation, that the former broker be informed of the details of the transfer.

Dishonored Checks [§17-521]

In the event of a dishonored check, licensees are not considered to have properly renewed their licenses until they pay both the original amount of the renewal fees and a collection fee of $25 for each dishonored check.

■ LICENSE TERM, TRANSFER, AND RENEWAL [§17-314]

A broker and the broker's affiliates' license renewal notices and application forms are mailed to the broker's main office not later than one month before licenses expire. The notices state

- the dates on which the current licenses expire;
- the dates by which the Commission must receive the renewal applications—when licensees use hard-copy (paper) applications for renewal; and
- the amount of the renewal fees.

Although the preferred mode of application for renewal is online—a method designed to produce instantaneous and less expensive processing—the Commission continues to accept and process hard-copy renewal and upgrade applications.

Continuing Education Requirements [§17-315]

Continuing education for license renewal is measured in **clock hours** with credit allowed only for approved, individual courses of not less than one and one-half and not more than six hours in length. A *clock hour* is defined in the Business Occupations and Professions Article as 50 minutes of actual class time for each 60-minute hour [§1-101].

Completion of the required number of continuing education hours in specific subjects is required for renewal of any level of license. The standard requirement is 15 hours of approved instruction. For licenses renewed on or before October 1, 2005, the 15 hours comprise at least three clock-hours of local, state, and federal legislative and regulatory updates, one and one-half hours in fair housing, and ten and one-half in other approved courses. All renewals after October 1, 2005, require—as part of the 15 hours—a three-clock-hour ethics course that includes the Maryland Real Estate Commission Code of Ethics and a discussion of flipping properties and predatory lending.

Licensees who have held a Maryland real estate license for ten years or more have a different requirement. If they renew their licenses on or before October 1, 2005, they will be required to complete only six clock hours (three in legislative update, one and one-half in fair housing, and one and one-half hours in another approved subject). From October 2, 2005, to October 1, 2006, their requirement will be seven and one-half hours, comprising three hours in legislative update, one and one-half hours in fair housing, and three in Real Estate Commission Code of Ethics and flipping and predatory lending practices. From October 2, 2006, to October 1, 2008, their renewal requirement will increase by another one and one-half hours of approved subject matter, for a total of nine hours. From October 2, 2008, onward, six *more* hours of approved subject matter will be added, for a total of 15 hours. From and after October 2, 2008, *all* licensees will be required to take 15 hours of continuing education. See Table 1.1a and 1.1b.

There are certain exceptions. Only seven and one-half hours are required for licensees who hold graduate degrees in law or real estate from accredited

TABLE 1.1a

Continuing Education Requirements

1. Licensees who have held an active Maryland real estate license ten years at the time of their renewal

Subject Matter	Renewal on or before Oct. 1, 2005	Renewal between Oct. 2, 2005, and Oct. 1, 2006	Renewal between Oct. 2, 2006, and Oct. 1, 2008	Renewal after Oct. 2, 2008
Legislative Update	3 hrs	3 hrs	3 hrs	3 hrs
Fair Housing (Licensees performing only commercial transactions may substitute Federal Americans with Disabilities Act)	1.5 hrs	1.5 hrs	1.5 hrs	1.5 hrs
Ethics, Flipping & Predatory Lending	0 hrs	3 hrs	3 hrs	3 hrs
Other Approved Courses	1.5 hrs	0 hrs	1.5 hrs	7.5 hrs
Total Hours Required	6 hrs	7.5 hrs	9 hrs	15 hrs

colleges or universities. Also, licensees who practice nonresidential brokerage exclusively may substitute one and one-half hours of instruction in the Federal Americans with Disabilities Act for any fair housing requirement.

In the Brokers Act, **nonresidential property** is defined in detail as

> *(1) real property improved by five or more single-family units; (2) improved and unimproved real property zoned for commercial, industrial, or nonresidential use by the local zoning authority of the county or municipality in which the property is located; and (3) unimproved real property zoned for improvement as multi-family units by the local zoning authority of the county or municipality in which the property is located, [but does not include]: (1) property zoned for agricultural use; or (2) single-family units, including a condominium or co-op unit, for sale or for lease, or otherwise conveyed or to be conveyed on a single basis.*

Renewal must be accomplished before licenses expire. Those renewing must pay to the Commission the required renewal fees and affirm that they have completed the required number of hours of continuing education. Those who have not completed the required number of hours and renewed their licenses before expiration are no longer properly licensed to provide brokerage services. Activities they perform during such a lapse in licensure may earn no compensation for them or their firms. A person whose license has expired may apply for reinstatement of that license at any time within four years after its expiration date.

TABLE 1.1b

Continuing Education Requirements (continued)

2. Licensees who have held an active Maryland real estate license fewer than ten years at the time of their renewal

Subject Matter	Renewal on or before Oct. 1, 2005	Renewal after Oct. 2, 2005
Legislative Update	3 hrs	3 hrs
Fair Housing (Licensees performing only commercial transations may substitute Federal Americans with Disabilities Act)	1.5 hrs	1.5 hrs
Ethics, Flipping & Predatory Lending	0 hrs	3 hrs
Other Approved Courses	10.5 hrs	7.5 hrs
Total Hours Required	15 hrs	15 hrs

There are several categories of subject matter approved for these courses:

A. Federal, State, or local legislative and regulatory changes
B. Antitrust law
C. Fair Housing law
D. Real estate ethics or professional standards
E. Disclosure
F. Professional enhancement for practicing licensees
G. Technology relating to real estate brokerage services (not more than three hours per renewal)

To be approved by the Commission, all continuing education course subject matter must relate to real estate.

Approved courses may be presented by the Maryland Association of REALTORS® or its member boards, the Real Estate Brokers of Baltimore City, Inc., or any similar professional association, or by an educational institution approved by the State Board of Higher Education. These courses must be taught by qualified instructors who are experienced in the real estate industry. The Commission's guidelines require that continuing education instructors have experience and expertise in the area or activity about which they are teaching.

When licensees complete each unit of study, the training institution that conducted the course issues certificates of completion to each student stating the

- number of clock hours,
- name and date of the course taken,
- code letter of the subject category, and
- the names of the teacher and/or the organization presenting the training.

The education provider also reports these data to the Commission.

The Commission may waive continuing education requirements for licensees who show good cause for being unable to meet the requirement.

**Inactive Status
[§17-316]**

The Commission will place the licenses of associate real estate brokers and real estate salespersons into inactive status when they are no longer affiliated with licensed real estate brokers and their license certificates and pocket cards are returned to the Commission.

A licensee whose license is on inactive status may not provide real estate brokerage services through that license. This prohibition includes accepting fees for referrals. An inactive licensee is not affiliated with any broker and may not be compensated by for any act of real estate brokerage. Individuals with inactive licenses may not belong to or be paid by a "referral company."

The placement of a license on inactive status does not affect the power of the Commission to suspend or revoke the license or to take any other disciplinary action against the licensee.

Unless an inactive license is reactivated, it expires four years after the date it is placed on inactive status. Renewal while on inactive status does not constitute reactivation. Subject to the four-year limitation, a license may be renewed while it is on inactive status without complying with the continuing education requirements. However, at the time of reactivation, all continuing education requirements not previously satisfied must be completed.

The Commission will reactivate the license of real estate brokers on inactive status and reissue license certificates and pocket cards to such brokers if they request reactivation and pay to the Commission the $10 reissuance fee. They must also meet the continuing education requirements that would have been necessary for renewal of licenses had they not been on inactive status. Salespersons and associate brokers returning from inactive status must meet the same requirements and must also submit an affiliation commitment, contingent on their reactivation, from a broker. While on inactive status, a salesperson or an associate broker has no broker.

**Display of Certificates;
Loss or Destruction
[§17-317]**

Licensed real estate brokers are required to display their license certificates at all times in a conspicuous place in their offices. The license certificates of licensees who are affiliated with a real estate broker must be displayed at the office location out of which each usually works.

The Commission must immediately be notified of the loss or destruction of a license certificate or pocket card. On receipt of an affidavit of loss or destruction and payment of the required fee ($5 for a lost or destroyed pocket card or license certificate), the Commission will issue appropriate duplicates.

Change of Name [§17-318]

When a licensee or a firm takes a new name, on receipt of the required application fee ($5), the old certificate, pocket card, and any required documentation, the Commission issues to the licensee a new license certificate and pocket card that reflect such change.

Licensure and the Deceased Broker [§17-319]

On the death of a licensed real estate broker, any adult member of the family may carry on the brokerage for up to six months to close and terminate the business. To do this, the certificate and pocket card of the deceased broker must be surrendered to the Commission. Any information required by the Commission must also be submitted.

Before the end of the six-month period for carrying on the business of a deceased real estate broker, an individual doing so may qualify for and receive from the Commission the license of the deceased broker, if the individual

- is a member of the immediate family of the decedent,
- has been continuously licensed as a real estate salesperson for the immediately preceding three years,
- passes the real estate broker examination required by this subtitle, and
- surrenders his or her real estate salesperson license certificate and pocket card to the Commission.

There must also have been compliance with the conditions for carrying on the business as stated in the first paragraph of this section.

A person receiving the reissued license of a deceased real estate broker may hold and use that license for as long as four years without meeting the 135-hour educational requirement. However, if the requirement has not been met within four years, the license automatically expires.

Return of Licenses; Terminating Affiliation [COMAR 09.11.01.08]

The license certificates and pocket cards of affiliates must be returned to the Commission by their brokers

- on the request of a real estate salesperson or associate real estate broker,
- on the death of the affiliate, or
- after a hearing before the Commission and on a finding that the license of a real estate salesperson or associate broker is to be suspended or revoked.

Real estate brokers are required to surrender to the Commission, promptly on demand, any such person's license that may be in their possession or control. Failure to do so is grounds for disciplinary action.

In the event of an affiliate's termination (discharge) a broker must

- immediately mail to the licensee, at the last known address of that individual, notice of such termination;
- submit written notice to the Commission, including a copy of the notice mailed to the licensee; and
- return the license certificate of the licensee to the Commission.

Licensing Out-of-State Applicants [§17-514]

The Commission will issue licenses only to nonresident applicants who file with the Commission a signed statement of **irrevocable consent.** By submitting this statement, applicants agree that suits and actions may be commenced against them without their actually being served papers notifying them of a forthcoming suit. They are consenting that official delivery of papers to the executive director of the Commission shall bind applicants in any action, suit, or proceeding brought against them, in any county in which the cause of action arose or the complaining party resides.

When serving process on the executive director of the Commission, persons filing must immediately send a copy of the filing, by certified mail, to the principal office of the person against whom the action is directed.

Note: The signature block on license examination applications contains these words: "If the address of this registration is not within the State of Maryland, I do hereby irrevocably consent that suits and actions may be commenced against me in the proper courts of the State of Maryland as required by the Maryland Annotated Code."

Maryland law states that if any nonresident real estate broker or other such licensee participates in any real estate transaction, divides a fee, and/or holds deposits from any such transaction in Maryland, that very act, is construed (considered) to give irrevocable consent.

■ PROCESSING COMPLAINTS

The Commission's Web site provides a form to be downloaded on which complaints against licensees may then be submitted. On the Commission's receipt of a properly completed complaint form, it sends a copy of the complaint to the broker of the company involved together with a letter from the Commission's executive director, stating that the broker must respond in writing with a full explanation of the allegations and what action the broker recommends. A broker's failure to respond to this inquiry may be considered grounds for disciplinary action. A chart indicating the steps in handling a complaint against a licensee is found in Appendix C of this book.

A copy of the executive director's letter is also sent to the complainant. Then, on receipt of the broker's response, a reply is sent to the complainant from the Commission, along with a copy of that response.

The Commission may commence proceedings on a complaint made by a Commission member or by other persons who must make such complaints under oath. Complaints must be in writing, state specifically the facts on which the complaint is based, and may be accompanied by documentary or other evidence.

After review of the content of the complaint, it may be referred for investigation, if it appears an infraction has occurred. A complaint not referred for investigation is considered dismissed. Within 30 days of such dismissal, any member of the Commission may file an exception disagreeing with the dismissal. If such exception is taken, the full Commission will hold a hearing to consider proceeding with an investigation.

If an exception is not filed, the dismissal is considered a final decision of the Commission, which means that any party aggrieved by the decision may appeal to the appropriate court. Decisions may not be appealed until they are final.

If the Commission or its designee, based on an investigation, determines that grounds exist for disciplinary action, the matter is referred for a hearing. Complaints not referred for a hearing after investigation must be dismissed. This has the same effect as a final decision: any party aggrieved by that dismissal may make judicial appeal.

Hearings and Notices

Except as otherwise provided in the State Government Article (as in situations where summary action is needed), before the Commission takes any final action, it gives the individual against whom the action is contemplated an opportunity for a hearing before the Commission or a hearing board.

At least ten days before the hearing, the hearing notice is served personally on the individuals against whom complaint has been made or is sent by certified mail to their last known addresses. If the individuals are licensees other than a broker, at least ten days before the hearing the Commission shall serve notice of the hearing to each real estate broker with whom the licensees are affiliated.

The individuals may have attorneys represent them at hearings. This does not mean that they can fail to appear and merely send their attorneys. If the individuals against whom the action is contemplated fail or refuse to appear, the Commission may proceed to hear and determine the matter without their presence. These hearings are open to the public.

Real Estate Hearing Board [§17-324]

The Commission establishes two or three real estate hearing boards—often called *panels*—each consisting of three Commission members. At least one member of each panel must be a professional member, and at least one must be a consumer member. From among each hearing board's members, the Commission designates a chairperson.

Referral of Cases

The Commission may order a hearing for any complaint that has been filed with the Commission and any other matter for which a hearing may be required.

Before deciding to hold a hearing, a panel will meet privately to

- review complaints and consider whether they provide a reasonable basis for disciplinary hearings, and
- review claims against the Guaranty Fund to determine what further action to take.

They meet in public to

■ hear licensees' responses to and defenses against complaints, and then
■ decide whether to authorize punitive actions against them.

Hearing boards exercise the same powers as, and conduct hearings for, the Commission. They report their decisions and actions to the Commission. Panels specifically advise the Commission of any action they take against licensees involved in monetary loss, misappropriation of funds, or fraud.

Hearing Regulations [COMAR 09.11.03]

COMAR—the Code of Maryland Regulations—provides for four types of hearings:

1. Judicial hearings
2. Applications for licensure
3. Revocation or suspension of licenses
4. Claims against the Guaranty Fund

Hearings are conducted under several levels of overlapping hearing regulations.

The decision of a hearing board is regarded as a *final decision* of the Commission. This means that any aggrieved party may *then* make a judicial appeal.

On dismissal of a complaint, the complainant and the licensee are notified in writing. The dismissal of a complaint after investigation is not reviewable further. Other complaints substantially based on the same facts are usually similarly dismissed.

Summary Actions [§17-328]

Summary actions are those taken before holding a hearing in order to protect the public against imminent loss. They are then *followed* by a hearing for which formal, timely notice is given.

Revocation after Actions of Other Agencies [§17-327]

The Commission may summarily order the revocation of the license of any licensee if the licensee is convicted of a violation of this title, the conviction is final, and the period for appeal has expired.

The license of any nonresident licensee may be revoked if the real estate regulatory agency of the state where the licensee is a resident revokes the license issued by that state and certifies the order of revocation to the Commission.

When the Commission orders a summary revocation under this section, it gives licensees written notice of the revocation and the finding on which it was based. After the revocation is effective, the Commission grants them an opportunity to be heard promptly either before the Commission or before a hearing board.

Rather than summarily order revocation of a license under this section, the Commission may elect not to revoke the license until after the licensee is given an opportunity for a hearing. If the Commission elects to give the licensee an opportunity for a hearing before revoking the license, the Commission gives notice and holds the hearing in the same manner as required for other hearings.

In any hearing held because of conviction or revocation by other agencies, the Commission considers only evidence of whether or not the alleged conviction or revocation in fact occurred. However, in such hearings a licensee may present matters in mitigation of the offense charged.

Summary Suspension for Trust Fund Violations [§17-328]

The Commission may—but is not required to—summarily order the suspension of a license if the licensee fails to

- account promptly for any funds held in trust or,
- on demand, fails to display to the Commission all records, books, and accounts of any funds held in trust.

The Commission gives the licensee notice and supporting reasons for its action and offers the opportunity to be heard later.

A summary suspension may start immediately, or at any later date set by the order, and shall continue until the licensee complies with the conditions set forth by the Commission in its order or until the Commission orders a different disposition after a hearing held under this section.

Judicial Review [§17-329]

When parties strongly disagree with a final decision of the Commission, they may appeal to a circuit court. Upon appeal, that court may set a bond not to exceed $50,000 and stay (delay) the suspension or revocation. The bond money would be for the use and benefit of any member of the public who might suffer financial loss because of any violation of the Brokers Act by the licensee.

Notice of Revocation or Suspension [§17-330]

Whenever a licensee's license is revoked or suspended and a stay is not ordered by the Commission or a court, the Commission notifies

- the licensee,
- the real estate broker with whom the licensee is affiliated,
- the Maryland Association of REALTORS®, and
- the local Board or Association of REALTORS® and the Realtist organization in the area of the licensee's office.

If the Commission revokes or suspends the license of a nonresident licensee, the Commission also notifies the Real Estate Commission or other licensing authority in the state where the licensee is a resident, reporting the cause for the revocation or suspension of the license. Table 1.2 clarifies some often-confused terms used in licensing.

TABLE 1.2

License Procedures

Process	Occasion
Renewal	Extends a license for another two-year term. Inactive licenses also require renewal.
Reissuance (Reactivation)	Licensee returns to active status and affiliates with a broker.
Reinstatement	Revives license that expired for lack of renewal, or restores license after suspension.

■ REAL ESTATE GUARANTY FUND (TITLE 17, SUBTITLE IV)

The Guaranty Fund exists to reimburse members of the public for actual financial losses at the hands of real estate licensees and their unlicensed employees. The maximum reimbursement for any claim is $25,000.

Use of Monies Collected

The Commission deposits all money collected for the Guaranty Fund with the State treasurer, who invests it, with the investment earnings credited to the Fund.

Initial Assessment for Fund

Before granting initial licenses to applicants, the Commission requires that they pay a $20 assessment that is credited to the Guaranty Fund. Regardless of how many times an individual applies to the Commission for one level of license, the Commission makes only one such assessment.

If the amount in the Guaranty Fund falls below $250,000, the Commission assesses all the individuals then holding licenses a fee—typically payable at renewal—sufficient to return the Guaranty Fund to that level.

Claims against the Fund

A person may recover compensation from the Guaranty Fund only for actual financial losses. Claims must be based on acts or omissions that occurred in the provision of real estate brokerage services by licensees or unlicensed employees of a licensed real estate broker. Claims must involve transactions that relate to real estate located in the State and be based on acts or omissions in which money or property is obtained from a person by theft, embezzlement, false pretenses, forgery, or an act that constitutes fraud or misrepresentation.

A claim against the Guaranty Fund must

■ be in writing and under oath,
■ state the amount of loss claimed,
■ state the facts on which the claim is based, and
■ be accompanied by documentation or other evidence that supports the claim.

At any claim hearing, the burden of proof shall be on the claimant to establish the validity of the claim.

A person may not recover from the Guaranty Fund any loss that relates to

- the purchase of any interest in a limited partnership that invests in real estate,
- a joint venture that is promoted by a real estate licensee for the purpose of investment in real estate, or
- the purchase of commercial paper secured by real estate.

A claim under the Guaranty Fund may not be filed by the spouse or by the personal representative of the spouse of the individual alleged to be responsible for the act or omission giving rise to the claim. Any claim must be filed with the Commission *within three years* of the loss or discovery of the loss.

Notice to Buyer

Real estate brokers must include in each sales contract a written notice that buyers are protected by the Guaranty Fund in an amount not exceeding $25,000. Although only buyers are mentioned in this notice, sellers may also submit claims.

Action by Commission on a Claim

The Commission must act promptly upon receiving claims by

- forwarding copies to licensees and/or unlicensed employees alleged to be responsible and to their brokers;
- requiring a written response, within ten days, from each of those individuals concerning the allegations set forth in the claim (this ten-day period is shorter than the 20 days required for response to other inquiries from the Commission);
- reviewing the claim and any responses to the claim; and
- conducting an investigation.

On the basis of its review of a claim and any investigation it conducts, the Commission either schedules a hearing or dismisses the claim.

Special Disposition of Smaller Claims

If the claim is $3,000 or less, the Commission, through a designated staff member such as its executive director, may issue a proposed order either to pay or to deny the claim. Both the claimant and the licensee receive a copy of this proposed order.

Within 30 days either the claimant or licensee may request a hearing or file written exceptions to the order. If either happens, the Commission must schedule a hearing on the claim. If no hearing is requested and no exceptions taken, the proposed order becomes a final order of the Commission.

Other Claims

The Commission gives notice of the hearing and opportunity to appear before the Commission to both the claimants and the licensees or unlicensed employees alleged to be responsible. The Commission must send the required notices to every party involved before conducting the hearing.

When the persons alleged to be responsible are licensees, the Commission may combine this hearing with disciplinary proceedings against licensees arising from the same facts alleged in a claim. A claimant may be *party* to that portion of the proceedings about the claim, but may be a *witness* only in the disciplinary portion.

The misdemeanor penalty for knowingly making a false statement or material misstatement of fact about a Guaranty Fund matter is a fine of not more than $5,000 or imprisonment not exceeding one year or both.

Payments by Guaranty Fund

If a claim proves valid, the Commission orders its payment by the Guaranty Fund. The amount of compensation recoverable from the Guaranty Fund is limited to the actual monetary loss incurred by the claimant. The payout may never be more than $25,000 for any one claim. The amount paid may not include

- losses other than those from the original transaction,
- commissions owed to a licensee acting as either a principal or an agent in a real estate transaction, or
- any attorney's fees incurred in seeking money from the Fund.

Payment is not made until either the time for seeking judicial review is over or any judicial stay has expired. The Commission orders payment of claims in the order in which they were awarded.

Reimbursement of Guaranty Fund

When payment is made from the Fund, the Commission immediately and without further proceedings suspends the licenses of the offending licensees. Licensees suspended in this way are not reinstated until they repay the full amounts owed to the Fund, plus interest, and make formal application for reinstatement. Reimbursement of the Fund does not affect any disciplinary actions imposed on licensees.

After payment of a claim by the Guaranty Fund, the licensee responsible is required to reimburse the Fund in full for the amount paid and for interest of at least 10 percent. (General Regulation .23 presently sets the rate at 12 percent.) The licensees responsible for the claim are **jointly and severally liable.** That is, each does not bear a proportionate share; each is responsible for the entire amount until the entire amount is paid.

If licensees do not reimburse the Guaranty Fund as provided, the Commission may have the State Collections Unit sue them for the amount that has not been reimbursed and seek liens against their real property.

■ PROHIBITED ACTS [§17-322]

After giving proper notice, conducting any needed investigation, holding the required hearing, and reaching its conclusions, the Commission is empowered to deny a license to any applicant, to reprimand licensees, and to suspend or revoke the licenses of any licensees who

- fraudulently obtain or attempt to obtain a license for themselves or others;
- fraudulently use licenses;
- directly or through other persons willfully make misrepresentations or knowingly make false promises;
- intentionally or negligently fail to disclose to any person with whom they deal a material fact that they know or should know that relates to property with which they deal;
- as affiliates, provide or attempt to provide real estate brokerage services on behalf of real estate brokers without informing in writing any other real estate broker under whom the affiliates are licensed;
- fail to follow the law concerning dual agency;
- retain or attempt to retain the services of any unlicensed individuals (in such a way as to evade the law prohibiting payment of a commission to an unlicensed individual);
- guarantee, authorize, or permit other persons to guarantee future profits from the resale of real property;
- solicit, sell, or offer to sell real property so as to influence or attempt to influence a prospective party to the sale of real property by offering prizes or free lots, conducting a lottery or contest, or advertising "free appraisals," unless prepared to appraise real estate free of charge for any person, for any purpose;
- accept a listing contract to sell real property that fails to provide a definite termination date that is effective automatically and may not require further notice from the either the buyer or the seller;
- accept a listing contract to sell real property that provides for a "net" return to a seller and leaves the licensees free to sell the real property at any price higher than the "net" price;
- knowingly solicit a party to an exclusive listing contract with another licensee to terminate that contract and enter a new contract with the licensees making the solicitation;
- solicit a party to a sales contract, lease, or agreement that was negotiated by other licensees to breach the contract, lease, or agreement for the purpose of substituting a new contract, lease, or agreement for which the licensees making the solicitation are either the real estate brokers or affiliated with those real estate brokers;
- for any transactions in which the licensees have served as or on behalf of a real estate broker, fail to furnish promptly to each party to the transaction copies of the listing contract to sell or rent real property, the contract of sale, or the lease agreement;
- for any transactions in which the licensees have served as or on behalf of a real estate broker, fail to keep copies of all executed listing contracts to sell or rent real property, contracts of sale, or lease agreements;
- whether or not acting for monetary gain, knowingly induce or attempt to induce persons to transfer real estate or discourage or attempt to discourage persons from buying real estate by making representations about the existing or potential proximity of real property owned or used by individuals of a particular race, color, religion, sex, handicap, familial status, or national origin; or by representing that the existing or potential proximity of real property owned or used by individuals of a particular

race, color, religion, or national origin will or may result in: the lowering of property values; a change in the racial, religious, or ethnic character of the block, neighborhood, or area; an increase in criminal or antisocial behavior in the area; or a decline in the quality of the schools serving the area;

- use any of the following material if it includes the name of an organization or association of which the licensees are not members: contract forms for the listing of real property for sale, rent, or exchange; contract forms for the sale, rent, or exchange of real property; or any advertising matter;
- as real estate brokers or affiliates, advertise the sale or rent of or an offer to buy real property while failing to disclose in the advertisement the name of the advertisers and the fact that the advertisers are real estate licensees;
- advertise in any misleading or untruthful manner;
- as affiliates, advertise the sale or rent of or an offer to buy real property in their names while failing to disclose in the advertisement the name of the real estate broker on whose behalf the affiliates are acting;
- for real estate brokerage services provided by associate real estate brokers or real estate salespersons, accept commissions or other valuable considerations from persons other than the real estate broker with whom they are affiliated;
- fail to account for or to remit promptly any money that comes into their possession;
- pay or receive a rebate, profit, compensation, or commission in violation of any provision of this act;
- under the laws of the United States or of any state, are convicted of felonies or misdemeanors that are directly related to their fitness and qualification to provide real estate brokerage services; or a crime that constitutes a violation of any provision of the Brokers Act;
- engage in conduct that demonstrates bad faith, incompetence, or untrustworthiness or that constitutes dishonest, fraudulent, or improper dealings;
- with actual knowledge of the violation, associate with licensees in a transaction or practice that violates any provision of the Brokers Act;
- fail as real estate brokers to exercise reasonable and adequate supervision over the provision of real estate brokerage services by other individuals on behalf of the broker;
- provide to any parties contracts that do not contain a notice of a buyer's right of selection, as required by the Brokers Act;
- require a buyer to employ a particular title insurance company, settlement company, escrow company, or title lawyer in violation of this act;
- fail to make the disclosure of representation as required by §17-528;
- violate any trust accounts provision of this act that relates to trust money;
- violate any other provision of this act;
- violate any regulation adopted under this act or any provision of the Code of Ethics; or
- violate §17-320(d) by failing as branch office managers to exercise reasonable and adequate supervision over the brokerage work of sales agents or associate brokers in their offices.

Instead of, or in addition to, suspension or revocation, the Commission may impose a penalty not exceeding $5,000 for each violation. To determine the amount of the penalty imposed, the Commission considers

- the seriousness of the violation,
- the harm caused by the violation,
- the good faith of the licensee, and
- any history of previous violations by the licensee.

The Commission pays any penalty collected into the General Fund of the State.

The Commission considers several facts when granting, denying, renewing, suspending, or revoking licenses, or reprimanding licensees, when the individuals concerned have been convicted of certain crimes. In the case of felonies and misdemeanors, they consider

- the nature of the crime, and
- the relationship of the crime to the activities authorized by the license.

In the case of felonies (crimes for which the maximum imprisonment could be more than one year), they consider

- the relevance of the conviction to the fitness and qualification of the applicants or licensees to provide real estate brokerage services,
- the length of time since the conviction, and
- the behavior and activities of the applicants or licensees before and after their convictions.

The Drug Enforcement Act of 1990 authorizes the Commission to impose sanctions upon licensees for a controlled substance offense.

A Maryland statute, Child Support—Enforcement Procedures, subjects licensees to having their licenses suspended and renewals denied if they are overdue in the payment of child support awarded by Maryland or any other state.

■ PROHIBITED ACTS PUNISHABLE BY IMPRISONMENT

There are real estate–related criminal offenses for which imprisonment of a person is a possible penalty. Note that the term *person* includes licensees, nonlicensees, individuals, and business entities such as corporations, partnerships, limited liability companies, and so forth. Although the Commission is empowered to pursue all violators of these provisions, including nonlicensees, and to impose monetary penalties of as much as $5,000, only a court can try, convict, and sentence an individual to prison.

In addition to the prohibitions and penalties enumerated above, the Brokers Act provides for fines not to exceed $5,000 and/or imprisonment not to exceed one year for the following acts:

1. Except as otherwise provided in the Brokers Act, a person may not provide, attempt to provide, or offer to provide real estate brokerage services unless licensed by the Commission.

2. Unless authorized under this act to provide real estate brokerage services, a person may not represent to the public by use of the title *Licensed Real Estate Broker, Licensed Associate Real Estate Broker,* or *Licensed Salesperson,* by other title, by description of services, methods, or procedures, or otherwise that the person is authorized to provide real estate brokerage services in the State.

3. Real estate brokers may not allow other licensees or any other unauthorized individuals to provide real estate brokerage services independently as real estate brokers. Real estate brokers may not retain unlicensed individuals to provide real estate brokerage services on their behalf. Licensed real estate brokers may not lend their license certificates or pocket cards to other individuals.

4. Licensees may not pay any form of compensation for the provision of real estate brokerage services to persons not licensed under the Brokers Act, except that payment may be made to individuals who are licensed in another state and who meet the requirements of this act. A professional service corporation formed under this act, and, after October 1, 2005, a limited liability company (LLC), may also receive such compensation. Note that corporations and partnerships are not authorized to receive such payments—only professional service corporations and (after October 1, 2005) LLCs.

5. Except as otherwise provided, licensees may not pay or offer to pay commissions to lawyers simply for the referral of persons as prospective parties to residential real estate transactions. Licensees may not solicit referral business from lawyers by a mass solicitation that offers to pay fees or commissions to the lawyers. This does not apply to payments or offers of payments to lawyers who hold a real estate broker license under this act or are otherwise entitled to a commission. Other than the considerations expressly prohibited, the law does not prohibit the payment or the offer of a payment of a commission by a licensee to a lawyer for other services that relate to real estate transactions.

6. In a real estate transaction involving a single-family dwelling, licensees or lawyers acting as real estate brokers may not require buyers, as a condition of settlement, to employ particular title insurance companies, settlement companies, escrow companies, mortgage lenders, financial institutions, or title lawyers. However, a seller may make owner financing a condition of sale.

7. Whether or not acting for monetary gain, persons may not knowingly induce or attempt to induce other persons to sell or rent dwellings or otherwise transfer real estate or knowingly discourage or attempt to discourage other persons from purchasing real estate by making representations regarding

   - the entry or prospective entry into a neighborhood of individuals of a particular race, color, sex, religion, or national origin;
   - the existing or potential proximity of real property owned or used by individuals of a particular race, color, sex, religion, or national origin; or

■ the existing or potential proximity of real property owned or used by individuals of a particular race, color, sex, religion, or national origin will or may result in the lowering of property values; a change in the racial, religious, or ethnic character of the block, neighborhood, or area; an increase in criminal or antisocial behavior in the area; or a decline in the quality of schools serving the area.

8. Persons may not provide financial assistance by loan, gift, or otherwise to other persons if they have actual knowledge that the financial assistance will be used in transactions that result from a fair housing violation.

9. If one of the purposes of the solicitation or attempted solicitation is to change the racial composition of a neighborhood, persons may not solicit or attempt to solicit the listing of residential properties for sale or lease by in-person door-to-door solicitation, telephone solicitation, or mass distribution of circulars.

10. A corporation, partnership, or any other association may not commit or cause any other person to commit any act that constitutes grounds for disciplinary action against a licensee under the Brokers Act. Violators are guilty of misdemeanors and, upon conviction, subject to a fine not exceeding $5,000.

11. In transactions involving residential property in Baltimore City:

■ All real estate brokers shall break down the properties listed in the registry by price categories established by the Commission. If a prospective buyer requests to see the registry, they shall allow the prospective buyer to see the part of the registry for the price category in which the prospective buyer indicates interest. This does not require a real estate broker who is a member of a multiple-listing service to disclose properties that are obtained from multiple listing.

■ Unless requested to do so by a prospective buyer or renter, real estate licensees may not fail or refuse to show any residential property that is available for sale, rent, or sublease to a prospective buyer or renter because of the race, color, sex, religion, age, or national origin of the prospective buyer or renter or the racial composition or character of the neighborhood where the property is located.

■ Licensees may not fail or refuse to show all available listed residential properties that are in a certain area and within a specified price range to a prospective buyer or renter who has requested to be shown all available properties that are in the area and within the specified price range.

■ If the representation is made because of the race, color, sex, religion, age, or national origin of the prospective buyer or renter, or because of the racial composition or character of the area where the property is located, real estate licensees may not represent to prospective buyers or renters that the available residential properties, prospective sites for a residence, or listings are limited to those already shown when, in fact, there is a residential property, a prospective site for a residence, or a listing that is available and within the price range specified by the prospective buyer or renter. A licensee may charge a reasonable fee for showing a residential property to a prospective buyer or renter.

- In Baltimore City and Baltimore County, real estate licensees may not mass-solicit listings by using the name or address of a present or previous client without the written consent of both parties to the contract involving that client.

    The Commission enforces the provisions of this section concerning Baltimore City. For this purpose, it receives complaints, conducts investigations, issues subpoenas, administers oaths, and holds hearings.

12. In transactions involving residential property in Montgomery County:

    - Real estate brokers shall maintain current and complete registries of all residential properties that they personally list for sale or rent in Montgomery County and, if members of a multiple-listing service, a registry of properties listed with the Montgomery County multiple-listing service.
    - Licensees may not refuse to show any residential property or prospective site for a residence that is available for sale, rent, or sublease to a prospective buyer or renter because of the race, color, religion, sex, marital status, national origin, physical or mental handicap of the prospective buyer or renter, or because of the composition or character of the neighborhood in which the property is located.

    The Commission enforces the provisions of this section concerning Montgomery County. For this purpose it receives complaints, conducts investigations, issues subpoenas, and holds hearings.

Maryland courts are required to report to the Commission, for appropriate action, all convictions of licensees for violation of this act with respect to blockbusting and discriminatory real estate practices in Baltimore City or Montgomery County.

■ REAL ESTATE BROKERAGE PRACTICE IN BALTIMORE CITY

Although Baltimore City does not issue or require a separate real estate license to perform real estate activities there, local law does regulate the activities of licensees who practice in that city. Many of the prohibited acts are similar, if not identical, to State law. The Baltimore City real estate license law is found in §132 of Article 19 of the Baltimore City Code under the title "Real Estate Practices."

■ MARYLAND SECURITIES ACT

The Maryland Securities Act requires licensing of persons engaged in the offer and sale of real estate-related securities, including limited partnership interests in real property. The Maryland Securities Commission regulates all activities construed to be securities-related business. To inquire if certain activities could be construed as securities-related business, contact the Maryland Securities Commissioner.

■ REAL ESTATE APPRAISERS ACT

Title 16 of the *Business Occupations and Professions* Article of the Annotated Code of Maryland establishes licensing and certification procedures for real estate appraisers and creates a nine-member State Commission of Real Estate Appraisers within the Department of Labor, Licensing, and Regulation to administer that act.

Individuals who are licensed to provide real estate brokerage services do not also need to be licensed as real estate appraisers when merely recommending a listing price or a purchase price for real estate, provided that the opinion is *not* called an *appraisal*. A competitive market analysis (CMA) is not an appraisal, and its preparation for a seller or purchaser does not require an appraisal license or certificate.

To receive a real estate appraiser's license or certification, an individual must complete mandated educational requirements, pass an examination developed by the State Commission of Real Estate Appraisers, and have accumulated 2,000 hours of acceptable appraisal work experience.

An individual may hold a real estate license and at the same time be a licensed or certified real estate appraiser. Such individuals should be extremely careful to avoid any conflicts of interest that could arise from providing real estate appraisal services in transactions in which they, their friends, their relatives, or those employed by their broker are also agents or principals.

Requirements for Preparing a CMA [COMAR 09.11.02.02.F]

The Real Estate Commission's Code of Ethics imposes specific requirements for licensees preparing a CMA for a prospect, customer, or client. This notice must appear conspicuously on the first page of the CMA:

COMPETITIVE MARKET ANALYSIS DISCLOSURE

This analysis is not an appraisal. It is intended only for the purpose of assisting buyers or sellers or prospective buyers or sellers in deciding the listing, offering, or sale price of the real property.

If a licensee includes a property in which the licensee has an interest as one of the comparables, that fact shall be disclosed to the client, prospective client, or customer.

■ BUILDING INSPECTIONS

Licensees are not required to be experts in building construction, but they should be alert to *red flags* that exist in a property with which they are dealing. **Red flags** are physical indications that there may be a defect in the property not readily apparent to a layperson or an inexperienced home purchaser. Red flags suggest the presence of latent defects. **Latent defects** are material facts that are not discoverable by ordinary inspection. When known by any party, they must be brought to the attention of all parties entering into a transaction. Parties should be strongly advised to seek the expert advice of a licensed home inspector or a licensed structural engineer.

Since October 1, 2001, Title 16 of the *Business Occupations and Professions* Article has required individuals who provide home inspections to be licensed by the State Commission of Real Estate Appraisers and Home Inspectors. It is unlawful to provide such inspections for consideration without this license. The penalty for doing so is a fine of not more than $5,000 per violation. Exempt from this requirement are state and local government inspectors and building code enforcement officials acting within the scope of their employment, as well as licensed construction professionals acting within the scope of their licenses when their services may be required in the building or remodeling of real property as long as they are not claiming to be licensed home inspectors.

■ CHANGES IN THE LICENSE LAW AND REGULATIONS

Changes are occasionally made in the Brokers Act and the regulations of the Commission. The material included in this chapter is current as of the date of publication. However, readers are cautioned to ascertain whether changes have been made since publication of this book. See the first two sections of this chapter for sources of updated information.

The General Assembly can make changes in the Brokers Act (Title 17), while the Commission can make changes in the its own Regulations and Code of Ethics (COMAR).

Before the Commission adopts, amends, or repeals regulations, it publishes notice of the proposed action in the *Maryland Register*, with an estimate of economic impact, a notice of opportunity for public comment on the proposal, and the text of the proposed changes. After 45 days, the Commission may take final action on the proposal. At that time, a report of its final action is published in the *Maryland Register*. The Commission's final action takes effect ten days after that notice appears, unless the Commission specifies a later date. Some significant recent changes to Title 17–The Brokers Act are found in Figure 1.2.

F I G U R E   1.2

Recent Changes to Title 17, Maryland Real Estate Broker's Act

Legislative Year	Section Changed*	Content of Change
2005	*Real Property Article* 10-702 SB 192	After October 1, 2005, the Property Disclosure/Disclaimer form required in one- to four-family residential sales must include **latent defects** of which the seller has actual knowledge. Latent defects are defined as material defects to the property or an improvement that a purchaser would not reasonably be expected to discover by a careful visual inspection and that would pose a direct threat to the health or safety of occupants of the property.
2005	17-512 HB 464	After October 1, 2005, salespersons and associate brokers in the same brokerage firm may form limited liability companies (LLCs). Their broker is permitted, at their request, to pay commissions they have earned to the LLC. Previously, only professional service companies qualified for such payment.
2005	17-211, 306, 307, 311, 312, 313, 314, 316, 317, and 318 *Business Regulation Article* 2-106 HB 865	Beginning July 1, 2006, fees paid to the Commission will be forwarded to the Comptroller to accumulate in a State Real Estate Commission Fund from which the Commission's operating expenses will then be paid. After July 1, 2007, the Commission is empowered to set almost every fee charged for license issuance, renewal, and so forth. Increases may not exceed 12.5 percent per year. Until then the fees remain as established by the General Assembly through statute, the present Title 17.
2004	17-527.2, 3 HB 701	Extended advertising requirements to brokers that were previously imposed only on affiliates. Changed term "trade name" to "designated name." Removed requirement that broker's name be at least as large as that of the affiliate who advertises; that requirement would have taken effect October 1, 2004. Related regulations are under consideration by the Commission.
2004	17-303(d) HB 1249 17-305(d) HB 1249	Added to **prelicensure** educational requirements for broker and for salesperson licenses: 3 hrs. real estate ethics approved by the Commission (as part of and not in addition to the present 60- and 135-hr. course requirements). The 3-hour course required biennially by the Associations of Realtors® does not satisfy this requirement.
2004	17-303, 305, 315 HB 1249	Mandated 3-clock-hour **ethics** course as part of required **continuing education.** *One 3-clock-hour ethics course that includes the Maryland Code of Ethics and a discussion of the practices of flipping and predatory lending.* Licensees renewing after October 1, 2005, must meet this requirement.
2004	17-315(a)(2)(i) HB 1249	Scheduled biennial increases in required **continuing education hours** for those holding licenses for 10 yrs. or more, from 6 to 9 to 15 hours. Although the exact dates on which these requirements will be imposed by the Commission on more-than-10-year licensees are not quite clear, licensees with fewer than 10 years of licensure will continue to have the 15-hr. requirement.
2004	17-315(s)(2)(ii) HB 1249	Allowed licensees with graduate degrees in law or in real estate to take a minimum 7.5 hrs. continuing education for each license renewal (rather than 9 or 15).
2004	17-315(b)(2)(i) HB 1349	Broadened the **subject matter** the Commission shall consider for approved **continuing education** to include *subject matter intended to assist a licensee in providing real estate brokerage services to the public in a more efficient and effective manner, provided that the subject matter is related to helping the public buy or sell real estate.*
2004	17-505 SB 366	Reduced broker vulnerability for "good-faith" distribution of earnest money deposits by giving broker "sole discretion" as to whether to make use of one of the optional distribution mechanisms.
2004	Real Property 8-203 (e) and (h) SB 372 HB 723	Changed rate of interest to be paid to tenants on their rental security deposits from 4 percent to 3 percent. Details how landlord shall deal with deposits of a tenant who has been evicted, etc. Gives such tenant a specified time to demand return of deposit and landlord 45 days to respond to the demand.

* Section changed in Title 17 unless noted otherwise. HB indicates House Bill; SB, Senate Bill.

Recent Changes to Title 17, Maryland Real Estate Broker's Act (continued)

Legislative Year	Section Changed*	Content of Change
2004	Real Property 14-117 (d) and (e) HB 1030	Set forth a required sales contract provision: "Chesapeake and Atlantic Coastal Bays Critical Area," intended to put purchasers on notice to investigate such possible limitations on the use of the subject property.
2003	17-536-17540	Established detailed requirements for persons licensed in another state to participate in commercial real estate transactions in Maryland by obtaining a temporary license.
2003	17-315	Commission will now accept photocopies, electronic mail certificates, and photocopies of such certificates as evidence of completion of continuing education courses.
2003	17-527.2(b)	Postponed deadline for earlier law regulating size of affiliates' names in ads from October 1, 2003, to October 1, 2004.
2003	Article Tax General 10-912	Required collection at settlement of funds from nonresident sellers of Maryland real property to apply to later-due taxes: 4.75 percent for nonresident individuals and 7 percent for nonresident entities.
2002	17-527.2	Defined "advertisement"; called name other than licensee's legal name a "trade name." Imposed requirement on salespersons and associate brokers that they conspicuously include in all advertising the full name (not just logo) and the name or trade name of the broker under whom they are licensed. Authorized granting of "trade name" to such affiliates for use in advertising as it appears on their license. (This has taken the form of nicknames.) Established October 1, 2003, as deadline for equal size requirement for name of licensee and name of brokerage.
2001	17-315 S 324	Added "and regulations" to the approved content for continuing education legislative update courses and removed the limitation "during the preceding 5 years." Also directed the Commission to adopt regulations for the conduct of continuous education by various forms of distance learning by January 1, 2003.
2001	17-322 HB 88	Added the penalty of "reprimand" to other existing penalties available to the Commission. Raised the maximum fine per violation of any part of Section 17-322 from $1,000 to $5,000.
2001	17-613(c) HB 88	In 17-613(c) set forth power of Commission to impose a $5,000 maximum penalty on any *person* (not just *licensee*) who violates any portion of Title 17 and established guidelines for imposition of this penalty similar to the existing ones for violation of Section 17-322.
2001	17-502 HB 460	Required deposit of earnest money deposits "promptly, but not more than 7 business days after the acceptance of a contract of sale by both parties" (rather than the former "within 3 days").
2001	Article 49B SB 205	Added "sexual orientation" to the previous list of protected groups [race, creed, sex, color, national origin, marital status, and disability (and familial status in regards to housing)] from being deprived of public accommodations and the services of any entity licensed by the Department of Labor, Licensing, and Regulation. Provided that group the same protections with respect to real estate transactions as is afforded to race, religion, etc. Added Sexual Orientation to list of exclusions from protection in rental of rooms in the owner's principal residence or apartment unit in an owner-occupied building of 5 or fewer apartments. (The former exclusions were "sex and marital status.")
2001	17-505 HB 83	Provided a fourth alternative for brokers to dispose of earnest deposits. This one relates to situation in which either buyer or seller fails to complete the transaction. Brokers communicate to both parties their decision to distribute deposits according to their understanding of the contract. Either party may refuse the plan. If neither does, the broker may proceed. Required that the contract that entrusts the earnest money to the broker contain a statement giving the broker permission to follow the plan outlined above, in the event that either party fails to complete the transaction that is the subject of that contract.

* Section changed in Title 17 unless noted otherwise. HB indicates House Bill; SB, Senate Bill.

QUESTIONS

1. Licensed salespersons may represent
   1. any owners who directly employ them.
   2. not more than one owner at one time.
   3. only brokers under whom they are licensed.
   4. any broker who is duly licensed.

2. License certificates issued for salespersons MUST be
   1. carried by them at all times.
   2. displayed by their brokers in their brokerage offices.
   3. retained by the Commission.
   4. displayed by them in their homes.

3. Brokers need NOT notify the Commission when
   1. salespersons resign.
   2. changes occur in the locations of their offices.
   3. changes occur in the names of their firms.
   4. changes occur in commission sharing.

4. As a licensed salesperson, you receive a lead from a friend who is not a real estate licensee. You split your commission with your friend.
   1. This is a violation of the license law.
   2. This is NOT a violation of the license law.
   3. This is a violation of the license law only if the seller is NOT informed.
   4. This is a violation of the license law only if your broker has NOT given written permission.

5. To be recognized by the IRS as "qualified real estate agents" and thus to receive the advantages of "self-employed" status, licensees must do all the following EXCEPT
   1. have a written employment contract with the broker agreeing to this status.
   2. be free from their broker's control of how their work is done.
   3. earn the preponderance of all income from the brokerage firm in the form of commissions.
   4. hold a real estate license.

6. Which of the following fees is paid biennially?
   1. Initial Guaranty Fund fee
   2. Broker's or salesperson's original license fee
   3. Broker's or salesperson's license renewal fee
   4. Guaranty Fund reassessment

7. In Maryland, the act of "blockbusting" is
   1. unethical but NOT prohibited by law.
   2. a felony.
   3. a misdemeanor.
   4. a legitimate listing technique.

8. Individuals found guilty of operating in the real estate business without a license may be fined by
   1. the district attorney.
   2. the Commission.
   3. the state or local Association of REALTORS®.
   4. the attorney general.

9. An unlicensed person improperly collecting a real estate commission is guilty of
   1. duress.
   2. a felony.
   3. a misdemeanor.
   4. fraud.

10. The Commission may revoke the license of any licensee who is found guilty of
    1. slandering competitors.
    2. intemperance.
    3. bad faith.
    4. puffing.

11. The maximum penalty for filing a false statement with the Commission in reference to a Guaranty Fund claim is
    1. not less than $200.
    2. not more than $200.
    3. $10,000 and not longer than two years' imprisonment.
    4. $5,000 and not longer than one year's imprisonment.

12. A license to provide residential real estate brokerage services can be issued only to a(n)
    1. corporation.
    2. limited liability company (LLC).
    3. partnership.
    4. individual.

13. Members of the Maryland Real Estate Commission are appointed by the
    1. Maryland Senate.
    2. Governor.
    3. House of Delegates.
    4. Executive Director of the Commission.

14. A salesperson license issued by the Commission on November 1 will expire
    1. one year from the date of issue.
    2. two years from the date of issue.
    3. April 30 of the next even-numbered year.
    4. March 1 of the next even-numbered year.

15. The main purpose of the Brokers Act is to
    1. raise revenue.
    2. protect the public interest.
    3. control salespersons.
    4. restrict competition.

16. The executive director of the Commission is
    1. appointed by the Governor.
    2. confirmed by the State Senate.
    3. appointed by the Secretary of Labor, Licensing, and Regulation.
    4. selected from the Maryland State Employees Classified System.

17. Ads placed by licensees seeking buyers for a listed property MUST include the
    1. name and address of the property owner.
    2. name of the listing salesperson.
    3. designated name of the broker.
    4. general location of the property.

18. The Guaranty Fund must be maintained at a minimum of
    1. $250,000.   3. $2,000.
    2. $25,000.   4. $200,000.

19. The Commission's Code of Ethics addresses relations with three groups. Which of the following is NOT one of those groups?
    1. Relations to the public
    2. Relations to the Commission
    3. Relations to the client
    4. Relations to fellow licensees

20. The Maryland Real Estate Commission is composed of
    1. five members.
    2. four persons who are not engaged in the real estate business and five licensed persons.
    3. four professional and four consumer members.
    4. representative brokers from real estate boards or associations throughout Maryland.

21. The Commission may refuse to issue a broker license to a Maryland resident who has filed a proper application and met the legal requirements
    1. after holding a hearing on the matter.
    2. if the applicant has been convicted of a traffic violation within the past year.
    3. without offering to hold a hearing on the matter.
    4. if the applicant has not reached the age of 21 years.

22. License fees are established by
    1. the Commission in Regulations.
    2. associations and boards of licensees.
    3. the Secretary of the Department of Labor, Licensing, and Regulation.
    4. the General Assembly by statute.

23. Which of the following is an act of real estate brokerage that requires a real estate brokerage license?
    1. A mortgage loan institution sells real estate acquired through foreclosure.
    2. A person offers to guide friends in the sale of their home, charging a consulting fee of $150.
    3. An attorney-at-law in a divorce action helps sell a house the couple owns for three percent commission.
    4. A property owner subdivides his land and sells five lots in one calendar year.

24. Fees paid for licenses finally go to the
    1. Maryland General Fund.
    2. testing service.
    3. Real Estate Board or Association active in the area.
    4. Comptroller of the State of Maryland.

25. Employees of the Commission
    1. include an Executive Director and field inspectors.
    2. must be licensed as brokers or salespeople while employed by the Commission.
    3. must have been licensed before being employed by the Commission.
    4. are permitted to perform acts of brokerage for which a license is required.

26. When brokers release salespersons, the licenses of the salespersons should be
    1. returned to the Commission by the brokers.
    2. returned to the Commission by the salespersons.
    3. removed from display but retained by the brokers.
    4. returned to the salespersons.

27. The Guaranty Fund protects a buyer for certain financial losses up to
    1. $250,000.   3. $2,500.
    2. $25,000.   4. an unlimited amount.

28. Which of the following statements pertaining to Maryland residential real estate licenses is NOT correct?
    1. Their holders are regulated by authority of the Business Occupations and Professions Article of the Maryland Annotated Code.
    2. They are issued and administered by the Maryland Real Estate Commission.
    3. They are not issued to corporations or associations.
    4. They are required for every person who sells real estate for consideration.

29. To deliver real estate brokerage services, a licensed real estate salesperson MUST
    1. be associated with a licensed real estate associate broker.
    2. perform real estate acts only on behalf of a licensed broker.
    3. be associated with a REALTOR®.
    4. operate a real estate business under his or her own name or designated name.

30. In performing which of these brokerage activities would a person be required to hold a valid real estate license?
    1. Developers selling new homes they have just built
    2. Attorneys-at-law performing acts of real estate brokerage in the course of other legal functions
    3. An attorney-in-fact acting under one power of attorney in the sale of several properties
    4. Trustees selling properties foreclosed under deeds of trust

REAL ESTATE AGENCY

■ OVERVIEW

While most of this chapter emphasizes only Maryland real estate law and practice, some general terms are also clarified here. On occasion, a brief restatement (in parentheses) may follow a technical term.

Topics addressed include the application of agency law to real estate brokerage; consumer confusion about various kinds of possible agency relationships; presumed buyer representation; various consent and disclosure forms; and the organization and management of brokerage firms, including advertising and handling of trust funds.

■ BROKERAGE AND AGENCY: NOT ALWAYS THE SAME

In general, **brokerage** involves bringing parties together and helping them negotiate contracts in return for a fee. Many kinds of brokers—commodity brokers, for instance—often do not actually represent either buyers or sellers. They merely *facilitate* transactions. The student should understand that performing certain kinds of brokerage does not always and everywhere require a broker to represent—be an agent of—either party. This book, however, describes brokerage that does involve agency.

■ AGENCY

Agency Duties
[§§17-528–17-535]

Maryland law sets forth almost all the agency duties of real estate licensees in the Maryland Real Estate Brokers Act. This statute—referred to throughout this book as the *Brokers Act*—is found in the *Business Occupations and Professions* Article of the Annotated Code of Maryland.

Detailed applications of the statute are found in the Code of Maryland Regulations (COMAR) in Sections 1 to 8 of Title 9, Subsection 11. COMAR is published in loose-leaf form. It is updated periodically and is available in many public libraries.

WWWeb.Link

Both are available for study and downloading from the Web site of the Maryland General Assembly: *www.mlis.state.md.us/*

Those sections of COMAR dealing with real estate brokerage can be found at *www.dsd.state.md.us/comar/subtitle_chapters/09_Chapters.htm#Subtitle11*

Students preparing for the salesperson or broker license exam may wish to download each part of Sections 1 and 2 entitled "General Regulations" and "Code of Ethics," paragraph by paragraph, and consolidate them into a single document for study.

Agency Relationships

Maryland real estate licensees, when acting as agents, owe their **clients** (the persons they represent) **fiduciary duties** as described in the principal text: Care, Obedience, Accounting, Loyalty, and Disclosure. Although these duties are few in number, they are in addition to the longer list of duties also owed to **customers** (third parties). Licensees owe *customers*, and other *third parties* honest and fair dealing, reasonable care, prompt presentation of all offers and counteroffers, honest answers to all questions (except those that are properly declared to be confidential by a client or are otherwise forbidden by law), and **affirmative** (voluntary) **disclosure** of material facts. See Table 2.1.

Important Terms: *Assist* versus *Represent*

Virtually all real estate brokerage companies in Maryland are willing to *assist* purchasers as *customers* in finding properties to purchase without representing them as *clients*. They will, however, offer purchasers client-level representation when engaged to do so. Licensed brokerage firms may also *represent* owners as *clients* in the sale of properties. Understanding the difference between *client-*

TABLE 2.1

Agents' Duties and Services to Customers and Clients

Duty or Service	To Their Principals (Clients)	To Third Parties (Customers)
Care	X	
Obedience	X	
Accounting	X	
Loyalty	X	
Disclosure of All Facts	X	
Magisterial Acts: Those Requiring the Exercise of Judgment	X	
Honesty and Fair Dealing	X	X
Reasonable Care and Skill in Performance	X	X
Affirmative Disclosure of Material Facts	X	X
Presentation of All Written Offers	X	X
Ministerial Acts: Those Actions of Service That Don't Require the Exercise of Judgment	X	X

level service and *customer-level service* is fundamental to effective and lawful provision of real estate brokerage services. Licensees **represent** clients. They **assist** customers.

■ THE CHALLENGE OF DUAL AGENCY

Origins of Buyer Representation

Until the early 1980s, Maryland residential real estate brokers usually represented client-sellers. Although buyers were typically regarded by law as third parties, they often—sometimes to their harm—regarded the salesperson assisting them as *their* agent.

Since then, consumers have become better informed. Today they typically demand that their "agent" actually *be* their agent—be on their team and deliver client-level service. They want a knowledgeable professional who will be loyal to them and will not only help them locate property to purchase but will also protect their interests, keep their confidence, and coach them in negotiations about price and many other matters throughout the transaction.

The Industry's Response to the Demand

Most firms throughout Maryland, in response to this growing demand, now offer representation to buyers—client-level service. These firms were already providing—and continue to provide—representation for client-sellers who list their properties with them.

The first example below illustrates a simple case of buyer representation.

■ **EXAMPLE 1**   Broker Norman, formally representing buyer Elizabeth, shows her a property listed by broker Eugene. Arturo is the owner/seller of that property and is, therefore, Eugene's client; he is receiving client-level service from Eugene's company and Elizabeth is receiving client-level service from Norman's. Both brokerage firms in this case are providing **single-agency service:** each broker is the agent of one party to this transaction.

■ **EXAMPLE 2**   A more complex situation has client-buyer Rebecca asking salesperson Brian to show her a property, owned by seller John, that is listed with Brian's broker, Yvonne. John is obviously already a client of Yvonne's company. So, at this moment, her company is being asked to represent parties on opposite sides of the same possible transaction. How can it give client service to both seller John and buyer Rebecca?

No individual (natural person) can possibly give total loyalty to opposing parties. That is the situation Yvonne's company is facing. Brian definitely wants both to sell his company's listing and to earn a fee for representing buyer-client Rebecca.

The Maryland Solution: Intracompany Agents (ICA) [§17-530]

The situation described in Example 2 above has such potential for conflict of interest that in the late 1990s Maryland wrote into the Broker Act certain actions that Brian's broker Yvonne is required to take if she wishes to keep both Rebecca and John as clients. The firm must first get the written consent of all parties to this dual agency. Then the company appoints two of its licensed affiliates to serve as **intracompany agents (ICAs).** (The term *intra* means *within*, as in *intra*mural games—those played *within* the *walls* of an institution.)

So Broker Yvonne appoints two affiliates, Viola and Brian, as ICAs of John and of Rebecca respectively. As broker, Yvonne is not permitted to appoint herself as one of those ICAs. The firm—if it has the informed consent of both buyer and seller—may now serve as agent of both parties in the contemplated transaction.

To maintain each side's confidentiality, the broker backs away from the transaction personally and lets the ICAs handle their respective clients. Each ICA will give her or his party **full client treatment,** which includes care, obedience, accounting, loyalty, and disclosure.

If Yvonne's company were very small and had only its broker and one other licensee, it could not perform the dual agency allowed by Maryland law. The law requires that the broker appoint two persons *other* than the broker to be ICAs. In a multioffice company, office managers, acting in the place of the broker and at the broker's direction, may *appoint* ICAs but not *serve as* ICAs.

Buyer Prospects' Representation Choices

On a *Buyer Representation Agreement* form, buyers are asked, among other things, to indicate whether they are willing to consider any property that will involve dual agency. Dual agency would arise if they, as client-purchasers, were shown a property listed with their buyer-broker's firm.

In addition, the company can show a client-buyer only those company listings whose owners also have consented to the possibility of dual agency when those properties were listed. The seller's consent must be confirmed when a specific situation involving dual agency arises; a Consent for Dual Agency form confirming assent must then indicate the specific property to be contracted for and the name of the specific prospect(s).

Buyers' consent to dual agency with respect to a specific property is made later, on their own *Consent for Dual Agency* form (Figure 2.1). This form will identify the buyers, the property, and the seller-owners by name.

■ A FIRM'S AGENCY OPTIONS IN REPRESENTATION

Licensed real estate brokers in Maryland, as in other states, may choose to operate as either *single-agency* or *dual-agency* companies. Those operating as single-agency companies typically choose to act as one of the following:

■ A **single-agency company** offering to represent either buyers or sellers, but not both, in any given transaction
■ An **exclusive-seller-agency company,** offering to represent only sellers in all transactions
■ An **exclusive-buyer-agency company,** offering to represent only buyers in all transactions

Single-agency companies offer to represent sellers while treating prospective buyers as customers (not clients) of that brokerage. They also do this when prospective buyers for the property are brought to them by *cooperating* agents, as described in Categories of Representation.

FIGURE 2.1

Commission's Consent for Dual Agency

STATE OF MARYLAND
REAL ESTATE COMMISSION

Consent For Dual Agency

(In this form, the word "seller" includes "landlord", "buyer" includes "tenant", and "purchase" or "sale" includes "lease.")

When Dual Agency May Occur

The possibility of dual agency arises when:

➢ The buyer is interested in a property listed by a real estate company; and

➢ The seller's agent and the buyer's agent work for that same real estate company.

Before the buyer and seller can proceed to be represented by a dual agent, they must both sign a Consent For Dual Agency. If they have previously signed a Consent For Dual Agency, they must affirm their consent for the sale of a particular property to a particular buyer.

Important Considerations Before Making a Decision About Dual Agency

☞   A dual agent does not exclusively represent either the seller or buyer and there may be a conflict of interest because the interests of the seller and buyer may be different or adverse.

☞ As a dual agent, the real estate company does not owe undivided loyalty to either the seller or buyer.

Your Choices Concerning Dual Agency

When a dual agency situation in fact arises, the buyer and seller have the following options:

1. **Consent in writing to dual agency.** If all parties consent in writing, the real estate company (the "dual agent") will assign one real estate agent from the company to represent the seller or landlord (the seller's "intra-company agent") and another agent from the company to represent the buyer or tenant (the buyer's "intra-company agent"). Intra-company agents may provide the same services to their clients as an exclusive seller's or buyer's agent, including advising their clients as to price and negotiation strategy.

2. **Do not consent to dual agency.** If either the buyer or the seller, or landlord or tenant, refuses to consent in writing to dual agency, the real estate company must terminate the agency agreement for that particular property with either the buyer or the seller, or both. If the seller's agreement is terminated, the seller must then either represent him or herself or arrange to be represented by an agent from another real estate company. If the buyer's agreement is terminated, the buyer or tenant may choose to enter into a written buyer agency agreement with an agent from a different company. Alternatively, the buyer or tenant may choose not be represented by an agent of his or her own but simply to receive assistance from the seller's agent, from another agent in that company, or from a cooperating agent from another company.

Provided by the Maryland Real Estate Commission

Commission's Consent for Dual Agency (continued)

Duties of a Dual Agent and Intra-Company Agent

Like other agents, dual agents and intra-company agents must keep confidential information about a client's bargaining position or motivations unless the client gives consent to disclose the information. For example, a dual agent or intra-company agent may not tell the other party, or the other party's agent, without consent of the client:

> ➤anything the client asks to be kept confidential*,
> ➤that the seller would accept a lower price or other terms,
> ➤the reasons why a party wants to sell or buy, or
> ➤that a party needs to sell or buy quickly

- However, like all agents, a dual agent and intra-company agent must disclose any material facts about a property to the other party.

How Dual Agents Are Paid

Only the dual agent receives compensation on the sale of a property listed by that company.

If a financial bonus is offered to an agent who sells property that is listed with his company, this fact must be disclosed in writing to both the buyer and seller.

I have read the above information, and I understand the terms of the dual agency. I understand that I do not have to consent to a dual agency, and that if I do not consent, there will not be a dual agency. I hereby voluntarily consent to have

_____act as dual agent for me as the:

(Firm Name)

❑   seller in the sale of the property at:_____.

❑   buyer in the purchase of any property listed for sale with the above-referenced firm.

_____   _____
Signature   Date   Signature   Date

AFFIRMATION

The undersigned Seller(s) hereby affirms consent to Dual Agency:

_____   _____
Signature   Date   Signature   Date

The undersigned Buyer(s) hereby affirms consent to dual agency:

_____   _____
Signature   Date   Property Location

_____
Signature   Date

The same single-agency companies may also offer to represent buyers in dealing with properties listed with other companies. What they have chosen *not* to do is offer to represent buyers and sellers *in the same property transaction.*

It is essential that each company decide which agency service or services it will offer and present that policy and its associated procedures to everyone in the organization. All persons affiliated with the company should be trained in the proper performance of these services. It is the responsibility of licensees who manage offices to ensure that these services are being performed according to the detailed requirements of the Brokers Act.

■ CATEGORIES OF REPRESENTATION [§17-530]

The Brokers Act and *Understanding Whom Real Estate Agents Represent*, the Maryland Real Estate Commission's relationship information form (Figure 2.2), recognize and define six kinds of agency representation in real estate brokerage: seller's agent, cooperating agent, buyer's agent, presumed buyer's agent, dual agent, and intracompany agent.

- **Seller's agents** are licensees who are affiliated with or acting as listing brokers for properties. They *represent* a seller and *assist* prospective buyers in the acquisition of real estate.
- **Cooperating agents** are a subtype of seller's agent. They are not affiliated with or acting as listing brokers for properties. Rather, they function as *subagents of the seller, representing* the seller through and under the seller's listing broker. They *assist* prospective buyers in the acquisition of real estate. This has long been a typical arrangement in transactions that involve a listing brokerage firm and a selling brokerage firm assisting a customer. However, it is becoming a less common practice.
- **Buyer's agents** are licensees who *represent* prospective buyers in the acquisition of real estate. When representing buyers in acquiring a property listed with another company, *buyer's agents are not subagents of the owner-seller.* Nor are they cooperating agents, as are described in the paragraph above.

There are two classes of buyer's agents. One class is the *presumed* buyer agent who has no express agreement to represent a prospect and who may make no claim for payment for this representation. The other class is the buyer agent *by written agreement.* This type may receive compensation for performance of the task set forth in the written agreement.

- **Dual agents** are *firms* (not individuals) that represent not only sellers but also prospective purchasers in the same property transaction. All parties must sign the Consent for Dual Agency form, presented in Figure 2.1, if dual agency is to proceed.
- **Intracompany agents** are a subtype under dual agents. They are pairs of licensees affiliated with a broker and assigned by their broker (or by their office manager) to deliver client-level service (one to the seller and one to the buyer) in the sale of a specific parcel of real estate listed with their company. They are acting on behalf of their firm, which is the dual agent. Both buyer and seller must have agreed to this arrangement for it to go forward.

F I G U R E 2.2

Commission's Relationship Information Form

State of Maryland
Real Estate Commission

Understanding Whom Real Estate Agents Represent

Before you decide to sell or buy or rent a home you need to consider the following information:

Agents Who Represent the Seller

Seller's Agent: A seller's agent works for the real estate company that lists and markets the property for the sellers, or landlords, and exclusively represents the sellers or landlords. That means that he or she may assist the buyer or tenant in purchasing or renting the property, but his or her duty of loyalty is only to the sellers or landlords. The seller pays the seller's agent's fees as specified in a written listing agreement.

Cooperating Agent: A cooperating agent works for a real estate company different from the company for which the seller's agent works. The cooperating agent can assist a buyer or tenant in purchasing or renting a property, but his or her duty of loyalty is only to the sellers or landlords. The cooperating agent's fees is paid by the sellers or landlords through the seller's agent's company.

Agents Who Represent the Buyer

Presumed Buyer's Agent (no written agreement): When a person goes to a real estate agent for assistance in finding a home to buy or rent, the agent is presumed to be representing the buyer and can show the buyer properties that are *not* listed by the agent's real estate company. A presumed buyer's agent may *not* make or prepare an offer or negotiate a sale for the buyer. The buyer does *not* have an obligation to pay anything to the presumed agent.

If for any reason the buyer does not want the agent to represent him or her as a presumed agent, either *initially* or *at any time*, the buyer can decline or terminate a presumed agency relationship simply by saying so.

Buyer's Agent (by written agreement): A buyer or tenant may enter into a written contract with a real estate agent which provides that the agent will represent the buyer or tenant in locating a property to buy or rent. The agent is then known as the buyer's agent. That agent assists the buyer in evaluating properties and preparing offers, and negotiates in the best interests of the buyer or tenant. The agent's fee is paid according to the written agreement between the agent and the buyer or tenant. If you as a buyer or tenant wish to have an agent represent you exclusively, you must enter into a written buyer agency agreement.

Dual Agents

The possibility of **dual agency** arises when the buyer's agent and the seller's agent both work for the same real estate company, and the buyer is interested in property listed by that company. The real estate company, or broker, is called the "dual agent." Dual agents do not act exclusively in the interests of either the seller or buyer, or landlord or tenant, and therefore cannot give undivided loyalty to either party. There may be a conflict of interest because the terms of the seller and buyer may be different or adverse.

If both seller and buyer, or landlord and tenant, agree to dual agency by signing a Consent For Dual Agency form, then the real estate company (the "dual agent") will assign one agent to represent the seller or landlord (the seller's "intra-company agent") and another agent to represent the buyer or tenant (the buyer's intra-company agent"). Intra-company agents may provide the same services to their clients as exclusive seller's or buyer's agents, including advising their clients as to price and negotiation strategy, provided the clients have both consented to be represented by dual agency.

Provided by the Maryland Real Estate Commission

Commission's Relationship Information Form (continued)

If either party does not agree to dual agency, the real estate company may withdraw the agency agreement for that particular property with either the buyer or seller, or both. If the seller's agreement is terminated, the seller must then either represent him or herself or arrange to be represented by an agent from another real estate company. If the buyer's agreement is terminated, the buyer or tenant may choose to enter into a written buyer agency agreement with an agent from a different company. Alternatively, the buyer or tenant may choose not to be represented by an agent of his or her own but simply to receive assistance from the seller's agent, from another agent in that company, or from a cooperating agent from another company.

No matter what type of agent you choose to work with, you have the following rights and responsibilities in selling or buying or renting property:

➤Real estate agents are obligated by law to treat all parties to a real estate transaction honestly and fairly. They must exercise reasonable care and diligence and maintain the confidentiality of clients. They must not discriminate in the offering of properties; they must promptly present each written offer or counteroffer to the other party; and they must answer questions truthfully.

➤Real estate agents must disclose all material facts that they know or should know relating to a property. An agent's duty to maintain confidentiality does not apply to the disclosure of material facts about a property.

➤All agreements with real estate agents should be in writing and should explain the duties and obligations of the agent. The agreement should explain how the agent will be paid and any fee-sharing agreements with other agents.

➤You have the responsibility to protect your own interests. You should carefully read all agreements to make sure they accurately reflect your understanding. A real estate agent is qualified to advise you on real estate matters only. If you need legal or tax advice, it is your responsibility to consult a licensed attorney or accountant.

Any complaints about a real estate agent may be filed with the Real Estate Commission at 500 North Calvert Street, Baltimore, MD 21202. (410) 230-6200.

This notice is information required by law and is **NOT A CONTRACT**

We, the ❑ Sellers/Landlord   ❑ Buyers/Tenants acknowledge receipt of a copy of this disclosure and that

_____ (firm name)

and_____(salesperson) are working as:

    ❑   seller/landlord's agent
    ❑   cooperating agent
    ❑   buyer's agent
    ❑   dual agent (See Consent Dual Agency form)
(You may check more than one box)

_____   _____
Signature   Date   Signature   Date

I certify that on this date I made the required agency disclosure to the individuals identified below and they were unable or unwilling to acknowledge receipt of a copy of this disclosure statement.

_____
Signature of agent   Date

_____   _____
Name of individual to whom disclosure was made   Name of individual to whom disclosure was made

■ PRESUMED BUYER'S AGENCY RELATIONSHIP [§17-533]

The Brokers Act has stated since January 1, 1999, that a licensee who assists a prospective buyer in finding property to buy—and is neither affiliated with nor acting as the broker of the listing company for the property shown—is *presumed by law* to be representing the purchaser. A licensee shall orally inform the prospect that the licensee represents him or her unless or until the prospect declines that representation. At the same time, the licensee should present the prospect with the Commission's form describing the various kinds of agents. It is extremely important to remember that neither (1) informing the prospect about buyer representation nor (2) presenting the agency disclosure form creates an express buyer-broker relationship for which compensation may be claimed. The licensee owes much to the prospect (presumed client), but the prospect owes nothing to the licensee.

Affiliates acting under presumed buyer representation may lawfully show prospects properties listed with other firms. But because the prospects have not agreed to *contractual* buyer representation, they are free to walk away and later buy through another firm any or all property they have been shown by the first firm. *Presumed clients* may walk away at any time while the licensee continues in the role of *presumed buyer representative*. They have all the freedom of customer-prospects and also the right to expect client-level service—all without any financial responsibility to the firm that is serving them. Of course, prospects being assisted as customers also are free to walk away from the company that has been assisting them, but they have had no claim to fiduciary duties—to client-level service.

Brokers should periodically reexamine and, where necessary, revise their policy and procedure manuals, office standard operating procedures, and all representation agreement forms to take into account the categories of representation in the present law including, of course, presumed buyer representation.

Before 1999, the statute presumed just the opposite—that the prospect was simply a customer. This significant reversal has caused considerable confusion among long-time agents.

Why was this change made? It is intended to protect the average poorly informed prospect. In the past most prospective buyers or tenants *thought* that the salesperson working with them was *their* agent and was "on their side." After all, the salesperson was polite and helpful and appeared knowledgeable. So they told the "agent" all their secrets. Now the law *requires* that the salesperson be on the prospect's team until either the prospect or the licensee expressly declines to continue this presumed relationship. This discourages a licensee from picking prospects' brains—learning their bargaining strategy and degree of urgency to find a property and then using that information against them by telling these things to a client-seller, giving that seller a considerable bargaining advantage. Such information is now considered *confidential*, even after the presumed agency ends.

Fiduciary Duties to a Presumed Client

During the period of presumed buyer representation, the licensee and that licensee's firm owe the potential buyer full fiduciary duties. One of those duties—loyalty—includes **confidentiality.** This means that whatever the presumed client says to the licensee must be treated as confidential from then on. This is true even if the presumed client (buyer prospect) walks away and never comes back. It is also true if the presumed client later refuses both presumed representation and contractual, formal representation. Confidentiality continues—even if the presumed client dies!

Disclosures made by the presumed client remain confidential even after termination of presumed agency. In addition, any facts learned from prospects during the period of presumed buyer representation must be kept confidential by the licensee and not be used to that client's disadvantage in any later negotiations.

To avoid this potential conflict-of-interest problem, some firms make it their policy for affiliates to decline presumed buyer representation very early in their contacts with prospects. This refusal to engage in presumed buyer representation can be made orally or in writing. Other firms leave the decision of whether to engage in presumed representation up to each affiliate.

Ending Presumed Representation

Other than by entering into a formal written buyer representation agreement, presumed agency representation of buyers ends only when one of these three things occurs:

1. The licensee or the buyers reject the presumed relationship. (This can be done orally.)
2. The buyers either begin negotiations or wish to draw up an offer for the purchase of a specific property listed with another firm.
3. The buyers wish to be shown a property listed with the licensee's own company.

Instance Number 1 may occur at any time before either the second or third instance occurs.

■ AGENCY DISCLOSURE: UNDERSTANDING WHOM REAL ESTATE AGENTS REPRESENT

Timing of Presentation [§17-530]

The Brokers Act requires that all licensees who are representing sellers disclose to buyers, or to the agents of the buyers, the fact that they (the licensees) are representing sellers. When they represent buyers, they are similarly required to disclose that fact to sellers or sellers' agents.

Under the Brokers Act, this disclosure must be made *no later than the first scheduled face-to-face meeting* with such parties. The author believes it is wiser to make the disclosure *at first contact*, as required of REALTORS® by their national organization, the National Association of REALTORS® (NAR), in its Code of Ethics. Perhaps one-third of all licensees in Maryland are not REALTORS® and are subject only to the Real Estate Commission's authority.

Again, the form that the Commission requires *all* licensees to use in disclosure of representation is presented in Figure 2.1.

This form is not a contract; it is an information piece on which signatures of prospects and licensee are requested. However, the prospects' signatures are *not required* for the presentation of the form to be effective. If the prospect will not sign it, the law allows the licensee alone to sign it, stating that the prospects could not or would not sign. Dates recorded on the form show that the disclosure was made in a timely way so as to satisfy the law.

What This Form Doesn't Do

There are two things that presenting this form *does not* do. It does not end presumed buyer representation and it does not create a formal buyer-representation contract. Though many licensees think that the form does one or both of those two things, it does neither.

Contents of Form

On this form, the buyers can see which of the four types of agent their salesperson is acting as in dealing with them. It is basically an information form about how real estate agents in general may work and how this salesperson, in particular, is working.

Decisions at Presentation

Buyers who receive this form may simply read it and, possibly, sign it. If they do not expressly reject presumed buyer representation at this point, the presumed representation continues. Buyers are free to reject both presumed and formal, written representation. If they do so, they continue *as customers* to be assisted in seeking a property to buy. They will then, of course, receive customer-level service.

If the buyers want *formal* buyer representation with its client-level service, they must enter into a written agreement with the licensee's firm to represent them as purchasers. Details of this form, the *Buyer Representation Agreement*, are found in Chapter 4.

■ THE CLIENT'S RIGHT OF CONFIDENTIALITY [§17-532]

Whatever **confidential information** a licensee learns from individuals while representing them—either under a formal representation agreement or as a presumed buyer representative—such as information about their personal finances, bargaining strategy, and motivations to buy or to sell, must of course be kept confidential throughout the conduct of the entire transaction. In addition, the confidentiality continues even after the agency ends, after a transaction is completed, even after a written agency agreement expires. Previously confidential information may be disclosed with the written permission of the former client or when the information has become public knowledge by the former client's publication of it.

Agents are forbidden, for example, to reveal confidential information to other clients whom they may later represent—or to other agents in their own company who may represent parties negotiating with the previous clients—or to use such "inside information" to the disadvantage of the previous clients.

When licensees later represent new clients in a transaction involving the former client, they must disclose to the new clients that they cannot reveal to them confidential matters about the old client.

The subject of confidentiality is so important that it deserves repeated explanation and clarification in a company's regular training sessions for sales personnel. Awareness of the need for greater confidentiality should reduce or even end casual office conversation about cases, clients, and customers.

Brokerage offices that practice dual agency should provide secure files, or other security arrangements, so that confidential information about buyers or sellers in the same transaction is kept segregated and does not fall into the hands of the intracompany agent representing an **adverse** (opposite) party. The broker—who is actually the dual agent—has full access to all this information but is forbidden by law to share it with adverse parties in any transaction unless required by court order or by the requirement to disclose newly discovered material facts. Of course, material facts should *never* be treated as confidential, because they must be revealed to all parties in every case.

■ AGENCY RELATIONSHIP NOT DETERMINED BY WHICH PARTY PAYS [§17-534]

Maryland law now clearly states that agency relationships and responsibilities are *not* determined by which party pays for brokerage services. Before 1998, when this principle was spelled out in the Brokers Act, it was already part of the common law but unknown to most licensees.

Application of This Principle

For example, when sellers pay—or agree to pay—a brokerage fee charged by a buyer broker, this payment does *not* make that broker the sellers' agent. This prevents a claim by the seller in this example that the licensee representing the buyer should have worked in that seller's best interest. It also prevents buyers from claiming that the licensee engaged to represent them was really under the control of the seller. Before the statute clarified this issue, such claims had been used (however improperly) to attack and seek rescission of sales agreements on the basis of "undisclosed dual agency."

This matter is *counterintuitive*—it goes against conventional wisdom and also against what many students have actually heard in previous classes. Pay particular attention to it.

> *The payment or promise of payment of compensation to a licensed real estate broker by a seller, lessor, buyer, or lessee, or by a licensee acting for a seller, lessor, buyer, or lessee: (1) is not determinative of whether a brokerage relationship has been created or exists; and (2) does not create or determine the existence of a brokerage relationship between a broker and a seller, lessor, buyer, lessee, or licensee.*

Worse yet, it is *not* necessary for a brokerage fee to be promised or paid to *create* an agency relationship with a licensee. Certain behaviors and statements of a licensee may properly be construed (interpreted) by a member of the public—and later by a court—to indicate that the licensee is indeed their agent, even without a formal agreement.

Consider this example: A licensee who says to a customer, "Trust me; I'll get you a great deal," is asking the customer to regard him or her as trustworthy and loyal, that is, as the customer's agent. If this occurs while the licensee is already serving as agent or subagent for the sellers in the same transaction, an undisclosed (probably unintended, but certainly unlawful) dual agency is created that may later prove to be the basis for rescission of sales contract, loss of commission, suit for damages, and disciplinary action by the Commission.

Last, but unfortunately not least, the person to whom the licensee owes loyalty (because of a careless remark) owes the licensee nothing for his or her trouble! This **implied agency,** like presumed representation, can amount to all work and no pay.

Remember: no individual licensee can *directly* and *personally* represent both parties to a residential transaction. When a brokerage firm is properly involved in a dual agency situation, its broker *is* the dual agent but does not directly and personally deal with the parties; the broker appoints intracompany agents to do so.

■ DISCLOSURE AND FAIRNESS [COMAR 09.11.02.02 A]

According to the Code of Ethics of the Commission, the obligation of absolute fidelity to the client's interest is primary, but it does not relieve licensees from the statutory obligation to deal fairly with all parties to a transaction and to reveal material facts.

Statutory attempts to guarantee fairness by requiring disclosures often miss their mark. This is because members of the public often receive so many lengthy and technical disclosures that they have little or no grasp of what is being disclosed! Hurrying prospects through the signing of disclosure forms and perhaps saying, "These are merely formalities required by law," amounts to an attempt to make the disclosures ineffective and must be avoided.

QUESTIONS

1. Real estate brokers' principals are their
   1. managers.
   2. clients.
   3. prospects.
   4. customers.

2. In handling a transaction involving any purchase and sale of residential real property, a real estate broker
   1. is the agent of the owner of the property being sold.
   2. may not act as the agent of the buyer.
   3. may not represent both buyer and seller in the same transaction without designating two intracompany agents.
   4. may not personally represent both buyer and seller unless both parties agree.

3. Arthur has been assigned by his broker, Marie, to work with Tony to provide buyer representation for the purchase of a property listed by Charise, a salesperson with Marie's company. Marie has named Charise to represent the seller. In this situation, which of the following is *TRUE*?
   1. Tony is a prospect; Arthur is his intracompany agent; Marie is a single agency broker; Charise is the intracompany agent for the seller.
   2. Tony is a client; Arthur is his intracompany agent; Marie is a disclosed dual agent; Charise is the intracompany agent of the purchaser.
   3. Tony is a customer; Arthur is his salesperson; Marie is an intracompany agent; Charise represents the seller.
   4. Tony is a client; Arthur is his intracompany agent; Marie is not a single agency broker; Charise is the intracompany agent for the seller.

4. Brokers who represent buyers of real estate
   1. are regarded by the law as dual agents in such transactions.
   2. must disclose this agency relationship to sellers.
   3. are in violation of the Brokers Act.
   4. will not be compensated.

5. Which of the following statements is *TRUE* concerning presumed buyer representation?
   1. Presumed buyer representation begins when a licensee shows a prospective purchaser a property listed by another brokerage firm.
   2. Presumed buyer representation ends when a licensee shows a prospective purchaser a property listed with another brokerage firm.
   3. A prospective purchaser who declines to enter into a buyer representation agreement is no longer owed confidentiality for matters discussed with the licensee who had been providing presumed buyer representation up to that point.
   4. A licensee is no longer the presumed buyer representative of a purchaser who makes an offer on a property.

6. Which statement concerning agency is *TRUE*?
   1. The broker is the agent of the party who is paying for his or her services.
   2. The broker is allowed to be a dual agent in a transaction if no harm is done.
   3. The salesperson may personally act as dual agent if both buyer and seller agree in writing.
   4. The broker who represents both buyer and seller in the same transaction must appoint two intracompany agents.

7. Agents' duties to their principals include
   1. disclosure of all facts.
   2. loyalty.
   3. presentation of all written offers.
   4. all of the above.

8. Under the Brokers Act, licensees who are representing sellers must disclose this fact to buyers or to the agents of the buyers
   1. at first contact.
   2. when an offer is made.
   3. not later than the first scheduled face-to-face meeting.
   4. when the buyer or agent of the buyer asks.

9. Which of the following does a licensee *NOT* owe to a customer?
   1. Due care
   2. Disclosure of material facts
   3. Obedience
   4. Honesty

10. Which of the following statements about agency is *TRUE* in Maryland?
    1. This State does not allow a brokerage firm to represent both buyer and seller in the same transaction.
    2. Dual agency in a transaction is permitted only in brokerage firms consisting of three or more licensees.
    3. Licensee Mary's performance of ministerial duties for a customer justifies the claim by that customer that Mary ". . . acted in a way that indicated she was my agent."
    4. The broker of a firm may act as one of the two intracompany agents required for dual agency.

3

REAL ESTATE BROKERAGE

■ OVERVIEW

In this chapter, you will be introduced to many requirements for proper conduct of real estate brokerage operations. They include forms of business organization through which services may be delivered; supervisory responsibilities of brokers and branch managers; evidences of reasonable and adequate supervision; activities that personal assistants may and may not engage in; how affiliates relate to the brokerage firm; and requirements for disclosing licensee identity in advertising. This information is not only basic to passing the state licensing examination, it is fundamental to proper conduct as new licensees.

■ BROKERAGE [§17-101]

As referenced in Chapter 1, the Brokers Act defines **real estate brokerage** as performing certain services *for another person in return for consideration*. These services are

- selling, buying, exchanging, or leasing real estate;
- collecting rent for the use of any real estate;
- giving assistance in locating or obtaining any residential real estate for purchase;
- regularly dealing in real estate or in leases or options on real estate;
- promoting the sale of real estate by listing it in a publication issued primarily for promoting real estate sales;
- subdividing land and selling the divided lots; and
- acting as consultant in any of these activities.

Title 09 of the Code of Maryland Regulations (COMAR) recites the numerous specific ways that the Brokers Act is to be applied to every aspect of providing brokerage services. Although relevant sections of COMAR have long been published in the same bound booklet with the Brokers Act, they come from a different source.

COMAR includes regulations created by the Real Estate Commission with the guidance of the Department of Labor, Licensing, and Regulation and under the authority of the Brokers Act. For licensees, these regulations have the *force of law* although they are "only" regulations.

■ ORGANIZATION OF BROKERAGE FIRMS [§17-321]

The Role of the Broker   The broker doesn't have to be a partner in the partnership that owns the firm; the broker doesn't have to be an officer, board member, or stockholder of the firm, or an officer of the limited liability company (LLC). Neither does the broker have to be the owner of a sole proprietorship to be its broker. Brokers may provide real estate brokerage services through any of the forms of business organization if they are employed by or have another contractual relationship with that firm and have been designated by the firm as its broker, personally responsible for the provision of real estate brokerage services.

Prior to delivering brokerage services through any one of the organizational forms, brokers must submit notice to the Real Estate Commission of their intention to do so. The notice must include

- the name of the real estate broker submitting the notice,
- a statement that the named individual has been designated as the broker of the firm,
- the address of the firm's principal place of business and of each proposed branch office,
- any designated name that the firm intends to use in conducting its business, and
- a list of all the licensed associate real estate brokers and licensed real estate salespersons who will be affiliated with the broker of the firm and any other information that the Commission may require by regulation.

The Commission maintains current information regarding every corporation, partnership, LLC, or sole proprietorship through which Maryland real estate brokerage services are provided.

Any individual who assists in providing brokerage services for a firm while associated with the firm as a partner, officer, shareholder, or in any other capacity must hold either a salesperson's or an associate broker's license, but company officers, shareholders, corporate board members, and so forth who do not personally involve themselves in providing brokerage services do not need to be licensed.

A brokerage firm—whether corporation, partnership, or LLC—that provides real estate brokerage services is not relieved from responsibility for the acts or omissions of its officers, partners, employees, or agents. The form of its organization does not shield it from such accountability.

Similarly, individuals who provide real estate brokerage services through—or on behalf of—corporations, partnerships, and so forth are not relieved of individual responsibility for their actions in providing those services because of the way they are affiliated with the firm, either as employees or nonemployees.

Limitation on Affiliates Interests' [§17-511]

Not more than 50 percent of ownership control in any form of business organization providing real estate brokerage services may be held directly or indirectly by salespersons or associate brokers or any combination thereof, including their immediate family members. Otherwise, affiliates might become able to control their principal, the broker, rather than the other way around. When affiliates apply for licenses or renewals, they report to the Commission the percentage of control they hold in the firm. This percentage must include other percentages held by immediate family members who are not themselves licensees in that firm. Immediate family members who are licensees will report their own percentages of ownership on their license applications.

Affiliation Arrangements [§17-321]

Brokers may provide brokerage services personally and/or through real estate salespersons or associate brokers licensed under them. Such affiliates typically are nonemployees (qualified real estate agents, as explained in Chapter 2), but employee status is also available. Qualified real estate agents (nonemployee affiliates) are often referred to as *independent contractors*, when, in fact, independent contractor status as defined by common law is a very elusive thing to describe or demonstrate. Qualified agent status is easy both to define and prove, as shown in Chapter 2 of this book. Any individual, including a licensed associate real estate broker, who provides real estate services on behalf of a real estate broker shall be considered a real estate salesperson with respect to the provision of those services. Licensed associate brokers have no more authority than salespersons and perform the duties of salespersons.

■ SUPERVISION [§17-320 AND COMAR 09.11.05]

Supervision means direction and review of professional real estate activities. Commission Regulation 5 requires that brokers supervise all licensees affiliated with them whether those affiliates are simply employees or are qualified real estate agents—self-employed **independent contractors.** Affiliates may not operate unsupervised no matter how they are affiliated with the firm.

There is a misunderstanding of this matter among many affiliates and some brokers, who dwell on the word *independent* in "independent contractor." Affiliates are in no way independent from their broker and the broker's supervision and control. Brokers can tell their affiliates not only what to do but how to do it. After all, the broker is responsible both to the Commission and to the courts for the conduct of their agents (affiliates). Salespersons and associate brokers are general agents of their broker; their broker is their principal.

There is a general legal rule that principals are responsible for the actions of their agents in the agents' performance of their duties. It follows that because brokers are responsible for the actions of their agents, they must have the authority to control them. Moreover, a broker cannot escape the duty to supervise by claiming, "My salespersons are independent contractors, so I can't tell them how to conduct their brokerage activities," or, "I can't be watching my agents all the time."

Brokers are also to direct and review the supervisory activities of each branch office manager. These **branch office managers** (who must be licensees with at least three years' active brokerage experience) are charged with responsibility to supervise the professional real estate activities of associate brokers and salespersons registered to their office. Brokers do not supervise affiliates in branch offices personally, but through their branch office managers. The supervisory duty of the branch manager is in *addition* to, rather than in place of, the supervision of the firm's broker.

Factors to be considered in determining reasonable and adequate supervision include but are not limited to availability of

- regular training or education sessions held at least once every two months;
- experienced supervisory personnel to review and discuss contract provisions, brokerage agreement provisions, and advertising;
- written procedures that give clear guidance for handling deposit monies and other funds;
- compliance with all fair housing laws and regulations;
- advertising requirements for real estate transactions;
- review of all contracts that have been signed by all parties;
- use and limitations of unlicensed personal assistants;
- disclosure of agency relationships by licensees in real estate transactions;
- obligation of all licensees to comply with the Broker Act, the Commission's Code of Ethics, and all applicable local, State, and federal laws and regulations;
- restrictions on the sale or lease of a licensee's real property and the purchase or leasing of real property by licensees for their personal use; and
- the unauthorized practice of law by a licensee.

In addition, the broker or office manager wishing to prove reasonable and adequate supervision must have evidence of

- affiliates' attendance at sales meetings;
- review of all executed contracts;
- review of all advertisements placed by any affiliate;
- compliance with the firm's written procedures and policies and distribution to affiliates of those written policies and procedures; and
- procedures for informing affiliates of new or changed real estate laws and regulations.

These examples of "reasonable and adequate" supervision impose a substantial burden on brokers to maintain a "paper trail" of many events and actions. When brokers charged with failure to provide such supervision cannot show evidence of meeting these requirements, they are presumed to have failed to supervise and the burden of proof of supervision falls on them.

■ PERSONAL ASSISTANTS

Some salespersons and associate brokers use personal assistants to help them in the conduct of their work. Some of these assistants hold real estate licenses, while others do not. Neither the Brokers Act nor COMAR makes specific mention of personal assistants. However, a 1994 memorandum from the Commission states, in pertinent part,

> *Licensees should be extremely careful in delegating responsibilities to others. They should also be aware that, under the Internal Revenue Code, a person whom they hire to assist them will most likely be considered an employee of the licensee who retained him or her and the licensee would be liable for complying with all IRS requirements on record keeping and payroll deduction, as well as being responsible for carrying workers' compensation insurance.*

The document urges seeking legal counsel for specific situations. Then, referring to individuals acting as personal assistants, the publication continues:

> [U]nlicensed persons, *as well as licensed agents from other firms employed by associate brokers or salespersons* [emphasis added] may not provide real estate brokerage services.

Presumably this prohibition on licensees' performing real estate brokerage services applies *when they are acting as personal assistants and employees of a licensee they are assisting.*

Duties of Personal Assistants

The Commission's guidelines specify what personal assistants may and may not do. Note that the word *licensee* as it appears below means a licensed associate broker or salesperson affiliated with the firm in which he or she is acting as a personal assistant. A licensed affiliate is regarded as "unlicensed" when assisting in a firm other than his or her own.

An **unlicensed personal assistant** *may*

- answer the telephone and forward calls to a licensee;
- submit listings and changes to a multiple-listing service;
- follow up on loan commitments after a contract has been negotiated;
- assemble documents for closing;
- secure documents (public information) from courthouse, public utilities, and so forth;
- have keys made for company listings;
- write ads for approval of licensee and supervising broker and place advertising;
- type contract forms at the direction of and for approval by licensee and supervising broker;
- compute commission checks;
- place signs on property;
- arrange the date and time of home inspection, termite inspection, mortgage application, well or septic inspection, presettlement walk-through, or settlement;

- prepare flyers and promotional information for approval by licensee and supervising broker;
- perform courier service, for example, delivering documents and picking up keys;
- schedule an open house;
- schedule appointments for licensee to show listed property; and
- accompany a licensee to an open house or showing

1. for security purposes, and
2. to hand out preprinted materials.

An unlicensed personal assistant *may not*

- prepare promotional materials or ads without the review and approval of the licensee they are assisting and the supervising broker or branch manager;
- show property;
- answer any questions on listings, title, financing, closing, and so forth;
- discuss or explain a contract, listing, lease, agreement, or other real estate document with anyone outside the brokerage;
- be paid on the basis of real estate activity, such as a percentage of commission, or any amount based on listings, sales, and so forth;
- negotiate or agree to any commission, split, management fee, or referral fee on behalf of a licensee;
- solicit property owners to list their property for sale, either in person or by telephone;
- solicit purchasers or lessees for the purchase or lease of real property;
- discuss with prospective purchasers or lessees the attributes or amenities of a property, whether at an open house or under any other circumstances;
- discuss with the owner of real property the terms and conditions of the real property offered for sale or lease;
- collect, receive, or hold deposit monies, rent, other monies, or anything else of value received from the owner of the real property or from a prospective purchaser or lessee;
- provide owners of real property or prospective purchasers or lessees with any advice, recommendations, or suggestions as to the sale, purchase, exchange, or leasing of the real property to be listed or real property presently available for sale or for lease; and
- hold himself or herself out in any manner, orally or in writing, as being licensed or affiliated with a particular company or real estate broker as a licensee.

A Possible Alternative   Some companies require that all personal help for an affiliate be delivered by a fellow licensee who works on the "buddy system" with the licensee being helped. Remuneration is paid by the firm's broker on an agreed-on apportionment of all commissions earned with the buddy's help. This way, the helper remains self-employed and the licensee receiving help has no administrative duties to perform on behalf of the helper—no withholding or reporting of income tax, Social Security, or Medicare; no contribution to the helper's

Social Security; and no premium for workers' compensation insurance on the helper. The broker remains the principal of both the licensee and the licensed buddy. The helping party is compensated from company commissions earned by their common effort.

■ SALES COMMISSION DISPUTES

The licensing law does not authorize the Real Estate Commission to arbitrate disputes between brokers or between brokers and salespersons over distribution of commissions. Such disputes should be submitted for arbitration to the respective Board or Association of REALTORS® if the parties to the dispute are members of the same board or to the Maryland Association of REALTORS® if the parties to the dispute are members of different boards or associations. Arbitration may be pursued through other agencies. To prevent commission disputes, the percentage and distribution of commissions should be agreed to in writing, especially those setting forth the agreement between brokers and their salespersons. Division of compensation between brokerage firms, however, is usually based on information in the published multiple listing.

■ PLACES OF BUSINESS–OFFICES [§17-517]

Each licensed real estate broker who is a *nonresident* of Maryland shall also maintain an office in Maryland if the state in which the nonresident broker resides requires that a resident of Maryland who is licensed in the other state maintain an office in that state.

The place of business in Maryland required by the Brokers Act for all broker licensees must be an office or headquarters where they and their employees and/or affiliates regularly transact real estate business. The Commission does not recognize mobile (rolling) offices. The broker's office is to be at a specific street address where investigators can readily find financial and other records. Records of the brokerage's transactions, including the records of the broker's escrow account, must be kept in a secured location at this stationary office. Commercial answering services, mechanical recording devices, or mail drops, singly or in combination, do not satisfy the requirement for an office. Brokers must display in their main offices their own licenses and the licenses of all their affiliates who work at that location.

The federal *Americans with Disabilities Act* requires that places of public accommodation make reasonable modifications to meet the needs of persons with disabilities. Real estate offices are such places. Access for the public should be barrier-free, and employees should be alerted to assist any physically challenged persons who visit an office. Moreover, every firm with 15 or more employees—and this includes affiliates—must make reasonable accommodation to the needs of any person with a disability who works for the firm.

Office Signs [§17-519]

A real estate broker must display a sign clearly visible to the public at each office and branch office that the real estate broker maintains. The sign must include the words *Realty, Real Estate,* or, where authorized by the respective trade associations, REALTOR® or *Realtist.*

Changes in Location [§17-520]

Within ten days of changing the location of any office, a real estate broker must submit

- written notice on a form provided by the Commission of such change in the address of the principal office and any branch office of the broker;
- the license certificate and pocket card of the broker or, for the branch office, its certificate; and
- the required fee.

Upon receipt of these things, the Commission issues a new certificate and card to the broker for the unexpired period of the broker's license or branch office certificate. If a real estate broker changes the address of the principal office or a branch office and fails to submit the required notice, the license of the broker is *automatically suspended* until the broker submits the required notice.

Branch Offices [§17-518]

Licensed real estate brokers may maintain branch offices in the State. They must appoint managers for each branch office who are either associate brokers or salespersons with three years of active experience. These managers must exercise reasonable and adequate supervision over the provision of real estate brokerage services by all affiliates working out of their branch offices. This responsibility is in addition to, not in lieu of, the responsibility of the broker. Licenses of all licensees working out of a branch office are displayed in that branch office together with a branch office certificate that shows, among other things, the name of the broker, as registered with the Commission, and the address of the main office.

Newly issued branch office certificates and their renewals are for two-year periods. There is a $5 fee for each certificate. Applications for branch office certificates must identify the individuals appointed as managers of the branch offices and be accompanied by payment of the required fees.

■ DISCLOSURE OF LICENSEE STATUS AND OF TEAM RELATIONSHIPS

Licensees within a company sometimes work with one another and also with nonlicensee support staff and call themselves a *group* or *team.* Licensees may not acquire an interest in or purchase, personally, for any member of their immediate family, their firm, any member of their firm, any unlicensed member of a brokerage group or team of which they are part, or any entity in which they have an ownership interest, property listed with them or their firm without making their true position known to the owner of the listed property.

When selling or leasing property in which licensees, their firm, or any member either of their immediate family, their firm, or any brokerage group or team of which they are a part have an ownership interest, licensees shall reveal that interest in writing to all parties to the transaction.

Moreover, when a licensee who is part of a group or team signs real estate documents, it must be in his or her own name and not in the name of the brokerage group or team.

■ ADVERTISING

Use of Designated Names [§§17-527.1, 17-527.2, 17-527.3]

A **designated name** is the name that appears on the license certificate of a licensee. Whenever brokers or affiliates, or individuals acting on their behalf, advertise in any medium, the advertisement must *meaningfully and conspicuously* present the designated name of that broker licensee as identified to the Commission. A franchise logo or a company logo, although it may appear in an advertisement, *does not satisfy* the requirement to identify the broker's firm. When an affiliate publishes his or her own name in an advertisement, it must be the full, legal name of the affiliate as shown on his or her pocket card and license certificate. The ad must *also* meaningfully and conspicuously display the designated name of the firm with which he or she is affiliated. Associate brokers and salespersons may not use their individual telephone numbers or e-mail addresses in advertisements unless the identified telephone number of their broker or branch office manager also appears in the advertisement. There is renewed emphasis on and active enforcement of these requirements.

The Broker Act states that **advertising** includes oral, print, and visual media. Its standards for advertising apply to

■ correspondence,
■ mailings,
■ newsletters and brochures,
■ business cards,
■ sale or lease sign riders,
■ promotional items,
■ automobile signage,
■ telephone directory listings,
■ radio and television announcements,
■ telephone solicitations, and
■ World Wide Web and Internet voice-overs.

Both the Brokers Act and COMAR require that all licensees show in all advertising the fact that they are licensees. This disclosure must be made even when the licensees are selling their own real property. Licensees may not advertise the listings held by other brokerage firms without prior approval by those firms.

Broker licensees using a franchise name in any advertising are required to include, clearly and unmistakably, their own name or their firm's designated name as registered with the Commission. Both brokers and their affiliates must make clear the designated name of the brokerage in every encounter—whether face to face or by radio, telephone, e-mail, or any other means.

Licensee "For Sale" signs displayed on property subject to ground rent must state the amount of the annual ground rent and the capitalization if the price of the property is shown. The lettering showing the ground rent and capitalization must be at least as large as the lettering showing the property sale price. The **capitalization** is the sum for which the land could be **redeemed**—purchased in fee—from its leasehold owner. Maryland ground rents are discussed in Chapter 13 of this book.

COMAR requires that a licensee obtain an owner's permission before placing signs on a property. Licensees should check local laws regarding the use of sale, directional, and open house signs on public property. They should also honor any restrictions imposed by cooperatives, condominiums, and homeowner associations. Licensees should familiarize themselves with HUD guidelines and rules concerning the use of the Equal Housing Opportunity logo or slogan in every display ad to avoid giving even the appearance of discriminatory practices.

■ FUNDS OF OTHERS HELD IN TRUST (TITLE 17, SUBTITLE V, PART I)

Trust money is defined as a deposit, payment, or other money that a person entrusts to a real estate broker to hold for the benefit of the owner or beneficial owner of that money and for a purpose that relates to a transaction involving real estate in this State.

The **beneficial owner** of funds in a trust account is that person, other than the owner (the source) of the trust money, for whose benefit a licensee holds the money. In summary, the *owner* of an earnest money deposit is the *purchaser* while the *beneficial owner* is the *seller*.

Management of Trust Money [§17-504]

The Brokers Act requires that when brokers receive trust money, such as earnest money deposits, and are not directed in writing to the contrary by the money's owner and beneficial owner, they must promptly deposit that money in a non–interest-bearing checking account, a non–interest-bearing savings account, or any combination of these accounts they maintain for that purpose in authorized financial institutions in Maryland. The account must be exclusively for the funds of others and contain none of the broker's or firm's funds. Real estate brokers may not use trust money for any purpose other than that for which it is entrusted to them.

Brokers are required to report the bank's name and the account's number to the Commission as soon as they start depositing trust monies there. If a licensee establishes another non–interest-bearing or special escrow account, changes an escrow account number, or transfers the account to another bank, the broker must notify the Commission in writing within ten days of such action. Trust monies from multiple transactions may be deposited in a single trust money account.

Associate real estate brokers or real estate salespersons who obtain trust money while providing real estate brokerage services shall immediately submit that money to the broker they represent.

Earnest monies must be deposited promptly, but in no event later than seven business days after acceptance of the contract by both parties. **Promptly** should be interpreted to mean "at the earliest opportunity."

Authorized Financial Institutions [§17-503]

Except when directed to the contrary in the fully signed purchase agreement, brokers must deposit all trust money in an escrow account in a financial institution located in the State whose deposits are insured by the Federal Deposit Insurance Corporation, the Federal Savings and Loan Insurance Corporation, the National Credit Union Administration, the State of Maryland Deposit Insurance Fund Corporation, or the Maryland Credit Union Insurance Corporation.

Disposition of Trust Money [§17-505]

The Brokers Act sets forth several options under which a broker may release earnest money held in trust. These choices address both situations in which the transaction goes smoothly to settlement and those where one or both parties dispute the distribution of the deposit when the transaction has collapsed.

The Brokers Act requires that real estate brokers maintain trust money in an authorized account until one of four things happens:

1. The real estate transaction is consummated or terminated.
2. The real estate broker receives proper written instructions from the owner and beneficial owner directing withdrawal or other disposition of the trust money.
3. A court directs disposition of funds after a broker's interpleader.
4. The owner or beneficial owner of the trust money fails to complete the real estate transaction for which the trust money was entrusted.

In the fourth instance, prior to distributing the trust money, the real estate broker shall notify both the owner and the beneficial owners (from here on the author will call them *the buyer* and *the seller*) of the broker's intention to distribute the trust money to the party who, in the broker's good-faith opinion, is entitled to receive it in accordance with the terms of the real estate contract. This notice must be delivered either in person or by a combination of certified mail, return receipt requested, *and* regular mail.

This notification shall state whether the trust money will be paid to the buyer or the seller and tell both that either of them may prevent distribution of the trust money by submitting a formal, written, similarly delivered protest within 30 days. If neither party submits a protest within that time, the trust money will be distributed in accordance with the real estate broker's notice.

The authority to make such good-faith disbursement of funds must be given in the purchase agreement that entrusted the funds to the broker at the time of offer and acceptance. Without such authority the broker may not use this process to dispose of the funds.

All notices and responses in this matter must either be hand-delivered to both the buyer and seller or to the broker or be sent by certified mail, return receipt requested, plus regular mail to all the parties involved. Brokers who receive a letter of protest may distribute the trust money in accordance with one of the other three alternatives. If no written protest is received, real estate brokers shall distribute the trust money in accordance with the terms of the notice sent earlier.

When the duty of real estate brokers to maintain trust money in an account terminates, they must promptly account for all trust money. Real estate brokers may invest trust money as the owners and beneficial owners of the trust money instruct in writing or as the real estate brokers, owners, and beneficial owners make written agreement.

Earnest money deposits that accompany offers to purchase are typically not deposited in the firm's trust account until the negotiation to purchase is completed. At any time prior to that completion, the broker is not only free but obliged to return the deposit to the offeror-buyer on that offeror's request. If the broker has deposited the offeror's check, no refund is usually made until the check clears.

Records to Be Kept Secure [§17-507]

Licensees must maintain in a secured area within their office adequate records of all real estate transactions engaged in by them in the course of brokerage. The records of transactions, including bank accounts or deposits referred to in these regulations, are to be available during usual business hours for inspection by the Commission, its field representatives, or its other employees.

Authority to Sign Trust Account Checks [COMAR 09.11.01.20]

The firm's real estate broker must be the signer, or at least one of the signers, on checks drawn on escrow accounts that the broker is required to maintain. The broker may designate an alternate signer to sign checks. This designated alternate signer, however, must be a licensee. A nonlicensee may be a required cosigner on the broker's escrow account, provided all checks are also signed by a designated licensee. At least one licensee must sign every check.

QUESTIONS

1. Any outdoor sign or advertisement displayed on property for sale subject to ground rent
   1. must, if price is shown, also show the annual ground rent but need not show any other details until inquiry is made by a prospective purchaser.
   2. must, if price is shown, show ground rent and cost of capitalization in lettering no smaller than the lettering used for the price.
   3. need show only leasehold price.
   4. need show only leasehold price and the phrase *plus GR*.

2. When licensees advertise real property they have listed for sale,
   1. the name of the salesperson may not be included in the advertisement unless the identity of the broker is also included.
   2. only the broker's name is permitted in advertisements.
   3. the price of the property must be included in all advertisements.
   4. members of multiple-listing services may advertise any of the services' listings.

3. The designated place of business for a real estate broker's office required by law may properly be a
   1. telephone answering service.
   2. post office box.
   3. van or recreational vehicle registered with the Motor Vehicle Administration.
   4. definite office location.

4. A real estate brokerage firm performing activities for which a real estate license is required may be operated by
   1. real estate salespersons.
   2. an associate broker.
   3. any person holding a valid real estate license issued by the State Real Estate Commission.
   4. a licensed real estate broker.

5. Advertising by a broker must include the
   1. designated name of that broker as registered with the Commission.
   2. name of the broker's REALTOR® board or association or Realtist organization.
   3. name of the licensed real estate broker.
   4. name of the licensee who listed the property.

6. In Maryland, the person primarily responsible for the real estate brokerage services provided through a corporation is the
   1. president of the corporation.
   2. licensed real estate broker of the firm.
   3. chairman of the board.
   4. majority stockholder of the corporation.

7. Salespersons may use their own names and phone numbers in advertising listed property if
   1. their broker affiliation is clearly shown and the firm's phone number clearly shown.
   2. their office manager's name is shown in letters at least half the size of the salespersons'.
   3. different colors for the broker's and salesperson's names are used.
   4. the broker gives permission.

8. When there are no instructions to the contrary from their owner and beneficial owner, the Brokers Act states that earnest money deposits
   1. may be commingled with the broker's funds.
   2. may be deposited in an insured and approved financial institution in Maryland.
   3. are to be placed in an interest-bearing account.
   4. may be withdrawn at any time prior to settlement as long as a licensee's signature appears on the escrow check.

9. A check drawn on a brokerage firm's escrow (trust) account
   1. must be signed by the associate broker of the firm using his or her designated name.
   2. must be signed by at least two licensees in the firm.
   3. may also be cosigned by an appointed non-licensee, if signed by a nonappointed licensee.
   4. does not need a second signature, if signed by the broker of the firm.

10. Unlicensed personal assistants may do all the following *EXCEPT*
    1. compute commission checks.
    2. submit listings and changes to a multiple-listing service.
    3. conduct an open house.
    4. schedule appointments for a licensee to show listed property.

4

LISTING AGREEMENTS AND BUYER REPRESENTATION AGREEMENTS

■ OVERVIEW

Maryland recognizes representation agreements between real estate brokers and sellers and also those between real estate brokers and buyers. (References to *buyers* and *sellers* should be understood, in this book, to apply to *tenants* and *landlords* whenever possible.)

Listings are agency agreements in which brokers agree to help sellers sell and sellers agree to compensate them for their service. These agreements may be either exclusive-right-to-sell, exclusive-agency, or open agreements as these terms are explained in the students' principal text.

The process of persuading a property owner to enter into such an agreement with a broker is called *listing a property*. It is typically done by affiliates (salespersons and associate brokers) on behalf of the broker. Although this procedure may later result in compensation for affiliates, only their broker and the client-seller are parties to the agreement. Moreover, the listing contract belongs to their broker.

Buyer representation agreements are agency agreements in which brokers agree to help buyers find property. They may be either exclusive buyer agency, exclusive-agency buyer agency, or open buyer agency agreements. These agreements are also typically arranged by affiliates but are contracts between their broker and the client-buyer and belong to their broker.

■ RESIDENTIAL BROKERAGE AGREEMENTS

No "Standard" Form

Realty industry boards and associations provide listing and buyer representation agreement forms for their members' use, but there is no standard form provided by either statute or regulation for either listing (seller representation) agreements or buyer representation agreements. However, the law has some specific requirements and prohibitions for whatever forms are used.

Required Provisions [§17-534]

All residential agency agreements—representing buyers or sellers, and open or exclusive—must be in writing and signed by the parties to the agreement. Copies are to be provided to all signers before the agreement is acted on by the firm.

Each agreement must state the duties and authority of the agent, the compensation to be paid to the agent, the performance that will call for such payment, and when payment is to be made. It also must state a definite date on which the agreement will end without further notice from either party. This makes it unlawful to include **automatic renewal provisions** in the agreement that would require a client to take any action to terminate representation at the end of the original term. Agency contracts may be extended only by signed, written extension agreements.

The agreement must set forth whether the agent is authorized to receive compensation from persons other than the client. Also, it must state whether the agent is authorized to cooperate with other brokers and share compensation with them. The agreement should either approve or refuse to approve compensation for cooperating agents (**subagents**) and/or for buyer brokers. In addition, the representation agreement must reveal the amount (usually expressed as a percentage) of the shared compensation with which other brokers will be compensated. Clients in agency agreements may not waive any of the above protective requirements in their contracts.

In their agency agreements (listings), most seller-principals can make choices with respect to dealing with buyer agents, subagents, and dual agents. These choices are indicated on the completed listing forms together with such routine issues as offering price, date of availability, acceptable forms of financing, and help with purchasers' closing costs.

Buyer-clients also indicate in their agency agreement whether they are open to negotiations that involve dual agency.

Net Listing Forbidden [§17-322(b) and COMAR 09.11.01.01 (b)]

Listings may not take the form of **net listing agreements** in which brokers retain all sale proceeds in excess of some minimum sales price agreed to by sellers.

Additional Offers: One Effect of *Silence* [§17-532(c)]

The Brokers Act states that when there is no express agreement to the contrary—that is, when there is *silence* about these matters—in the brokerage agreement, listing brokers

- *are not* required to seek additional offers for a listed property that becomes subject to a contract of sale, but
- *are* required to present additional written offers and counteroffers on a property that is "under contract" that come to the broker's firm.

Most listing agreements provided by associations in the industry do address these choices directly in the preprinted listing form, usually in a way that imposes the least burden on the brokerage firm. These forms do not require further showing and call for no presentation of later offers.

■ OTHER PROVISIONS

Ministerial Acts [§17-528, §17-532]

Ministerial acts are acts performed by a licensee that do not involve discretion or the exercise of judgment by that licensee. They may be performed on behalf of both clients and third parties (nonclients) before, during, and after the writing of a contract agreement. When agency agreements authorize agents to perform ministerial acts on behalf of third parties, those acts cannot be construed (interpreted) to violate the agents' duty of loyalty to their clients. Neither may they be construed to indicate an agency agreement between the nonclient and the licensee performing those acts.

Copies of Agency Agreements [§17-322(b) 15,16; COMAR 09.11.01.12]

Licensees must give copies of agency agreements with seller-clients to those clients before beginning to carry out the tasks assigned in the agreements. Licensees must also keep copies of all such agency agreements indefinitely. Although the statute and regulations do not make a parallel requirement for handling buyer representation agreements, it is clearly wise to apply the same standards to handling documents created for such agency.

Disclosure and Disclaimer Statement [§17-322(e) and COMAR 09.11.02.02(J)]

At the time of listing a residential property for sale, brokers are to present the Residential Property Disclosure and Disclaimer Statement to sellers for their completion and signature. They should warn sellers that neither disclosure nor disclaimer relieves them of the legal requirement to make voluntary disclosure to purchasers of all material property defects. Failure by either a buyer's or seller's broker to present this form to the buyer before presentation of a written offer opens the offending licensee to disciplinary action because that failure could result in a contract's becoming void or voidable.

Licensee Responsibilities for Disclosure [§17-530(b) and §17-533(i)]

Licensees already representing either a seller or a buyer must, at the first scheduled face-to-face meeting with the other party, disclose in writing their existing agency relationship, using the Relationship Information Form mandated by the Commission. (See Figure 2.2 in Chapter 2 of this book.) This is true even when representing a "presumed" client. In addition, a licensee serving in the capacity of presumed buyer agent must—at least orally—disclose that fact to the presumed client at the first opportunity and present the Relationship Information Form to that buyer.

An offer to purchase shall not be presented until the licensee has made sure that purchasers have received a copy of the *Maryland Residential Property Disclosure and Disclaimer Statement*. (See Figure 4.1.) Many agents leave multiple

FIGURE 4.1

Property Disclosure and Disclaimer Statement

MARYLAND RESIDENTIAL PROPERTY DISCLOSURE AND DISCLAIMER STATEMENT

Property Address: _____

Legal Description: _____

NOTICE TO SELLER AND PURCHASER

Section 10-702 of the Real Property Article, *Annotated Code of Maryland*, requires the owner of certain residential real property to furnish to the purchaser either (a) a RESIDENTIAL PROPERTY DISCLAIMER STATEMENT stating that the owner is selling the property "as is" and makes no representations or warranties as to the condition of the property or any improvements on the real property, except as otherwise provided in the contract of sale, or (b) a RESIDENTIAL PROPERTY DISCLOSURE STATEMENT disclosing defects or other information about the condition of the real property actually known by the owner. Certain transfers of residential property are excluded from this requirement (see the exemptions listed below).

10-702. EXEMPTIONS. The following are specifically excluded from the provisions of §10-702:

1. The initial sale of single family residential real property:
   A. that has never been occupied; or
   B. for which a certificate of occupancy has been issued within 1 year before the seller and buyer enter into a contract of sale;
2. A transfer that is exempt from the transfer tax under §13-207 of the Tax-Property Article, except land installment contracts of sales under §13-207(a) (11) of the Tax-Property Article and options to purchase real property under §13-207(a)(12) of the Tax-Property Article;
3. A sale by a lender or an affiliate or subsidiary of a lender that acquired the real property by foreclosure or deed in lieu of foreclosure;
4. A sheriff's sale, tax sale, or sale by foreclosure, partition, or by court appointed trustee;
5. A transfer by a fiduciary in the course of the administration of a decedent's estate, guardianship, conservatorship, or trust;
6. A transfer of single family residential real property to be converted by the buyer into use other than residential use or to be demolished; or
7. A sale of unimproved real property.

MARYLAND RESIDENTIAL PROPERTY DISCLOSURE STATEMENT

NOTICE TO OWNERS: Complete and sign this statement only if you elect to disclose defects or other information about the condition of the property actually known by you; otherwise, sign the Residential Property Disclaimer Statement. You may wish to obtain professional advice or inspections of the property; however, you are not required to undertake or provide any independent investigation or inspection of the property in order to make the disclosure set forth below. The disclosure is based on your personal knowledge of the condition of the property at the time of the signing of this statement.

NOTICE TO PURCHASERS: The information provided is the representation of the Owners and is based upon the actual knowledge of Owners as of the date noted. Disclosure by the Owners is not a substitute for an inspection by an independent home inspection company, and you may wish to obtain such an inspection. The information contained in this statement is not a warranty by the Owners as to the condition of the property of which the Owners have no knowledge or other conditions of which the Owners have no actual knowledge.

How long have you owned the property? _____

Property System: Water, Sewage, Heating & Air Conditioning (Answer all that apply)

Water Supply	❑ Public	❑ Well	❑ Other _____		
Sewage Disposal	❑ Public	❑ Septic System approved for _____(# bedrooms)			
Garbage Disposal	❑ Yes	❑ No			
Dishwasher	❑ Yes	❑No			
Heating	❑ Oil	❑ Natural Gas	❑ Electric	❑ Heat Pump Age ____	❑ Other _____
Air Conditioning	❑ Oil	❑ Natural Gas	❑Electric	❑ Heat Pump Age ____	❑ Other _____
Hot Water	❑ Oil	❑ Natural Gas	❑Electric Capacity _____ Age____	❑ Other _____	

Page 1 of 4

FIGURE 4.1

Property Disclosure and Disclaimer Statement (continued)

Please indicate your actual knowledge with respect to the following:

1. Foundation: Any settlement or other problems?   ❏ Yes   ❏ No   ❏ Unknown
Comments:_____

2. Basement: Any leaks or evidence of moisture?   ❏ Yes   ❏ No   ❏ Unknown   ❏ Does Not Apply
Comments:_____

3. Roof: Any leaks or evidence of moisture?   ❏ Yes   ❏ No   ❏ Unknown
    Type of Roof:_____Age_____
Comments:_____
    Is there any existing fire retardant treated plywood?   ❏ Yes   ❏ No   ❏ Unknown
Comments:_____

4. Other Structural Systems, including exterior walls and floors:
Comments:_____
    Any defects (structural or otherwise)?   ❏ Yes   ❏ No   ❏ Unknown
Comments:_____

5. Plumbing system: Is the system in operating condition?   ❏ Yes   ❏ No   ❏ Unknown
Comments:_____

6. Heating Systems: Is heat supplied to all finished rooms?   ❏ Yes   ❏ No   ❏ Unknown
Comments:_____
    Is the system in operating condition?   ❏ Yes   ❏ No   ❏ Unknown
Comments:_____

7. Air Conditioning System: Is cooling supplied to all finished rooms? ❏Yes ❏ No ❏ Unknown ❏ Does Not Apply
Comments:_____
    Is the system in operating condition? ❏ Yes   ❏ No   ❏ Unknown   ❏ Does Not Apply
Comments:_____

8. Electric Systems: Are there any problems with electrical fuses, circuit breakers, outlets or wiring?
    ❏ Yes   ❏ No.   ❏ Unknown
Comments:_____
    Will the smoke detectors provide an alarm in the event of a power outage? ❏Yes   ❏ No   ❏ Does Not Apply
Comments:_____

9. Septic Systems: Is the septic system functioning properly? ❏ Yes ❏ No ❏ Unknown ❏ Does Not Apply
    When was the system last pumped? Date_____   ❏ Unknown
Comments:_____

10. Water Supply: Any problem with water supply?   ❏ Yes   ❏ No   ❏ Unknown
Comments:_____
    Home water treatment system: ❏ Yes   ❏ No   ❏ Unknown
Comments:_____
    Fire sprinkler system: ❏ Yes   ❏ No   ❏ Unknown   ❏ Does Not Apply
Comments:_____
    Are the systems in operating condition?   ❏ Yes   ❏ No   ❏ Unknown
Comments:_____

11. Insulation:
    In exterior walls?   ❏ Yes   ❏ No   ❏Unknown
    In ceiling/attic?   ❏ Yes   ❏ No   ❏ Unknown
    In any other areas?   ❏ Yes   ❏ No   Where?_____
Comments:_____

12. Exterior Drainage: Does water stand on the property for more than 24 hours after a heavy rain?
    ❏ Yes   ❏ No   ❏ Unknown
Comments_____
    Are gutters and downspouts in good repair? ❏ Yes   ❏ No   ❏ Unknown
Comments:_____

Provided by the Maryland Real Estate Commission

F I G U R E   4.1

Property Disclosure and Disclaimer Statement (continued)

13. Wood-destroying inspects: Any infestation and/or prior damage? ❑ Yes   ❑ No   ❑ Unknown
Comments:_____
        Any treatments or repairs? ❑ Yes   ❑ No   ❑ Unknown
        Any warranties?   ❑ Yes   ❑ No   ❑ Unknown
Comments:_____

14. Are there any hazardous or regulated materials (including, but not limited to, licensed landfills, asbestos, radon gas, lead-based paint, underground storage tanks, or other contamination) on the property? ❑ Yes ❑ No ❑Unknown
If yes, specify below
Comments:_____

15. Are there any zoning violations, nonconforming uses, violation of building restrictions or setback requirements or any recorded or unrecorded easement, except for utilities, on or affecting the property? ❑ Yes ❑ No ❑ Unknown
If yes, specify below
Comments:_____

16. Is the property located in a flood zone, conservation area, wetland area, Chesapeake Bay critical area or Designated Historic District?
        ❑ Yes   ❑ No   ❑ Unknown   If yes, specify below
Comments:_____

17. Is the property subject to any restriction imposed by a Home Owners Association or any other type of community association? ❑ Yes   ❑ No   ❑ Unknown   If yes, specify below
Comments:_____

18. Are there any other material defects affecting the physical condition of the property? ❑ Yes ❑ No ❑Unknown
Comments:_____

NOTE: Owner(s) may wish to disclose the condition of other buildings on the property on a separate RESIDENTIAL PROPERTY DISCLOSURE STATEMENT.

The owner(s) acknowledge having carefully examined this statement, including any comments, and verify that it is complete and accurate as of the date signed. The owner(s) further acknowledge that they have been informed of their rights and obligations under §10-702 of the Maryland Real Property Article.

Owner _____ Date _____

Owner _____ Date _____

The purchaser(s) acknowledge receipt of a copy of this disclosure statement and further acknowledge that they have been informed of their rights and obligations under §10-702 of the Maryland Real Property Article.

Purchaser _____ Date_____

Purchaser_____ Date_____

Page 3 of 4

Provided by the Maryland Real Estate Commission

F I G U R E 4.1

Property Disclosure and Disclaimer Statement (continued)

MARYLAND RESIDENTIAL PROPERTY DISCLAIMER STATEMENT

NOTICE TO OWNER(S): Sign this statement only if you elect to sell the property without representation and warranties as to its condition, except as otherwise provided in the contract of sale; otherwise, complete and sign the RESIDENTIAL PROPERTY DISCLOSURE STATEMENT.

The undersigned owner(s) of the real property described above make no representations or warranties as to the condition of the real property or any improvements thereon, and the purchaser will be receiving the real property "as is" with all defects which may exist, except as otherwise provided in the real estate contract of sale. The owner(s) acknowledge having carefully examined this statement and further acknowledge that they have been informed of their rights and obligations under §10-702 of the Maryland Real Property Article.

Owner _____   Date_____

Owner_____   Date_____

The purchaser(s) acknowledge receipt of a copy of this disclaimer statement and further acknowledge that they have been informed of their rights and obligations under §10-702 of the Maryland Real Property Article.

Purchaser _____   Date_____

Purchaser _____   Date_____

Page 4 of 4

FORM: DLLR/REC/P/10-1-01Rev

Provided by the Maryland Real Estate Commission

copies of the form on a table in the for-sale property. Although this may indicate willingness to disclose, it does not take the place of obtaining a properly dated receipt for delivery of the form.

They must also provide to buyers on behalf of client-sellers the federal lead-paint disclosure form for properties built before January 1, 1978 (i.e., in 1977 or earlier), that buyers are considering. If the buyers are clients and the sellers are not represented by any licensee, it is the responsibility of the buyer's agent to procure any required lead-paint disclosure form and present it to buyer before presenting any offer from that buyer. There is one specific form for rental and a different one for sale properties. It is vitally important to use the correct one, because use of the wrong one is regarded by federal law as utter failure to meet the requirement and is subject to harsh penalties—up to $10,000 each—for repeated, deliberate violations. In addition to the appropriate form, prospective purchasers and tenants must be given the government booklet *Protect Your Family from Lead in Your Home*.

■ LISTING AGREEMENT PROPERTY INFORMATION

In agency agreements for the sale of a property, the age of the house, area of the lot, zoning of the property, taxes, and other detailed property information should appear in the portion of listing agreements that will be published. If accurate data are not available from the owner, the listing licensee should obtain correct data from public records or personal inspection. Estimates of such information and "educated guesses" are totally unacceptable.

Listing licensees should also examine any existing house location survey of the property, not what information it shows regarding property lines and improvements, and attempt to determine if it is thorough and up-to-date. Accurate information, responsibly presented in the listing, reduces chances for confusion and uncertainty when the property is shown and a contract offer prepared.

When describing the condition of the property in remarks distributed through the multiple-listing service (MLS), licensees must be careful not to say anything that buyers may later consider misrepresentation. Licensees must also take care not to insert information into the MLS that betrays sellers' confidentiality. *This obligation of confidentiality does not extend to material facts.*

Material Facts [§17-322(b)4 and COMAR 09.11.02.01(d)]

To prevent error and misrepresentation, the Commission's Code of Ethics requires that licensees make reasonable efforts to discover all material facts about each property they list. A **material fact** includes any negative information about a property that is not readily visible to or discoverable by a prudent purchaser and that would tend to discourage such a purchaser from going forward with a purchase. The Brokers Act requires that licensees disclose such information that they know, or should know, to each prospective buyer. This is a demanding requirement.

Stigmatized Property [§17-322.1]

A licensee may not be held personally liable for failure to disclose that an owner or occupant of the property is, was, or is suspected of being infected with human immunodeficiency virus (HIV) or diagnosed with acquired immunodeficiency syndrome (AIDS). In fact, it is a violation of federal and state law to communicate information about the alleged presence of such diseases, even when asked.

Moreover, Maryland statutes declare that the occurrence of a homicide, suicide, natural death, accidental death, or felony on a property is not a material fact that sellers or their agents are required to disclose. Therefore, failure to disclose them is not a basis for disciplinary action by the Commission or for a civil suit.

A licensee needs the express permission of sellers to reveal any of these latter, nonmedical facts to prospective purchasers or their agents, because such disclosure might impede the sale of the listed property. Notice that even when sellers have given permission to answer questions about these matters, under the Brokers Act licensees are not required to volunteer the information as they would be in the case of material facts. But to meet the requirement of truthfulness, they must answer prospects' questions about these matters when given sellers' permission.

Some licensees also consider it prudent to get their client-sellers' approval to *affirmatively*—that is, voluntarily and without being asked—*disclose* certain facts such as the reported history of homicide, suicide, natural death, accidental death, or felony on the subject property. They do this to prevent buyers, who often learn these facts on their own between contract and settlement, from trying to escape their contracts. If the buyers are reconciled to the facts before they sign their offer, they may be less likely to renege on (refuse to honor) their commitment.

■ RESIDENTIAL PROPERTY AND DISCLOSURE AND DISCLAIMER FORM [REAL PROPERTY ARTICLE 10-702]

The Broker Act directs the Commission to provide the Residential Property Disclosure and Disclaimer Statement (Figure 4.1) and require its use in residential transactions by all brokerage firms in Maryland. There are occasional additions to the form. Licensees are urged always to use the most current form. Failure to do so will likely expose seller-clients to the risk of rescission of sales contracts. Incidentally, sellers, although marketing their own residential property without broker assistance, are still required to present this form to purchasers before the offer to purchase is submitted.

Seller Disclosure

At the time a listing agreement is prepared and executed, this important document is to be completed by the sellers. This instrument affects all parties to a sales transaction. On this form, sellers choose whether to disclose the condition of a large number of physical features of the listed property. If they choose to make such disclosure, they should complete the form.

A **completed form** is one in which sellers respond to every inquiry on the Statement, even if only to say *unknown* or *not applicable*. By leaving even one response blank, the sellers fail to meet the obligations imposed by Maryland law. Such failure also enables the buyers to rescind the contract in the same way as if they had not been given the Disclosure and Disclaimer Form at all.

Disclaimer—"As Is"

If sellers choose not to disclose, they must complete the portion of the form that makes this refusal and states that they are selling the property "as is" except as otherwise provided in the sales contract. This four-page form—whichever portion is completed—signed and dated by the purchasers, is attached to and moves forward with the contract offer. Contrary to popular belief, use of the term *as is* does not free the sellers or their agents from the required affirmative (voluntary) disclosure of material facts.

Either disclosing or disclaiming may be more appropriate under certain market conditions— such as a buyers' market or a sellers' market—but licensees should not coach sellers in this choice. They should certainly not suggest use of the disclaimer as a means of withholding material facts. Nor should they guide the sellers' answer to any question in the Disclosure portion.

If sellers need guidance in these decisions and answers, they should turn to competent legal counsel and/or other technical experts. The responses are to be the representations of the owners, not the licensee.

Listing agents should obtain from sellers the completed Maryland Residential Property Disclosure and Disclaimer Statements at the time of taking listings. Listing licensees must inform sellers of their rights and obligations arising from this form. Completion of this form is required in all sales of residential properties containing four or fewer single-family units. (There are seven situations in which single-family properties being sold do not require the use of the form. These limited situations are listed in the preprinted Disclosure and Disclaimer Statement introductory paragraphs.)

Duty to Provide Purchasers with Statement

Maryland statutes make it the duty of sellers, even when selling their single-family residential real property "For Sale by Owner" (FSBO), to complete and deliver to each purchaser, upon or before entering into a contract of sale, a Disclosure and Disclaimer Statement in which either the Disclosure or the Disclaimer is completed. When sellers are represented by a licensee, it becomes the duty of that licensee to provide them with the form and explain to them their obligation to complete it for delivery to each buyer-prospect.

It is then the duty of a licensee representing client-buyers to explain their rights and obligations with respect to this form. If the buyer is not represented by a licensee, this duty falls on the licensee representing the owner-seller. The rights and obligations of all parties are listed in this form.

When listing licensees learn that prospective purchasers are planning to make an offer, they must make every effort to provide them with the Disclosure and

Disclaimer Statement in a timely manner. This can be done personally or through the buyers' broker.

When listing agents do not know in advance that an offer is forthcoming, they should present the completed Disclosure and Disclaimer Statement to the purchasers or their agent immediately when an offer is produced. The purchasers can then reconsider their offer in the light of the Disclosure and Disclaimer Statement before releasing the offer for presentation.

Effect of a Properly Completed Statement

When purchasers do receive the Disclosure and Disclaimer Statement before or on entering into the contract, they may not later rescind the contract of sale based on the information contained in the Disclosure and Disclaimer Statement.

Purchasers who do not receive this Disclosure and Disclaimer Statement before they enter into a sales contract retain the right to rescind the contract either for five days after they finally receive the form, until they apply for a loan, or until they occupy the property, whichever is earliest.

If purchasers never get a Disclosure and Disclaimer Statement and are never warned by a lender of the loss of their right to rescind, they may rescind at any time before settlement or before presettlement occupancy.

■ TERMINATION OF AGREEMENT [§17-322(10), §17-534]

Maryland law sets no minimum or maximum time periods for agency agreements. The term of such an agreement is negotiable between client and broker. Every listing and every buyer representation agreement must contain a definite termination date on which it will end without further notice from either party. Automatic extension provisions violate this law.

Unless the agency agreement states the contrary, licensees have no further obligations or duties to clients after termination, expiration, or completion of performance of the brokerage relationship, except to account for all trust monies and to keep confidential all personal and financial information about the clients or other matters that clients request be kept confidential.

Death of an **owner in severalty** (sole ownership) would normally terminate a listing agreement by operation of law. However, death of one owner, when a married couple has held title as tenants by the entirety, may not necessarily terminate a listing. It is prudent to have the language of a listing form reviewed by a firm's legal counsel to clarify whether such an agency agreement will be binding on a deceased seller's estate.

Licensees may withdraw from representing either buyer-clients or seller-clients who refuse to consent to disclosed dual agency and may terminate brokerage relationships with them. However, the Brokers Act states that dual agents, simply by making required disclosures of the existence of dual agency, have not thereby terminated their brokerage relationships.

In this State, a trustee sale, foreclosure sale, tax sale, or condemnation proceeding involving the listed property will generally terminate a listing.

■ DETERMINING AMOUNT AND DISTRIBUTION OF BROKERAGE FEES

Antitrust Compliance [*Commercial Law* Article §11-204]

Brokers (typically working through licensees affiliated with them) negotiate their compensation with the sellers *in each transaction*. The amount or commission rate charged in a transaction is not set by any law, regulation, association, or board. Clients and brokers negotiate rates. To suggest otherwise is a violation of federal and state antitrust laws and can bring severe penalties. Commission splits between and among brokers in cooperating situations are similarly negotiable. Commission schedules within brokerage firms are established by negotiation between the broker and the affiliates licensed under them.

Agency Relationship Not Created by Payment of Fee [§17-534(d)]

The Brokers Act specifically states that payments or promises to pay compensation to licensees do not determine that brokerage (agency) relationships have been created or exist, nor do they create brokerage relationships. Contrary to a long-held notion, *those who pay agents are not made clients of those agents just because of the payment.*

When Fee Earned and When Paid [Real Property §14-105]

Maryland law indicates that, unless there is a previous agreement to the contrary, listing brokers have earned their commissions when sellers accept and sign enforceable contracts of sale. Recent court cases have debated the definition of the term *enforceable*. Sellers typically pay brokerage commissions at settlement, using proceeds arising from the settlement. Brokers and homeowners may, however, agree at the time of listing that if settlement does not take place, no commission is due.

Agency Agreement Basic to Claim [§17-516]

According to the Brokers Act, persons performing brokerage services may not maintain an action (sue) for commission unless they had authority to provide those services at the time both of offering to perform and of performing the services.

Dual Agency Option

Licensees procuring a listing should introduce the sellers to the possibility of potential buyers' also being represented by their company. They should explain the concept of "intracompany agents" as outlined in the Brokers Act and seek the sellers' decision as to whether they will accept dual agency. Their response can be reflected in the provisions of the listing agreement itself.

Cooperation among Brokers [COMAR 09.11.02.03(b)]

The Code of Ethics states that brokers shall cooperate with other brokers on property listed exclusively by their firms whenever it is in the interest of their clients. The cooperating companies may then share commissions on a previously agreed-on basis. Negotiations concerning property subject to exclusive listings must be carried on solely through listing brokers.

In the listing interview, the broker must present to sellers the Relationship Information Form required by the Commission. (See Chapter 2.) Using the explanations contained in that form, the sellers may decide what, if any, relationship(s) they want their listing contract to permit with other real estate firms. Will it be cooperation with subagency? Will it be buyer brokerage? Will it be whichever of the two "happens"?

Sellers should be made to understand that licensees from other companies who represent a purchaser will not be representing them. Sellers should also decide if—and how—the commission they pay will be shared with another company if no subagency occurs when dealing with another brokerage. Many listing forms allow sellers to authorize their broker to work with and compensate buyer brokers by sharing part of the brokerage fee.

On the listing data form brokers submit to the MLS, they should show how sellers have decided to choose from among their representation options. They also will show the amount of the cooperating commission, if subagency is invited.

Listing to Be Signed [COMAR 09.11.01.12]

When all relevant data have been entered on the listing form, all persons who have an ownership interest in the property must sign it. Alternatively, persons who have proper authorization from the owners—such as attorneys-in-fact, acting under a properly drafted power of attorney—may sign the listing for them. Competent legal counsel should be consulted in approaching such situations. It is the responsibility of the listing agent to make sure that the signatures of all required parties are on a listing. A listing becomes effective on the date of the last required signature.

When separated or divorcing couples holding title as tenants by the entireties wish to list property, the author recommends consultation with the attorneys representing the parties. Because divorced parties may each retain interests, both their signatures likely will be necessary for an enforceable listing.

When sellers are corporations, trustees, guardians of minors, or personal representatives, documentation of the authority of persons signing the listing is often required. A licensee faced with such situations is urged to seek competent legal guidance.

Common Source Information Companies [§17-535]

The Brokers Act states that licensees who make use of common source information companies, such as MLSs, are not considered to be agents of those services or companies simply by virtue of their use of data from those companies. Licensees who participate in such companies are not thereby considered to be the agents or subagents of any client of another broker by reason of such participation. These information services may not restrict access to their services to licensees based on the level of their licenses.

Industry Forms [§17-312(17)]

The word REALTOR® and its related logo appear in the printed portion of many MLS listing and other contract forms. Licensees who use any form that bears the name of an organization of which they are not members violate the Brokers Act.

Several Boards and Associations of REALTORS® offer MLSs serving specific geographic areas. Listing contract forms and numerous addenda are available from local real estate boards, associations, and MLSs for the exclusive use of their members. There are often special forms for different types of property: residential for sale, commercial/industrial for sale or lease, income property, farms, commercial office rental, residential lots, unimproved land, condominiums, cooperatives, and businesses. Although the brokerage industry has produced forms for statewide use and regional use within the State, licensees should be alert to differences that still exist among those forms and between those forms and the forms unique to certain brokerage firms.

■ LOCAL REQUIREMENTS

Licensees should familiarize themselves with and conform to all relevant county and municipal requirements in areas where they provide real estate services. For instance, Baltimore County zoning regulations require "development plan notice and conveyances" to be provided to any purchaser of a home in any area covered by an approved development plan. In other counties, air traffic patterns are part of the information that prospective purchasers must receive. In 1998, Montgomery County greatly restricted the use of signs. That county has established special licensing requirements for persons who wish to post any signs in residential areas within that jurisdiction. Client-sellers should be made aware of any requirements that will impact their transaction.

■ OUT-OF-STATE LISTINGS

Maryland licensees are not authorized to show out-of-state property properly listed and advertised in Maryland unless they also have valid licenses issued in the state where the property is located and comply with all laws of that state.

QUESTIONS

1. Broker use of which type of residential listing agreement is illegal in Maryland?
   1. "Net"
   2. Exclusive-agency
   3. Open
   4. Exclusive-right-to-sell

2. A seller should complete the Residential Property Disclosure and Disclaimer Statement
   1. at settlement.
   2. when an offer is received.
   3. when the property is being listed.
   4. after a sales contract has been signed.

3. When purchasers receive no Residential Property Disclosure and Disclaimer Statement either before, at, or after entering into a purchase agreement, the
   1. contract is void by action of law after three days.
   2. purchasers may rescind the contract before they apply for a mortgage loan.
   3. contract is voidable by the purchaser for five days.
   4. lender has five days to tell the purchaser of the right to void the agreement.

4. Sellers must receive a copy of their listing agreement
   1. if they request it.
   2. before the broker advertises the property or offers it for sale.
   3. within 15 days after acceptance by the broker.
   4. only when a buyer is found.

5. To show a property located in the State of Virginia that is multiple-listed with a Maryland brokerage, a Maryland licensee MUST
   1. hold a Virginia real estate license.
   2. be a member of Maryland's multiple-listing service.
   3. be a Maryland broker licensee.
   4. hold a multiple-state license certificate.

6. A listing agreement form published by a multiple-listing service may be used by any
   1. broker or salesperson licensed by the Commission.
   2. member of any Board or Association of REALTORS®.
   3. licensed member of the organization that operates that listing system.
   4. licensee.

7. A listing on Maryland residential property
   1. may contain an automatic renewal provision.
   2. may be parol.
   3. must be in writing and signed by all parties.
   4. may leave the commission fee to be negotiated at the time an offer is made.

8. Purchasers who receive the Residential Property Disclosure and Disclaimer Statement before signing their contract offer may
   1. rescind the contract at any time up to three days after signing.
   2. rescind the contract at any time up to five days after signing.
   3. rescind at any time prior to settlement or to taking occupancy.
   4. not rescind the contract based on any facts the statement discloses.

9. The amount or rate of commission on a real estate sale
   1. must be stated in the listing agreement.
   2. is established by the Commission.
   3. is established by the local real estate Board or Association of REALTORS®.
   4. is established by law.

10. In Maryland, a residential listing agreement
    1. does not create an agency.
    2. may be oral.
    3. must be in writing.
    4. need not contain a definite termination date.

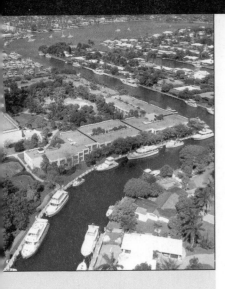

CHAPTER FIVE

INTERESTS IN REAL ESTATE

■ OVERVIEW

Freehold estates, such as fee simple absolute, fee determinable, fee conditional, and life estates—as well as future interests, such as remainder and reversion—are recognized in Maryland. Leasehold estates for years, from period to period, at will, and at sufferance are also recognized. In addition, the ground rent system, as described in Chapter 13 of this book, is found in several areas.

The legal life estates dower and curtesy have been abolished, and there is no homestead exemption in Maryland.

■ EASEMENT BY PRESCRIPTION AND ADVERSE POSSESSION

An **easement by prescription** may be acquired in Maryland when an adverse user makes use of another's land for the required period—20 years. Notice that the term *prescriptive* comes from what is *prescribed* by statute. **Adverse possession** for a similar, prescribed period, can also ripen into a claim for ownership. However, it must be not only open, hostile, continuous, and notorious occupancy but also under *claim of right* or *color of title*.

By requiring such claim or color, Maryland rejects *squatters' rights*. Squatters have no claim to land other than squatting on it; they are trespassers. Claim of right or color of title arises in a situation where an innocent buyer is deeded property by a person thought to be its owner but later proved not to be. Such an innocent buyer is said to be a *bona fide purchaser* (BFP) for value. Consult competent legal counsel in cases involving prescriptive easements and adverse possession.

■ RIPARIAN RIGHTS

Owners of real estate bordering a navigable body of water in Maryland have the common-law right to make a landing, wharf, or pier for their own use or for the use of the public. The right to make such an improvement is also subject to state and federal rules and regulations. The owner who makes such improvement owns the pier over the water but not the water beneath it.

Title to land beyond the mean (average) high-water mark of navigable waters, as well as to the waters themselves, belongs to the public. Regardless of the property descriptions in owners' deeds, they legally own their riparian property as far as the mean high-water mark. **High-water mark** is defined as the highest elevation of water in the usual, regular, periodic ebb and flow of the tide, not including storms or floods.

■ AGRICULTURAL LAND PRESERVATION EASEMENT

The Maryland Agricultural Land Preservation Foundation exists to purchase easements on land in certain areas for the purpose of restricting land to agricultural use. Details are contained in the *Agriculture* Article of the Annotated Code of Maryland. The State is actively purchasing development rights and seeking to slow residential subdivision of agricultural land. The State's purchases of these easements are funded in large part by the revenues produced by the real estate transfer tax. Further discussion is found in Chapter 14 of this book.

QUESTIONS

1. Easements to restrict land to agricultural use may be purchased by the
   1. Maryland Land Development Corporation.
   2. Maryland Department of Assessments and Taxation.
   3. Maryland Agricultural Land Preservation Foundation.
   4. Maryland Environmental Department.

2. In Maryland a person may acquire an easement over another person's land only
   1. after 10 years' continuous use.
   2. after 15 years' intermittent use.
   3. after 20 years' continuous use.
   4. if it is an easement by necessity.

3. Which of the following is recognized in Maryland?
   1. Dower
   2. Homestead exemption
   3. Curtesy
   4. Easement by prescription

4. Jefferson Thomas owns several acres of land in Maryland. His property is divided by a navigable river. Thomas has the right to
   1. build a pier on one of the riverbanks, subject to state and federal laws.
   2. construct a dam across the river to divert the waters into an artificial lake on his property.
   3. construct a wharf without state approval.
   4. make use only of the dry land.

5. Funds to purchase agricultural easements come from
   1. general (ad valorem) tax revenues.
   2. special assessments for this specific purpose.
   3. fines on developers who overdevelop agricultural land.
   4. transfer taxes imposed at the time of real estate transfers.

CHAPTER SIX

6

HOW OWNERSHIP
IS HELD

■ OVERVIEW

Maryland law recognizes ownership in severalty and various forms of co-ownership: tenancy in common, joint tenancy, tenancy by the entirety, partnership, and trust—all as described in the principal text. It also provides for condominium, time-share, and cooperative ownership.

■ FORMS OF CONCURRENT OWNERSHIP (CO-OWNERSHIP)

Tenancy in Common and Joint Tenancy

Unless the deed clearly specifies otherwise, a conveyance of Maryland real estate to two or more persons normally creates **tenancy in common.** To create a **joint tenancy,** it is necessary to use such words as ". . . to Fred Donaldson and Sam Roberts, as joint tenants and not as tenants in common." One might also add the phrase "with right of survivorship." However, a deed to a husband and wife is presumed to create a tenancy by the entirety unless it specifies tenancy in common or joint tenancy.

Tenancy by the Entirety

In Maryland, only a legally married husband and wife can own property as **tenants by the entirety.** (Common-law marriages cannot be established in Maryland but are recognized as valid if established in other jurisdictions that recognize and permit them.) Both husband and wife must sign a deed to convey property they hold as tenants by the entirety. Neither spouse who owns Maryland real property as a tenant by the entirety may petition a court for its partition.

Tenants by the entirety may grant their property back to themselves as either tenants in common or joint tenants, or they can grant the entire property either to one spouse or the other. They can do this without having ownership pass through the hands of a third ("straw") party. They can also deed their property into a trust. Competent legal assistance is always important in such transfers.

A tenancy by the entirety is terminated by the death of either spouse with the survivor holding the property in severalty. Notice that *severalty* appropriately describes the condition of being severed (separated) from others—and owning by oneself.

Although Maryland is not a community property state, at the time of divorce the Property Disposition in Divorce and Annulment statute has many of the same effects as community property rules that govern in other states.

On divorce or other legal termination of the marriage, tenants by the entirety are considered tenants in common, by operation of law. But when divorce occurs, causing the former couple's ownership to change to tenancy in common by action of law, a court may still delay any **partition proceeding** (division of the property by one against the other's will) for a period as long as three years. Normally, a tenancy in common, like joint tenancy, can be partitioned at any time by one tenant (owner) without the agreement of the other. The ban on partition after divorce can occur if the property is to be occupied as the "family home" by the custodial spouse with minor children.

Trust

The provisions of the *Uniform Partnership Act* apply in Maryland. The statute allows a corporation (as well as an individual) to become a member of a partnership. Also, the **real estate investment trust (REIT),** a form of unincorporated trust or association, has been recognized in Maryland since 1963. The procedures for forming or dealing with a REIT are legally complex. Brokerage licensees in any way involved with a REIT should strongly urge their clients to use legal counsel. The licensees themselves may be required by law to hold securities licenses to engage in such activities. The *Maryland Securities Act*, found in the Maryland Corporations and Associations Article, requires a securities license for persons engaged in selling securities that are real estate-related.

■ CONDOMINIUMS [REAL PROPERTY ARTICLE, TITLE 11]

Detailed provisions of the *Maryland Condominium Act* are contained in Title 11 of the *Real Property* Article of the Annotated Code of Maryland. Any licensee involved with condominium sales or development should obtain a complete copy of the law and seek competent legal advice. The Condominium Act is enforced by the Division of Consumer Protection in the Office of the Attorney General.

Definitions

A **condominium** is a property subject to a plan of organization called a *regime*. It is governed by a **council of unit owners,** which is either an unincorporated body or an unincorporated nonstock corporation. Persons who subject their property to a condominium regime are called *developers*. A condominium **unit** is a space described in three dimensions in the declaration and on the condominium plat.

All the parts of a condominium other than its units are **common elements.** There are **limited common elements,** identified in the declaration or described on the condominium plat, reserved for the exclusive use of one or more, but fewer than all, of the unit owners. **General common elements** are all the common elements except the limited common elements. The expenses and profits of the council of unit owners are called *common expenses* and *common profits*.

Converting Property to a Condominium

To create a condominium the property owner must expressly declare the intention to do so by recording a declaration, bylaws, and a plat of the proposed site. These documents must comply with statutory requirements. When this has been done, the property is then said to be under a condominium regime, and the owner is its developer. The declaration is indexed on the county records under both the name of the developer and the name of the condominium. The condominium regime must be registered with the Secretary of State before a condominium unit may be sold or even offered for sale. The declaration may subsequently be amended within certain limits only by the written consent of 80 percent of the unit owners at the time of amendment.

Public Offering Statement

A contract for the initial sale of a residential condominium unit to a member of the general public is not enforceable by the seller until the purchaser is given a copy of the Public Offering Statement registered with the Secretary of State. This Statement contains the proposed contract for purchase of units; the declaration, bylaws, rules, and regulations; proposed property management agreements; insurance policies; and maintenance agreements, as well as a proposed budget and financial reports. Many other items make this an extensive package for purchasers to read, study, and understand.

Whether they read the Statement or not, buyers may make written rescission of a purchase contract, without stating any reason, within 15 days after they receive it. They may also rescind that agreement within five days following receipt of any later, substantial amendments that the seller may make to the Statement. Buyers who rescind within these time limits are entitled to prompt return of all deposits.

Buyers who proceed to settlement lose their rights to terminate. However, sellers remain liable to buyers for one year for any damages suffered as a result of the sellers' failure to disclose material facts or their making any false or misleading statements. A purchaser's right to rescind or cancel under the Condominium Act may not be waived in the contract of sale.

Conversion of Residential Rental Facility

Before a residential rental facility can be converted to condominium ownership, tenants must be given notice in the form prescribed by law. This notice is also registered with the Secretary of State at the same time as the Public Offering Statement. A tenant may not be required to vacate the premises prior to the expiration of 180 days from the giving of notice, except for breach of the lease. However, the tenant may terminate the lease, without penalty for termination, by providing at least 30 days' written notice to the landlord after receiving proper notice of conversion. There are many other statutory requirements that protect tenants during conversion of a rental property to condominium.

Ownership of Units and Interests in Common Elements

In addition to exclusive ownership of a condominium unit, each unit owner has a right to share a defined, undivided percentage interest in the common elements of the property. Unit owners' undivided interests in the common elements cannot be partitioned or separated from the unit to which each percentage is assigned. All unit owners in a condominium are members of the council of unit owners. It is considered a legal entity even if unincorporated.

Organization: Declaration, Bylaws, Rules and Regulations

In addition to federal, state, and local laws and ordinances, a condominium is governed according to its declaration, bylaws, and rules and regulations. The rules must conform to the bylaws, the bylaws must conform to the declaration and the declaration is subject to the statute. In Maryland the statute—in some states called a *horizontal property act*—is called the *Maryland Condominium Act*.

The recorded declaration must contain at least the name by which the condominium is to be identified, including or followed by the phrase "a condominium." It must also contain a description of the land and buildings, with a statement of the owner's intent to establish a condominium regime; a general description and number of each unit, its perimeter, location, and other identifying data; a general description of the common elements and the units to which their use is restricted initially; the percentage interest in common areas related to each unit; and the number of votes at meetings of the council of unit owners that go with each unit. These related common elements and voting rights are **appurtenances,** that is, things of value that attach to a property.

At the least, the **bylaws** must express the form of administration; whether the council is to be incorporated; whether the council's duties may be delegated to a board of directors or manager, and what powers the owners have in directors' selection and removal; the council's mailing address; the procedure to be followed in council meetings; and the manner of assessing and collecting unit owners' respective shares of the common expenses. By law, the council of unit owners must be established within 60 days after the initial sale of units representing 50 percent of votes in the condominium. Bylaws of a condominium are recorded at the same time as its declaration. Unless higher percentages are required in the bylaws, they may be amended by the affirmative vote of unit owners having at least $66^2/_3$ percent of the votes in the council of unit owners.

In addition to rules set forth by the developer and recorded in the Public Offering Statement, the council of unit owners (or the board of directors, if so authorized in the bylaws) can pass rules to govern the condominium by majority vote at any properly advertised meeting held for that purpose. The bylaws specify what body originates and changes rules. They also define a quorum for the meeting at which rules are voted upon. A simple majority of those present and voting adopts rules. However, if 15 percent of *all owners* petition to disapprove the rule change, a special meeting of the council of unit owners is called. The rule change can be disapproved at that meeting if 50 percent of those owners present and voting vote for its disapproval. But among those voting for disapproval there must be at least 33 percent of the total votes possible if every unit owner had been present and voting.

Termination of Regime

Unless taken by eminent domain, a condominium regime may be terminated only by agreement of at least 80 percent of the unit owners, *or more if so specified in the declaration*. Upon termination of the regime, *and unless otherwise provided in the deed of termination*, the unit owners become tenants in common, with each owning an interest equal to the former percentage interest in the common elements.

Common Expenses, Taxes, Assessments, Liens

Unit owners are responsible for their percentage share of the common expenses of the council of unit owners. Assessments against each unit owner for common expenses are unrecorded liens on their units. A lien may be foreclosed in the same manner as a mortgage or deed of trust if it is recorded and action to foreclose it is brought within three years.

If the condominium is intended for residential use, the council of unit owners is required to maintain property insurance on common elements and units and comprehensive general liability insurance, including medical, in amounts set by the declaration, master deed, or the council.

Each unit is taxed as a separate and distinct entity on the county tax records. A delinquent tax on a specific unit will not affect the title to any other unit on which all taxes and assessments are paid.

Under the Consumer Protection Act of the *Commercial Law* Article of the Annotated Code of Maryland, certain condominium disputes will be investigated by the Division of Consumer Protection of the Office of the Attorney General, which is authorized to administer a program of voluntary mediation of condominium disputes involving unit owners, boards of directors, and/or councils of unit owners.

Resale of Unit

A contract for the resale of a unit by a unit owner other than a developer is not enforceable unless that contract contains, in conspicuous type, a notice in the form specified in the Condominium Act (Section 11-135). The unit owner is required to furnish four things to the purchaser not less than 15 days prior to the closing:

1. A copy of the declaration (other than the plat).
2. The bylaws.
3. The rules or regulations of the condominium.
4. A certificate containing statements concerning such things as monthly expenses, proposed capital improvements, fees payable by unit owners, financial statements of the condominium, insurance coverage, and much more. This certificate is to be provided by the council of unit owners within 20 days of such request by the sellers. Sellers pay the council (or its management company) for costs of preparing the certificate. This cost can easily exceed one hundred dollars. The council must only charge the seller the amount the certificate actually cost to prepare; no profit or markup is allowed.

Once resale purchasers receive these condominium documents ("condo docs"), they have seven days to give written notice rescinding their contract to purchase without stating any reason. This right is waived if they proceed to closing before the seven-day period elapses.

Condominium resale contracts must contain the required clauses and disclosures to ensure compliance with the act. Some local real estate boards and associations make available to their members a *Condominium Contract of Sale* and *Condominium Listing Contract. The contract for resale is voidable by the purchaser for seven days after the certificate* (number 4 above) *has been provided or until conveyance of the unit has been made,* whichever comes first.

Renting a Condominium Unit in Montgomery County

In Montgomery County, before a tenant executes a lease for an initial term of 125 days or more, the owner of any residential rental property within any condominium or development is required to provide to the prospective tenant—to the extent applicable—a copy of the rules, declaration, and recorded covenants and restrictions that limit or affect the use and occupancy of the property or common areas and under which the owner and the tenant are also obligated.

■ TIME-SHARE OWNERSHIP

There are two principal forms of time-sharing: the right-to-use (time-share license) method and the purchase-of-fractional-interest (time-share estate) method. In the **time-share license** form, owners of interests in vacation properties, including condominiums, hotels, motels, marinas, and boats, may trade their vacation periods and facilities either directly or indirectly through space banks that are maintained by firms established to help time-sharers swap vacation facilities. In the **time-share estate,** widely used in Maryland in the Eastern Shore and western areas, the customers buy fractional interests for designated time periods in a resort condominium, either on a rental (estate for years) or permanent (fee simple) basis. The fee simple buyer receives a deed for a share of the property. Mortgages or deeds of trust are accepted for the unpaid portion of the purchase price. Contracts, settlements, and all other matters are similar to purchases of condominium units.

The State Securities Commission requires that anyone offering part ownership or interest in condominiums must disclose the inherent risks of such an investment. Limited-use resort securities must comply with the registration and antifraud requirements of the State Securities Act.

The Time-Sharing Act [*Real Property*, Article Title 11A]

The *Maryland Real Estate Time-Sharing Act* provides for the creation, sale, lease, management, and termination of time-share interests; registration of certain documents; registration of time-share developers with the Commission; and certain bonding requirements. Certain advertising and promotional practices are prohibited. Developers are required to prepare Public Offering Statements describing time-share projects regulated by the Secretary of State. Certain protections for purchasers are provided, such as sales contract cancellation periods and disclosures of information, warranties, and exchange programs. Terms generally relating to time-share interests in real estate are defined. The following sections highlight some main points of the act. Any licensee involved in time-share sales or development should obtain a complete copy of the act or seek competent legal advice. Time-share developers and persons selling time-share estates are also subject to the provisions of the License Law.

Preventing Creation of a Time-Share.   The owners of at least 34 percent of the units in a condominium may sign and record a land record document within the county of the project's locale, stating an intent to limit time-shares in the project. Thereafter, no person or other entity may become a developer of more than one unit in the project.

Property owners in a residential community governed by recorded covenants and restrictions may prohibit time-shares on any property subject to those covenants and restrictions by amending them by a majority vote (or by any greater percentage required by the covenants and restrictions).

Public Offering Statement.   Upon or before the signing of a sales contract, the developers—or other owner-sellers—who offer time-shares for their own accounts must deliver to each purchaser a Public Offering Statement. This could apply to real estate licensees selling their own time-shares.

The requirements for disclosure under the Time-Sharing Act differ substantially from those required under the Condominium Act.

A time-share owner who is not associated with the developer of a time-share project is exempt from filing and disseminating a Public Offering Statement.

Conversions.   A developer desiring to convert a building more than five years old into a time-share project is required to include an engineer's report in the Public Offering Statement and to give any tenant or subtenant at least 120 days' notice of the intention to convert the building to a time-share project.

Cancellation Rights.   *First purchasers* of time-shares have the right to cancel the sales contract until midnight *of the tenth calendar day* following whichever occurs latest: (1) the contract date; (2) the day on which the time-share purchaser received the last of all documents required as part of the Public Offering Statement; or (3) the date on which either the time-share unit meets all building requirements and is ready for occupancy or the developer obtains a payment and performance bond and files the bond with the Commission. This right of cancellation cannot be waived.

Unlike the law concerning condominiums, *no closing on a time-share can occur until the purchaser's cancellation period has expired.* If closing is held prior to the cancellation period, the closing is voidable at the option of the purchaser for a period of one year after the expiration of the cancellation period.

Resale Disclosures.   An owner selling his or her time-share is required to furnish to the purchaser before execution of the contract or transfer of title or use

- a copy of the time-share instrument and
- a resale certificate containing the information required by the Time-Sharing Act.

The purchaser may cancel the contract to purchase at any time *within seven days after receipt of the resale certificate* without reason and without liability and is then entitled to the return of any deposits made under the contract.

Deposits.   All purchase money received by a developer from a purchaser must be deposited in an escrow account designed solely for that purpose with a financial institution whose accounts are insured by a government agency. The funds remain there until the end of the ten-day cancellation period or any later time provided for in the contract. Purchase money may be released to the developer, provided the developer maintains a surety bond. No claim can be made against the Real Estate Guaranty Fund if a loss is covered by that bond.

Warranties.   All time-share units sold by developers have implied warranties of three years for common elements and one year for units with respect to structural components and heating and cooling systems. In addition, the developer must warrant to a purchaser of a time-share that any existing use of the time-share unit that will continue does not violate any law.

Sales Contract.   The statute requires contracts for the first sale of time-shares to use specific language to disclose cancellation rights. Contracts must also show the estimated completion date of each unit and each common element as well as estimates of the time-share expenses and facility fees. All this is intended to disclose the total financial obligation being incurred by purchasers.

Exchange Programs.   The Time-Sharing Act requires detailed information concerning each exchange program a developer makes available for purchasers' use. To comply with the act, each exchange company offering an exchange program is required to file the required information with the Commission on an annual basis.

Registration.   The Time-Sharing Act requires that developers, with certain exceptions, register with the Commission. A developer may not offer a time-share to the public until the developer has received a certificate of registration as a time-share developer. The developer is required to file certain documents and material with the Commission. The Time-Sharing Act gives the Commission the authority to

- issue regulations and orders consistent with the act,
- investigate possible violations of the act and subpoena witnesses and documents in connection with the investigations,
- bring suit against violators,
- order violators to correct conditions resulting from the violation, and
- revoke the registration of any developer who is convicted of violating the act.

In addition, the Secretary of State is authorized to adopt regulations necessary to implement and enforce the provisions of the act pertaining to Public Offering Statements. A violation of the act could provide grounds for the suspension or revocation of a broker's or salesperson's license under the Brokers Act.

Project Broker. Developers are required to designate licensed real estate brokers as project brokers for each time-share project. Each time-share project is considered a separate real estate office for purposes of the Brokers Act. Any person who sells, advertises, or offers for sale any time-share must be a licensed broker, an associate broker, or a salesperson, or be exempt from licensure under Title 17. An unlicensed person may be employed by a developer or project broker to contact, but not solicit, prospective buyers so long as the unlicensed person

- performs only clerical tasks,
- schedules only those appointments induced by others, or
- prepares or distributes only promotional materials.

Time-Share Regulations [COMAR 09.11.04]

Regulations governing time-shares require that records be maintained of names and addresses of all personnel retained for sale of time-share estates, including agents, employees, and licensees, whether employees or independent contractors. Records must also be made and kept of all sales transactions, of estates conveyed and encumbrances on them, and of amounts of purchase money held for such sales. The Commission may require certification of such amounts by a certified public accountant. Developers must also maintain bonding in prescribed amounts for deposit monies being held.

Time-share marketing statements about the characteristics of the time-share project or estate may not be false, inaccurate, or misleading. A developer may not indicate that an improvement will be placed in a time-share project unless the developer has sufficient finances and bona fide intentions to complete the improvement. Statements used in the marketing of time-share estates located in Maryland may not induce a prospective purchaser to leave the State for the purpose of executing a contract for sale when to do so would circumvent the provisions of Maryland law. No one may advertise or represent that the Commission has approved or recommended any time-share project or estate offered for sale.

■ MARYLAND COOPERATIVE HOUSING CORPORATION ACT [CORPORATIONS AND ASSOCIATIONS ARTICLE, TITLES 5-6B]

The Maryland Cooperative Housing Act provides for conditions, contracts, rights, and requirements relative to the development and sale of interests in cooperatives. Detailed provisions are contained in statutes. A member of the cooperative receives a **proprietary lease,** an agreement with the cooperative housing corporation that gives the member an exclusive possessory interest in a unit and a possessory interest in common with other members in that portion of a cooperative project not constituting units. It creates a legal relationship of landlord and tenant between the corporation and the member.

■ MARYLAND HOMEOWNERS ASSOCIATION ACT [REAL PROPERTY ARTICLE §11B]

This act sets forth conditions, rights, and requirements regulating homeowner's associations (HOAs) in the State.

For sales contracts to be binding on purchasers, sellers must make disclosure showing that the property is subject to an HOA; listing the rights, responsibilities, and obligations of purchasers; and disclosing purchasers' rights of rescission if the *Maryland Homeowners Association Act* (MHAA) information is not provided to them by sellers in a timely manner. This information recites factual details pertaining to disclosures that must include liability, warranties, meetings, books, and records. Time periods for rescission vary with the number of lots in the HOA and between initial sale and resale of properties.

■ CANCELLATION PERIODS

Because it is important for real estate licensees to know the cancellation periods allowed by law for various types of condominium and time-share sales contracts, they are summarized in Table 6.1.

T A B L E 6.1

Cancellation Periods in Various Sale Situations

Type of Sale	Period for Cancellation	After
Condominium by Developer	15 days	Receipt of Certificate (Certificate also must be received not less than 15 days prior to closing.)
Condominium by Developer	5 additional days	Receipt of any later amendments to Public Offering Statement
Condominium by Resale	7 days	Receipt of Resale Certificate (This certificate must also be received not less than 15 days prior to closing.)
Time-Share by Developer	10 days	Contract, receipt of last required disclosure document, or receipt of occupancy permit, whichever is last. A settlement performed before the end of a cancellation period is unlawful and voidable by purchaser.
Time-Share by Resale	7 days	Receipt of Certificate
HOA	Varies by number of lots and whether original or resale	n/a

QUESTIONS

1. Which of the following forms of ownership is *NOT* usually recognized in Maryland?
   1. Tenancy in common
   2. Community property
   3. Trust
   4. Ownership in severalty

2. In Maryland, a deed that conveys ownership to "Karen and David Munoz, husband and wife," but does *NOT* specify the form of ownership
   1. automatically creates a tenancy in common.
   2. must be redrawn before the property is sold, specifying the form of ownership.
   3. creates a tenancy by the entirety.
   4. creates an ownership in severalty.

3. Which of the following is *NOT* true? In Maryland, a tenancy by the entirety
   1. may be held only by a husband and wife.
   2. continues after the death of one of the owners.
   3. gives each individual possession of the entire estate.
   4. may not be partitioned.

4. A time-share developer is required to
   1. register with the State Real Estate Commission.
   2. register with the State Treasurer.
   3. register with the local Board or Association of REALTORS®.
   4. be a licensed real estate broker.

5. The bylaws of a condominium can be changed or altered by
   1. the manager of the property.
   2. a two-thirds vote of the unit owners.
   3. the council of unit owners by majority vote.
   4. a simple majority of unit owners.

6. A developer who proposes to convert a residential rental facility to a condominium regime must register with the
   1. office of the Attorney General.
   2. local Board of REALTORS®.
   3. Secretary of State.
   4. Maryland Real Estate Commission.

7. A developer selling a newly built condominium unit to an original purchaser
   1. is liable for damages as a result of misleading statements for five years after the sale.
   2. is subject to the seller's voiding the contract if the developer fails to deliver a Public Offering Statement.
   3. is protected by the doctrine of caveat emptor from liability for misleading statements.
   4. must file a Public Offering Statement with the State Real Estate Commission.

8. Purchasers of time-shares from the developer
   1. have a right to cancel the contract only if the seller has misrepresented material facts.
   2. have ten days in which to cancel the sale for any reason.
   3. must close the sale within ten days after signing the sales contract.
   4. must obtain a payment and performance bond to ensure their compliance with the contract.

9. A contract for resale of a condominium by its owner (other than its developer) is *NOT* enforceable unless the owner furnishes the buyer, not later than 15 days prior to the closing,
   1. a copy of the declaration.
   2. the rules and regulations.
   3. a statement regarding monthly expenses, proposed capital improvements, other fees, financial statements of the condominium, and insurance details.
   4. all of the above.

10. Should a dispute develop between a unit owner, board of directors, and/or council of unit owners, parties may apply for mediation to the
    1. local Board of REALTORS®.
    2. office of the county state's attorney.
    3. office of the Attorney General.
    4. local Board of Development and Planning.

CHAPTER SEVEN

LEGAL DESCRIPTIONS

■ OVERVIEW

Two of the methods of property description presented in the student's principal text are in common use in Maryland. They are the **metes-and-bounds** and **recorded plat of subdivision** methods. Maryland was never included in the federal government's rectangular survey system.

At the very least, a description that identifies land "with reasonable certainty" is required in a contract for sale of realty. Postal address alone is usually not an adequate legal description except for such short residential leaseholds as one or two years.

■ EXAMPLES OF LEGAL DESCRIPTIONS USED IN CONTRACTS

Metes and Bounds

■ "Beginning at an iron pipe set on the northeast side of Annapolis Street at a point located South 38° 45' East, 200 feet from where the northeast side of Annapolis Street intersects the southeast side of Giddings Avenue—all as shown on Aldridge's Revised and Corrected Plat of West Annapolis recorded among the Land Records of Anne Arundel County in JCB Liber 4, Folio 297; and running thence and at right angles to Annapolis Street, North 51° 15' East, 150 feet to a pipe; thence South 38° 45' East 50 feet to a pipe; thence South 51° 15' West, 150 feet to a pipe on the northeast side of Annapolis Street; thence with same, North 38° 45' West, 50 feet to the place of beginning."

■ "That certain parcel of real estate located in Worcester County, Maryland, being on the east side of Farm Lane, north of Jerry Road, being further known as the Arthur R. Jackson property, consisting of one acre, more or less, with the improvements thereon, previously conveyed by deed of Robert Allen, grantor, recorded in FWH Liber 29, Folio 1312, the exact boundaries and acreage to be determined by means of a survey, which has been ordered to be prepared by Johnson and Landsman, surveyors, Snow Hill."

Recorded Plat of Subdivision

■ "Lot #16, Block #3 of the Plat of Melville Development Corporation as surveyed by John Walmer, Catonsville, Maryland, August 15, 1968, as recorded in FWH Liber 295, Folio 1720, in the County of Ridge, State of Maryland."

■ SURVEY MARKERS

Surveyors are governed by the *Maryland Professional Land Surveyors Act*. They are licensed by the State Board for Professional Land Surveyors. The Board specifies that they use specific types of stakes, markers, monuments, or other landmarks in their work.

It is a **misdemeanor**—a crime less than a felony, for which a prison term of not more than one year may be imposed—to intentionally move, damage, or obliterate any markers on property belonging to another person if the marker was put in place by a civil engineer, surveyor, real estate appraiser, or members of their teams. The exception is when the marker interferes with proper use of the land. A fine of not more than $500 can be imposed upon conviction.

If there is a dispute over any boundary line or if the bounds mentioned in a document are lost, the circuit court of the county where the property is located may be petitioned to establish the boundary lines or the location of the missing bounds. These experts' fees are considered costs in the proceeding.

■ LOCATION DRAWINGS AND BOUNDARY SURVEYS

The Office of the Secretary of Licensing and Regulation, through its Board for Professional Land Surveyors, requires that surveyors have a signed election form requesting either a location drawing or a boundary survey from the party ordering the survey. *This election (choice) should be made by purchasers at the time of forming their agreement to purchase*.

The **boundary survey** identifies property boundary lines and corners sufficiently well to establish the physical position and extent of the boundaries, including visible indications of rights that may arise from prescription or adverse possession. It is needed for an owner having a fence placed or other improvements erected. It reports that monuments have either been located or placed on the property.

A **location drawing** provides a plat of the property that shows the location of any improvements. It costs less than a boundary survey but is often sufficient for most residential resales and refinancing situations.

A description of each type and of its uses, limitations, and costs appears on the election form. The form electing which survey is being ordered is typically submitted by the title, settlement, or law office preparing for settlement.

■ SUBDIVISION PLATS

Subdividers must have plats of proposed subdivisions prepared by a licensed surveyor and approved and recorded by local authorities before offering them for sale. Reference to a recorded subdivision plat may be part of a sufficient legal description. No distances on a subdivision plat may be marked "more or less" except those lines that begin, terminate, or bind on a body of water.

QUESTIONS

1. In Maryland contracts, lot, block, section, and similar references to a subdivision plat
   1. are permitted in individual lot descriptions when the plat was properly recorded.
   2. must be prepared by licensed real estate brokers.
   3. are not sufficient for sales agreements but are good enough for listings.
   4. are sufficient for listings but not for sales agreements.

2. A location drawing
   1. is essentially the same as a boundary survey.
   2. is appropriate for typical residential resales.
   3. costs more than a boundary survey.
   4. can properly be used for placing fences and other improvements.

3. Which of the following is MOST likely to be a sufficient legal description?
   1. 142 Pinehurst Road, Ocean Pines
   2. That lot fronting 100 feet on Pinehurst and being 250 feet deep
   3. That two acres, shown on attached plat of subdivision survey as prepared by Landsman & Co., surveyors of Catonsville, Maryland
   4. 1776-B Liberty St., Snow Hill, Md., being the northern half of a duplex

4. "Beginning at the intersection of the east line of Goodrich Boulevard and the south line of Jasmine Lane and running south along the east line of Goodrich Boulevard a distance of 230 feet; thence easterly parallel to the north line of Wolf Road, a distance of 195 feet; thence northeasterly on a course of N 22°E, a distance of 135 feet; and thence northwesterly along the south line of Jasmine Lane to the point of beginning." This legal description is an example of a
   1. block description.
   2. rectangular survey.
   3. subdivision description.
   4. metes-and-bounds description.

5. Legal real property descriptions in Maryland
   1. employ the rectangular survey system.
   2. consist of the street or mailing addresses of the properties.
   3. are based on recorded plats of subdivision or metes-and-bounds data.
   4. consist of the post office box numbers.

CHAPTER EIGHT

REAL ESTATE TAXES AND OTHER LIENS

■ OVERVIEW

Maryland property taxes are levied by and for the support of the county and city governments as well as local special taxing districts. A number of counties also impose **impact fees** on developers in addition to property taxes on owners. The impact fees are levied on new residential units to pay for additional public facilities and services for the use and benefit of new residents. They increase the initial cost of home ownership because developers pass along to purchasers the cost of the fees.

■ ASSESSMENT

Real property is assessed for tax purposes by the State Department of Assessments and Taxation. There are local offices of that department in Baltimore City and in each Maryland county.

In 2001, Maryland's general (ad valorem) tax assessment ratio was raised from 40 percent to 100 percent of the market value estimated by triennial assessment. The effect of raising the assessment ratio and lowering the tax rate was revenue-neutral, and so required no increase in the taxes to be paid. The purpose of the change was to make property tax rates in the State appear competitive with those in surrounding jurisdictions in hopes of attracting prospective residents and employers. (See Table 8.1.)

The procedure for assessing property in Maryland, the **triennial assessment,** is based on a three-year cycle in which one-third of all properties are revalued every year for tax purposes.

Each county has been organized into three principal assessing areas to coincide with the years of the assessment cycle. The areas generally have similar density and other common characteristics and are reviewed on a rotating basis. By the end of a three-year period, all properties will have been physically reviewed and valued once; then a new cycle commences.

TABLE 8.1

County Tax Rates

	2004–2005 (Fiscal 2005) County Tax Rates		
Counties and Baltimore County	**Real Property Tax Rate in Dollars per $100 of Assessment***	**Transfer Tax Rate The Consideration Payable Multiplied by This Rate†**		**Recordation Tax Quoted in Dollars per $500 of Transaction Amount**
Allegany	1.0007	0.20%	0.002	3.00
Anne Arundel	0.941	1.00%	0.010	3.50
Baltimore City	2.328	1.50%	0.015	5.00
Baltimore County	1.115	1.50%	0.015	2.50
Calvert	0.892	0.00%	0.000	5.00
Caroline	0.952	0.50%	0.005	5.00
Carroll	1.048	0.00%	0.000	5.00
Cecil	0.980	0.00%	0.000	3.30
Charles	1.026	0.00%	0.000	5.00
Dorchester	0.930	0.75%	0.0075	5.00
Frederick	1.000	0.00%	0.000	5.00
Garrett	1.036	1.00%	0.010	3.50
Harford	1.092	1.00%	0.010	3.30
Howard	1.044	1.00%	0.010	2.50
Kent	1.012	0.50%	0.005	3.30
Montgomery	0.734	1.00%	0.010	3.45
Prince George's	0.960	1.40%	0.014	2.20
Queen Anne's	0.926	0.50%	0.050	3.30
St. Mary's	0.878	1.00%	0.010	4.00
Somerset	1.010	0.00%	0.000	3.30
Talbot	0.540	1.00%	0.010	3.30
Washington	0.948	0.50%	0.005	3.80
Wicomico	1.025	0.00%	0.000	3.50
Worcester	0.730	0.50%	0.050	3.30
Allegany	1.0007	0.20%	0.002	3.00

* To this add any municipal tax.
† This is in addition to State Transfer Tax Rate of 0.5%.

This information is found at *http://www.dat.state.md.us*

An inspection of the exterior premises always accompanies a revaluation. If changes in zoning or use occur, or if additions or extensive improvements to property have been made, the property may be revalued out of sequence.

Real property assessment is further controlled by a **phase-in provision,** designed to take some of the financial sting out of inflation. For the one-third of all real properties reassessed in a particular year, one-third of any increase in value is added in that year, and the balance is added in equal increments over the following two years in the three-year cycle. For example, a property increasing in value from $72,000 to $84,000 would have a value for tax purposes of $76,000 the first year, $80,000 the second year, and $84,000 the third year.

If, on completion of the triennial review, the value of a property is found to have changed, the owner is sent a **notice of reassessment** that shows the property's assessment for the next three years; no other notice is sent until the new cycle begins three years later. Taxpayers who believe that their assessments are improper may appeal within 45 days of receiving notice of assessment.

■ PAYMENT

Taxes on residential property are paid in two equal installments. The first payment is due July 1, but can be paid without penalty as late as September 30. The second, due January 1, can be paid without penalty as late as January 31. One of the purposes of the two-payment arrangement is to reduce the amount of ad valorem tax "set asides" needed by purchasers at settlement. The statute creating the two-payment system requires that counties prepare their data processing systems for quarterly payments that may be authorized by future legislation.

Lenders who accept responsibility to pay property taxes on the mortgaged properties collect the required funds in expense (escrow) accounts. They are required to pay those taxes within 45 days after the earlier of the following: (1) the first due date after their receipt of the tax bill or (2) after funds collected by the lender are sufficient to pay the amount of taxes and interest due. Lenders who fail to pay taxes as provided above must bear any additional costs of penalties and interest.

■ PROPERTY TAX RELIEF

The **Homestead Tax Credit** is designed to protect owner-occupied residence assessments from the effects of rapid inflation. It automatically provides a credit against the real estate tax if the assessment on a dwelling increases over the previous year by more than a certain percentage determined by the state legislature. The credit equals the amount by which the reassessment exceeds the established percentage and applies if certain other conditions were met during the previous calendar year.

Because the Homestead Tax Credit does not take into account homeowners' ability to pay, the state legislature devised what is popularly known as the **circuit breaker.** After taking into account homeowners' net worth, gross annual income, and assessed value of their property, this program, for homeowners of all ages, sets limits on the amount of residential property tax due. This relief must be applied for each year.

The owners of unsold and unrented single-dwelling units or newly constructed or substantially rehabilitated commercial properties may be entitled to *tax credits* not exceeding the property taxes on the improvements. The credit applies for no more than one year immediately following construction or substantial rehabilitation.

Special provision has also been made for **senior tenants,** age 60 or older, to receive as much as $600 from the State to offset property taxes. Asset and income limits are among certain restrictions that apply.

The residential property *owned by a veteran* with a permanent, 100 percent, service-connected disability is exempt from property tax. The 100 percent disability may result from blindness or some other disabling cause. This benefit is retained by the *unremarried surviving spouse* of the deceased, disabled veteran as well. Application for this benefit must be accompanied by documentation of veteran status, 100 percent disability, and ownership of the property.

Assessment on a residence *owned by an individual who is legally blind* is reduced by $15,000. The property must be the individual's legal residence and not be occupied by more than two families. The *unremarried surviving spouse* of a blind individual receives the same benefit. No individual may claim both the exemption for the blind and the exemption for the disabled veteran.

■ TRANSFER AND RECORDATION TAXES

Except as discussed in the following paragraph, in every written or oral agreement for the sale or other disposition of property it is presumed, in the absence of any contrary provision in the agreement or the law, that the parties to the agreement intended that the cost of any recordation tax or any State or local transfer tax be shared equally between the grantor and grantee. This presumption does not apply to mortgages or deeds of trust. (Refer to Table 8.1.)

First-Time Maryland Homebuyers

The law provides that first-time homebuyers will not pay the State transfer tax. In a transfer involving such a buyer, the State transfer tax of 0.5 percent is reduced to 0.25 percent, and must be paid by the seller. Furthermore, unless the parties in such a transaction agree to the contrary, the recordation taxes and local transfer taxes are to be paid by the seller. **First-time homebuyers** are defined in the law as *purchasers who have never before owned and occupied a principal residence in this State, will occupy the property as their principal residence, and/or meet certain other requirements.*

■ CORPORATE FRANCHISE TAX

Most corporations are taxed annually on their franchise or right to do business in the State. The annual tax ($300 in 2004) becomes a general lien on the property or the corporation and can be enforced against it. When a broker files for a real estate license and the brokerage is a corporation, the Commission requires that a copy of the brokerage's Articles of Incorporation be filed also.

■ PROPERTY TAX ASSESSMENTS, AGRICULTURAL USE

Lands that are actively devoted to farm or agricultural use are favorably assessed on the basis of those uses rather than their probably more intensive highest and best use.

Agricultural Use Assessment

The State Department of Assessments and Taxation establishes criteria for the purpose of determining whether land qualifies for assessment as agricultural use. The State's purpose is to slow the conversion of farm lands into more intensive, nonfarm uses.

Agricultural Transfer Tax

The Agricultural Transfer Tax, ranging from 3 percent to 5 percent of the consideration, funds the state's Agricultural Land Preservation Program. The tax is based on multiple factors: the size of the tract, improvements that may be in place, and the value of the land reflected in the consideration. The tax is waived in a transfer in which the purchaser promises to keep the land in agricultural use for five tax years. The tax is more fully discussed in Chapter 10 of this book.

The Agricultural Transfer Tax is calculated by the Assessments Office and is payable at the time the property transfer takes place. Negotiation about which party will pay should be reflected in the contract of sale. A full discussion of this tax is found at the Maryland State Department of Assessment and Taxation Web site.

 **WWWeb.Link**

http://www.dat.state.md.us/sdatweb/agtransf.html

■ AD VALOREM TAX DELINQUENCY AND REDEMPTION

This tax is due in two payments: one on July 1 and the other on January 1 each year. Taxes that are not paid by September 30, and by January 31 under the two-payment system, are considered delinquent, bear interest as provided by law, and are subject to a real estate tax sale held by the county treasurer.

The dates and rules regarding such sales are made by each county. Tax-delinquent properties sold at a tax sale are not conveyed immediately to the buyer. There is a six-month **statutory period of redemption** during which the delinquent taxpayer may redeem the property by paying the county treasurer the amount of the delinquent tax plus the accumulated interest in penalties and related legal fees. The annual interest rate for redemption is established by law by various jurisdictions. In some cases, it is as high as 20 percent. If no redemption is made during the six-month period, the tax sale buyer may apply to the court for the issuance of a deed to the property. Unpaid taxes create a priority lien on real property.

Ad valorem taxes on a parcel of property that remain unpaid for longer than three years, perhaps because the lien on the property did not sell at tax sales, are no longer collectible. There is a three-year limitation of actions on this tax. Only the most recent three years' taxes remain a lien on any property. A number of tax program pamphlets are available in each county Tax Assessment Office.

■ MECHANICS' LIENS

Mechanics' liens, as discussed in the main textbook, are authorized by law in many states to protect the rights of contractors, suppliers, and other persons engaged to improve real estate. After the completion of work on Maryland real estate, contractors or suppliers have six months in which to record a notice of their lien. They then have one year from the date of recording to petition the courts to enforce the lien in the event such petition was not included when the lien was recorded.

It is unlawful for **unperformed** (executory) **contracts** between contractors and subcontractors relating to construction, alteration, or repair of a building, structure, or improvement to contain a provision that waives or requires that the subcontractor waive the right to claim a mechanic's lien.

Buyers purchasing properties that have been recently improved or constructed should seek protection against possible outstanding mechanics' liens. In the usual purchase of real estate, the attorney for the buyer has responsibility to ascertain that the property being purchased is free from unpaid taxes and mechanics' or other outstanding liens.

Release of Lien

When a lien on real property is satisfied, lienholders are required to mail or deliver a release of the lien within seven days after receiving payment. The release may be in the form of the original note, marked "paid" or "canceled." If lienholders fail to provide such a release after demand by the payor, the payor may bring action in the circuit court. In such an action, the lienholders or their agent may be liable for delivery of the release, as well as for all costs and expenses of the action.

QUESTIONS

1. In Maryland, real estate taxes are imposed by
   1. cities.
   2. special taxing districts.
   3. counties.
   4. all of the above.

2. All residential real property in Maryland is
   1. reassessed for tax purposes each year.
   2. assessed for tax purposes at the property's full market value.
   3. reassessed for tax purposes every other year.
   4. reassessed at time of resale.

3. Peter and Jayne Janney own a contracting firm in Maryland. On February 1, 2002, Arch Chandler hired the Janney firm to construct an addition to his five-bedroom house. The Janneys finished work on the project on March 15; it is now April 15, and the Janneys have not yet been paid. Based on this situation, which of the following is correct? The Janneys have until
   1. August 1 to record a notice of lien.
   2. August 1 to enforce their mechanic's lien.
   3. September 15 to record a mechanic's lien.
   4. October 15 to enforce a mechanic's lien.

4. Ollie Akers has chosen to make semiannual real estate tax payments on the home he occupies. Which of the following statements is *FALSE*?
   1. Ollie's payments will be due July 1 and January 1 of each tax year.
   2. Ollie's first semiannual payment becomes late if paid after September 30.
   3. Ollie's second semiannual payment becomes late if paid after January 31.
   4. Ollie's second semiannual payment becomes late if paid after March 31.

5. Ted Bolton has never before owned a principal residence in Maryland. He will settle on the purchase of a $100,000 home to occupy here in April. How will the State transfer tax be apportioned at settlement?
   1. Bolton will pay $0 and sellers will pay $500.
   2. Bolton will pay $250 and sellers will pay $250.
   3. Bolton will pay $0 and sellers will pay $250.
   4. The apportionment will be whatever Bolton and the sellers agree in the contract of sale.

CHAPTER NINE

REAL ESTATE CONTRACTS

■ OVERVIEW

In Maryland, real estate contracts are used, among other things, for sales, rentals, options, and installment sales. This chapter discusses various contract issues, including age requirements for valid contracts, the Statute of Frauds, mandatory clauses for residential resales, and limitation of actions on contract enforcement in this state. It also presents the industry-created sales contract now available for REALTOR® use throughout Maryland (Figure 9.1). Students who go on to practice real estate brokerage as REALTORS® are advised always to use the latest version of such contracts and their addenda.

■ GENERAL CONTRACT RULES: COMPETENCY, STATUTE OF FRAUDS, LIMITATION OF ACTIONS

Competency

Under Maryland law, a person reaches the age of majority and has the capacity to enter into a valid real estate contract at age 18. However, minors married to persons who have reached the age of majority may enter into valid real estate contracts jointly with their spouses.

Statute of Frauds

To be legally enforceable under Maryland's Statute of Frauds, all contracts for the transfer of any interest in real property for more than one year must be in writing and signed by the parties. Any **oral (parol) transfer** of an interest in real property for more than one year can convey no more than a tenancy at will. Maryland laws require a 30-day notice to vacate under a tenancy at will.

The Maryland Statute of Frauds does not require a lease for a term of one year or less to be in writing to be enforceable. The year is measured from the date the lease is entered into rather than the date on which occupancy begins. Regardless of these interesting facts, all licensees are bound by Commission regulations to reduce to signed, written form *all agreements* that they help negotiate.

Limitation of Actions (Statute of Limitations)

Suits to enforce a simple contract must be filed within three years. For contracts signed "under seal," however, the time limit is 12 years. Mention of the word *seal* or use of the phrase *witness my seal* in the body of a contract together with use of the letters L.S. (standing for the Latin phrase *locus sigilli*) in the signature block create a **contract under seal.** Such a contract is called a **specialty contract.**

■ CONTRACTS FOR THE SALE OF REAL ESTATE

Real estate sales contracts and other contract forms must always be drafted by attorneys. Licensees are authorized only to insert required information into these forms. Licensees who draft their own clauses or phrases could be accused of the misdemeanor *unauthorized practice of law.* Under Maryland law the maximum penalty for such "unauthorized practice" is a fine of not more than $5,000 and/or imprisonment for not more than one year.

Although licensees, unless otherwise licensed to do so, cannot act as attorneys in their brokerage activities, they should nevertheless emphasize to buyers and sellers that a signed sales contract is legally binding. Buyers and sellers should obtain legal counsel to interpret and approve the provisions of contracts. It is grossly misleading, and probably an example of the unauthorized practice of law, to give false assurance to the parties, such as, "Don't worry; there will be an attorney at settlement," as if that would protect them from errors made in their earlier contract negotiations.

To reduce confusion arising from the use of a wide variety of contract forms, the Maryland Association of REALTORS® (MAR), working with its member associations and boards throughout the State, prepares a contract form that its members may use in residential sale transactions statewide. The MAR, with the aid of its legal counsel, also provides contract language for 20 or more addenda. All these forms are copyrighted by the MAR and may not be altered or modified without the prior written express consent of that Association. MAR member-brokers are free either to use the statewide forms—as long as they make no changes in their wording—or to have counsel draft forms for their particular firms' use. Nonmember-brokers may not use the forms. A sample of the MAR's Residential Sales Contract is shown in Figure 9.1.

Information That Must Be Included

In certain circumstances, Maryland statutes require that licensees include specific information in contracts. Other information is required in *all* contracts of sale, even when the sellers are not licensees and are simply selling their own property. Unless otherwise specifically agreed, a contract of sale is generally not made invalid by omission of "required" disclosures such as those discussed below.

All contracts for the sale of improved residential real property must disclose *the estimated cost of any deferred water and sewer charges* for which the purchaser may become liable. Violation of this disclosure requirement entitles the initial purchaser of the improved property to recover from the seller two times the amount of deferred charges the purchaser would be obligated to pay during the five years of payments following the sale.

FIGURE 9.1

Maryland Association of REALTORS® Residential Sales Contract

RESIDENTIAL CONTRACT OF SALE

This is a Legally Binding Contract; If Not Understood, Seek Competent Legal Advice.
THIS FORM IS DESIGNED AND INTENDED FOR THE SALE AND PURCHASE OF IMPROVED SINGLE FAMILY RESIDENTIAL REAL ESTATE LOCATED IN MARYLAND ONLY. *FOR OTHER TYPES OF PROPERTY INCLUDE APPROPRIATE ADDENDA.*

BROKER: _____ BRANCH OFFICE: _____
OFFICE PHONE: _____ FAX: _____ BROKER/AGENT ID: _____
SALES ASSOCIATE: _____ E-Mail: _____ PHONE: _____
ACTING AS: ☐ SELLER AGENT (WHETHER "COOPERATING AGENT" OR "SELLING AGENT"), OR
☐ BUYER AGENT; OR
☐ INTRA - COMPANY AGENT WITH BROKER AS DUAL AGENT

IN COOPERATION WITH

BROKER: _____ BRANCH OFFICE: _____
OFFICE PHONE: _____ FAX: _____ BROKER/AGENT ID: _____
SALES ASSOCIATE: _____ E-Mail: _____ PHONE: _____
ACTING AS: ☐ LISTING BROKER AND SELLER AGENT; OR
☐ INTRA - COMPANY AGENT WITH BROKER AS DUAL AGENT

TIME IS OF THE ESSENCE. Time is of the essence of this Contract. The failure of Seller or Buyer to perform any act as provided in this Contract by a prescribed date or within a prescribed time period shall be a default under this Contract and the non defaulting party, upon written notice to the defaulting party, may declare this Contract null and void and of no further legal force and effect. In such event, all Deposit(s) shall be disbursed in accordance with Paragraph 22 of this Contract.

As used in this Contract, and in any addendum or addenda to this Contract, the term "days" shall mean consecutive calendar days, including Saturdays, Sundays, and holidays, whether federal, state, local or religious. A day shall be measured from 12:00:01 a.m. to and including 11:59:59 p.m. E.S.T. For the purposes of calculating days, the count of "days" shall begin on the day following the day upon which any act or notice as provided in this Contract, or any addendum or addenda to this Contract, was required to be performed or made.

1. **DATE OF OFFER:** _____
2. **SELLER:**   NAME: _____
   ADDRESS: _____ ZIP: _____

3. **BUYER:**   NAME: _____
   ADDRESS: _____ ZIP: _____
4. **PROPERTY DESCRIPTION:** Seller does sell to Buyer and Buyer does purchase from Seller, all of the following described Property (hereinafter "Property") known as _____
_____ located in _____
City/County, Maryland, Zip _____ together with the improvements thereon, and all rights and appurtenances thereto belonging.
5. **PURCHASE PRICE:** The purchase price is _____
Dollars ($_____).
6. **SETTLEMENT:** Date of Settlement _____ or sooner if agreed to in writing by both parties.
7. **ESTATE:** The Property is being conveyed: ____ in fee simple or _____ subject to an annual ground rent, now existing or to be created, in the amount of _____Dollars ($_____) payable semi-annually, as now or to be recorded among the Land Records of _____ City/County, Maryland. If the Property is subject to ground rent and the ground rent is not timely paid, the owner of the reversionary interest (i.e., the person to whom the ground rent is payable) may bring an action of ejectment against the leasehold owner pursuant to Section 8-402.2 of the Real Property Article, Annotated Code of Maryland (as amended).

Buyer _____/_____   Page 1 of 10   Revision #9   10/04   Seller _____/_____

FIGURE 9.1

Maryland Association of REALTORS® Residential Sales Contract (continued)

Residential Contract of Sale

As a result of this action, the owner of the reversionary interest may obtain title to the Property in fee, discharged from the lease.

8. SETTLEMENT COSTS: NOTICE TO BUYER: BUYER HAS THE RIGHT TO SELECT BUYER'S OWN TITLE INSURANCE COMPANY, TITLE LAWYER, SETTLEMENT COMPANY, ESCROW COMPANY, MORTGAGE LENDER, OR FINANCIAL INSTITUTION AS DEFINED IN THE FINANCIAL INSTITUTIONS ARTICLE, ANNOTATED CODE OF MARYLAND. BUYER ACKNOWLEDGES THAT SELLER MAY NOT BE PROHIBITED FROM OFFERING OWNER FINANCING AS A CONDITION OF SETTLEMENT. Buyer agrees to pay all other settlement costs and charges including, but not limited to, all Lender's fees in connection herewith, including title examination and title insurance fees, all document preparation and recording fees, notary fees, survey fees where required, and all recording charges, except those incident to clearing existing encumbrances or title defects, except if Buyer is a Veteran obtaining VA financing, those prohibited to be paid by a Veteran obtaining VA financing or except if Buyer is obtaining FHA financing, those prohibited to be paid by a Buyer obtaining FHA financing, which prohibited charges shall be paid by Seller.

9. TRANSFER CHARGES: SECTION 14-104 OF THE REAL PROPERTY ARTICLE OF THE ANNOTATED CODE OF MARYLAND PROVIDES THAT, UNLESS OTHERWISE NEGOTIATED IN THE CONTRACT OR PROVIDED BY STATE OR LOCAL LAW, THE COST OF ANY RECORDATION TAX OR ANY STATE OR LOCAL TRANSFER TAX SHALL BE SHARED EQUALLY BETWEEN THE BUYER AND SELLER. Unless otherwise provided by an addendum to this Contract, the costs of state and local transfer and recordation taxes (other than agricultural land transfer tax) shall be shared equally by Buyer and Seller. (If First-Time Maryland Home Buyer: See Transfer and Recordation Tax Addendum.)

10. ADJUSTMENTS: Ground rent, homeowner's association fees, rent and water rent shall be adjusted and apportioned as of date of settlement; and all taxes, general or special, and all other public or governmental charges or assessments against the Property which are or may be payable on a periodic basis, including Metropolitan District Sanitary Commission or other benefit charges, assessments, liens or encumbrances for sewer, water, drainage, paving, or other public improvements completed or commenced on or prior to the date hereof, or subsequent thereto, are to be adjusted and apportioned as of the date of settlement and are to be assumed and paid thereafter by Buyer, whether assessments have been levied or not as of date of settlement if applicable by local law. Any heating or cooking fuels remaining in supply tank(s) at time of settlement shall become the property of Buyer.

11. TERMITE INSPECTION: Buyer, at Buyer's expense, (if VA, then at Seller's expense) is authorized to obtain a written report from a Maryland licensed pest control company that, based on a careful visual inspection, there is no evidence of termite or other wood-destroying insect infestation in the residence or within three (3) feet of the residence; and damage due to previous infestation has been repaired. The provisions of this paragraph also shall apply to (1) the garage or within three (3) feet of the garage (whether attached or detached), (2) any outbuildings located within three feet of the residence or garage and (3) a maximum of ten (10) linear feet of the nearest portion of a fence on Seller's Property within three feet of the residence or garage. If there is evidence of present infestation as described above, or if damage caused by present or prior infestation is discovered, Seller, at Seller's expense, shall repair any damage caused by present or prior infestation and have the present infestation treated by a licensed pest control company. If the cost of treatment and repair of such damage exceeds 2% of the purchase price, Seller may, at Seller's option, cancel this Contract, unless Buyer, at Buyer's option should choose to pay for the cost of treatment and repairs exceeding 2% of the purchase price, then this Contract shall remain in full force and effect. If such report reveals damage for which the cost of treatment and repair exceeds 2% of the purchase price, Seller's decision regarding treatment and repair of damage shall be communicated in writing to Buyer within five (5) days from receipt of the report, after which Buyer shall respond to Seller in writing with Buyer's decision within three (3) days from receipt of Seller's notification of Seller's decision. If Seller does not notify Buyer in writing of Seller's decision within five (5) days from receipt of report, Buyer may, at Buyer's option, pay for the cost of treatment and repairs exceeding 2% of the purchase price. If Buyer does not want to pay for the cost of treatment and repairs exceeding 2% of the purchase price, Buyer may terminate this Contract upon written notice delivered to Seller. In the event this Contract is terminated under the terms of this paragraph, the Deposit(s) shall be disbursed in accordance with the Deposit(s) paragraph of this Contract.

12. CONDITION OF PROPERTY AND POSSESSION: At settlement, Seller shall deliver possession of the Property and shall deliver the Property vacant, clear of trash and debris, broom clean and in substantially the same condition as existed on the date of Contract Acceptance. All electrical, heating, air conditioning (if any), plumbing (including well and septic), and any other mechanical systems and related equipment, appliances and smoke detector(s) included in this Contract shall be in working condition. Buyer reserves the right to inspect the Property within five (5) days prior to settlement. **EXCEPT AS OTHERWISE SPECIFIED IN THIS CONTRACT, INCLUDING THIS PARAGRAPH 12, THE PROPERTY IS SOLD "AS IS".** The obligations of Seller as provided in this Paragraph 12

Buyer _____/_____   Page 2 of 10 Revision #9   10/04   Seller _____/_____

FIGURE 9.1

Maryland Association of REALTORS® Residential Sales Contract (continued)

Residential Contract of Sale

shall be in addition to any Disclosure and Disclaimer Statement as required by Section 10-702, Real Property Article, Annotated Code of Maryland **AND** any provision(s) of any inspection contingency or contingencies addendum or addenda made a part of this Contract.

13. SALE/SETTLEMENT OR LEASE OF OTHER REAL ESTATE: Neither this Contract nor the granting of Buyer's loan referred to herein is to be conditioned or contingent in any manner upon the sale, settlement and/or lease of any other real estate unless a contingency for the sale, settlement and/or lease of other real estate is contained in an addendum to this Contract. Unless this Contract is expressly contingent upon the sale, settlement and/or lease of any other real estate, Buyer shall neither apply for nor accept a financing loan commitment which is contingent upon or requires as a pre-condition to funding that any other real estate be sold, settled and/or leased.

14. BUYER RESPONSIBILITY: If Buyer has misrepresented Buyer's financial ability to consummate the purchase of the Property, or if this Contract is contingent upon Buyer securing a written commitment for financing and Buyer fails to apply for such financing within the time period herein specified, or fails to pursue financing diligently and in good faith, or if Buyer makes any misrepresentations in any document relating to financing, or takes (or fails to take) any action which causes Buyer's disqualification for financing, then Buyer shall be in default; and Seller may elect by written notice to Buyer, to terminate this Contract and/or pursue the remedies set forth under the **"Default"** Paragraph 16.

15. SELLER RESPONSIBILITY: Seller agrees to keep existing mortgages free of default until settlement. All violation notices or requirements noted or issued by any governmental authority, or actions in any court on account thereof, against or affecting the Property at the date of settlement of this Contract, shall be complied with by Seller and the Property conveyed free thereof.

16. DEFAULT: Buyer and Seller are required and agree to make full settlement in accordance with the terms of this Contract and acknowledge that failure to do so constitutes a breach hereof. If Buyer fails to make full settlement or is in default due to Buyer's failure to comply with the terms, covenants and conditions of this Contract, the Deposit(s) may be retained by Seller as long as a release of Deposit(s) agreement is signed and executed by all parties, expressing that said Deposit(s) may be retained by Seller. In the event the parties do not agree to execute a release of Deposit(s), Buyer and Seller shall have all legal and equitable remedies. If Seller fails to make full settlement or is in default due to Seller's failure to comply with the terms, covenants and conditions of this Contract, Buyer shall be entitled to pursue such rights and remedies as may be available, at law or in equity, including, without limitation, an action for specific performance of this Contract and/or monetary damages. In the event of any litigation or dispute between Buyer and Seller concerning the release of the Deposit(s), Broker's sole responsibility may be met, at Broker's option, by paying the Deposit(s) into the court in which such litigation is pending, or by paying the Deposit(s) into the court of proper jurisdiction by an action of interpleader. Buyer and Seller agree that, upon Broker's payment of the Deposit(s) into the court, neither Buyer nor Seller shall have any further right, claim, demand or action against Broker regarding the release of the Deposit(s); and Buyer and Seller, jointly and severally, shall indemnify and hold Broker harmless from any and all such rights, claims, demands or actions. In the event of such dispute and election by Broker to file an action of interpleader as herein provided, Buyer and Seller further agree and hereby expressly and irrevocably authorize Broker to deduct from the Deposit(s) all costs incurred by Broker in the filing and maintenance of such action of interpleader including but not limited to filing fees, court costs, service of process fees and attorneys' fees, provided that the amount deducted shall not exceed the lesser of $500 or the amount of the Deposit(s) held by Broker. All such fees and costs authorized herein to be deducted may be deducted by Broker from the Deposit(s) prior to paying the balance of the Deposit(s) to the court. Buyer and Seller further agree and expressly declare that all such fees and costs so deducted shall be the exclusive property of Broker. If the amount deducted by Broker is less than the total of all of the costs incurred by Broker in filing and maintaining the interpleader action, then Buyer and Seller jointly, and severally, agree to reimburse Broker for all such excess costs upon the conclusion of the interpleader action.

17. MEDIATION OF DISPUTES: Mediation is a process by which the parties attempt to resolve a dispute or claim with the assistance of a neutral mediator who is authorized to facilitate the resolution of the dispute. The mediator has no authority to make an award, to impose a resolution of the dispute or claim upon the parties or to require the parties to continue mediation if the parties do not desire to do so. Buyer and Seller agree that any dispute or claim arising out of or from this Contract or the transaction which is the subject of this Contract shall be mediated through the Maryland Association of REALTORS®, Inc. or its member local boards/associations in accordance with the established Mediation Rules and Guidelines of the Association or through such other mediator or mediation service as mutually agreed upon by Buyer and Seller, in writing. Unless otherwise agreed in writing by the parties, mediation fees, costs and expenses shall be divided and paid equally by the parties to the mediation. If either party elects to have an attorney present that party shall pay his or her own attorney's fees. BUYER AND SELLER FURTHER AGREE THAT THE OBLIGATION OF BUYER AND SELLER TO MEDIATE AS HEREIN PROVIDED SHALL APPLY TO ALL DISPUTES AND CLAIMS ARISING WHETHER PRIOR TO, DURING OR WITHIN ONE (1) YEAR

Buyer _____/_____   Page 3 of 10   Revision #9   10/04   Seller _____/_____

Maryland Association of REALTORS® Residential Sales Contract (continued)

Residential Contract of Sale

FOLLOWING THE ACTUAL CONTRACT SETTLEMENT DATE OR WHEN SETTLEMENT SHOULD HAVE OCCURRED. BUYER AND SELLER AGREE THAT NEITHER PARTY SHALL INITIATE OR COMMENCE ANY ACTION IN ANY COURT OR BEFORE ANY ADMINISTRATIVE AGENCY, WITHOUT FIRST SUBMITTING THE DISPUTE OR CLAIM TO MEDIATION AS HEREIN PROVIDED. IN THE EVENT BUYER AND/OR SELLER SHALL INITIATE OR COMMENCE ANY ACTION IN ANY COURT OR BEFORE ANY ADMINISTRATIVE AGENCY WITHOUT FIRST SUBMITTING THE DISPUTE OR CLAIM TO MEDIATION AS HEREIN PROVIDED, THE PARTY INITIATING OR COMMENCING SUCH ACTION AGREES TO PAY ALL COSTS AND EXPENSES, INCLUDING REASONABLE ATTORNEYS' FEES, INCURRED TO ENFORCE THE OBLIGATION AS PROVIDED HEREIN TO FIRST MEDIATE THE DISPUTE OR CLAIM BY ANY PERSON OR ENTITY WITH WHOM OR WITH WHICH THE PARTY WAS REQUIRED TO MEDIATE. THE PROVISIONS OF THIS PARAGRAPH SHALL SURVIVE CLOSING AND SHALL NOT BE DEEMED TO HAVE BEEN EXTINGUISHED BY MERGER WITH THE DEED.

18. PAYMENT TERMS: The payment of the purchase price shall be made by Buyer as follows:
(a) An initial Deposit(s) by way of _____ in the amount of _____
Dollars ($ _____) at the time of this offer. (b) An additional Deposit(s) by way of _____
_____ in the amount of _____ Dollars
($_____) to be paid within _____ (____) days from the Date of Contract Acceptance. (c) The purchase price less any and all Deposit(s) shall be paid in full by Buyer in cash, wired funds, bank check, certified check or other payment acceptable to the settlement officer at settlement. (d) All Deposit(s) will be held in escrow by: _____ .

19. FINANCING: This Contract is contingent upon Buyer obtaining a written commitment for a loan secured by the Property as follows:

(Mark) ☐ Assumption Addendum
☐ Conventional Loan as follows:
     Loan Amount $ _____
     Term of Note _____ Years
     Amortization _____ Years
     Interest Rate _____ %
     Loan Program _____

☐ FHA Financing Addendum
☐ Gift of Funds Contingency Addendum
☐ Owner Financing Addendum
☐ VA Financing Addendum
☐ OTHER: _____

☐ No Financing Contingency

20. FINANCING APPLICATION AND COMMITMENT: Buyer agrees to make written application for the financing as herein described within _____ (____) days from the Date of Contract Acceptance. If such written financing commitment is not obtained by Buyer within _____ (____) days from the Date of Contract Acceptance, Seller, at Seller's election and upon written notice to Buyer, may declare this Contract null and void and of no further legal effect, and all Deposit(s) shall be disbursed in accordance with the Deposit(s) paragraph of this Contract. If Buyer has complied with all of Buyer's obligations under this Contract, including those with respect to applying for financing and seeking to obtain financing, then the release of Deposit(s) agreement shall provide that Deposit(s) shall be returned to Buyer.

21. ALTERNATE FINANCING: Provided Buyer timely and diligently pursues the financing described in Paragraph 19 **"Financing"**; Paragraph 20 **"Financing Application and Commitment"**; and the provisions of Paragraph 14 **"Buyer Responsibility"**, Buyer, at Buyer's election, may also apply for alternate financing. If Buyer, at Buyers sole option, obtains a written commitment for financing in which the loan amount, term of note, amortization period, interest rate, down payment or loan program differ from the financing as described in Paragraph 19 above, or any addendum to this Contract, the provision of Paragraph 19 or any addendum to this Contract shall be deemed to have been fully satisfied. Such alternate financing may not increase costs to Seller or exceed the time allowed to secure the financing commitment as provided in Paragraph 20 above, or any addendum to this Contract.

22. DEPOSIT(S): Buyer hereby authorizes and directs Broker as specified in Paragraph 18-d of this Contract to hold the initial Deposit(s) instrument without negotiation or Deposit(s) until the parties have executed and accepted this Contract. Upon acceptance, the initial Deposit(s) and additional Deposit(s) (the "Deposit(s)"), if any, shall be placed in escrow as provided below and in accordance with the requirements of Section 17-502(b)(1), Business Occupations and Professions Article, Annotated Code of Maryland. If Seller does not execute and accept this Contract, the initial Deposit(s) instrument shall be promptly returned to Buyer. Brokers may charge a fee for establishing an interest bearing account. Buyer and Seller instruct Broker to place the Deposit(s) in: **(Mark One)**

    ☐ A non-interest bearing account.
OR ☐ An interest bearing account, the interest on which, in absence of default by Buyer, shall accrue to the benefit of Buyer.

Buyer _____/_____   Page 4 of 10 Revision #9 10/04   Seller _____/_____

Maryland Association of REALTORS® Residential Sales Contract (continued)

Residential Contract of Sale

The Deposit(s) shall be disbursed by Broker at settlement. In the event this Contract shall be terminated or settlement does not occur, Buyer and Seller agree that the Deposit(s) shall be disbursed by Broker only in accordance with a release of Deposit(s) agreement executed by Buyer and Seller. In the event Buyer and/or Seller fail to complete the real estate transaction in accordance with the terms and conditions of this Contract, and either Buyer or Seller shall be unable or unwilling to execute a release of Deposit(s) agreement, Buyer and Seller hereby acknowledge and agree that Broker may distribute the Deposit(s) in accordance with the provisions of Section 17-505(b)(1), Business Occupations and Professions Articles, Annotated Code of Maryland.

23. CONVENTIONAL LOAN LENDER FEES/CHARGES: Buyer agrees to pay loan origination/loan discount fees of _____ % of the loan amount, and Seller agrees to pay loan origination/loan discount fees of _____ % of the loan amount. Buyer shall receive the benefit of any reduction in said fees. All loan insurance premiums as required by Lender shall be paid by Buyer. If the existing loan is to be transferred to/assumed by Buyer, Buyer agrees to pay all fees and charges required by Lender.

24. INCLUSIONS/EXCLUSIONS: Included in the purchase price are all permanently attached fixtures, including all smoke detectors. Certain other **now existing items** which may be considered personal property, whether installed or stored upon the property, are included if box below is marked.

INCLUDED
☐ Alarm System
☐ Built-in Microwave
☐ Ceiling Fan(s) # ___
☐ Central Vacuum
☐ Clothes Dryer
☐ Clothes Washer
☐ Cooktop
☐ Dishwasher
☐ Drapery/Curtain Rods
☐ Draperies/Curtains
☐ Electronic Air Filter

INCLUDED
☐ Exhaust Fan(s) # ___
☐ Exist. W/W Carpet
☐ Fireplace Screen/Doors
☐ Freezer
☐ Furnace Humidifier
☐ Garage Opener(s) #___ w/remote(s) #___
☐ Garbage Disposer
☐ Hot Tub, Equip. & Cover
☐ Intercom
☐ Playground Equipment

INCLUDED
☐ Pool, Equip. & Cover
☐ Refrigerator(s) # ___ w/ice maker
☐ Satellite Dish
☐ Screens
☐ Shades/Blinds
☐ Storage Shed(s) # ___
☐ Storm Doors
☐ Storm Windows
☐ Stove or Range
☐ T.V. Antenna

INCLUDED
☐ Trash Compactor
☐ Wall Oven(s) # ____
☐ Water Filter
☐ Water Softener
☐ Window A/C Unit(s) # ____
☐ Window Fan(s) # ____
☐ Wood Stove

ADDITIONAL INCLUSIONS (SPECIFY): _____

ADDITIONAL EXCLUSIONS (SPECIFY): _____

25. AGENCY CONFIRMATION: Buyer and Seller each confirm that disclosure of the agency relationships as described in this Contract conforms with the agency relationships previously agreed to in writing.

26. BROKER'S FEE: All parties irrevocably instruct the settlement agent to collect the fee or compensation and disburse same according to the terms and conditions provided in the listing agreement and/or agency representation agreement. Settlement shall not be a condition precedent to payment of compensation.

27. BROKER LIABILITY: Brokers, their agents, subagents and employees do not assume any responsibility for the condition of the Property or for the performance of this Contract by any or all parties hereto. By signing this Contract, Buyer and Seller acknowledge that they have not relied on any representations made by Brokers, or any agents, subagents or employees of Brokers, except those representations expressly set forth in this Contract.

28. ATTORNEY'S FEES: In any action or proceeding between Buyer and Seller based, in whole or in part, upon the performance or non-performance of the terms and conditions of this Contract, including, but not limited to, breach of contract, negligence, misrepresentation or fraud, the prevailing party in such action or proceeding shall be entitled to receive reasonable attorney's fees from the other party as determined by the court or arbitrator. In any action or proceeding between Buyer and Seller and/or between Buyer and Broker(s) and/or Seller and Broker(s) resulting in Broker(s) being made a party to such action or proceeding, including, but not limited to, any litigation, arbitration, or complaint and claim before the Maryland Real Estate Commission, whether as defendant, cross-defendant, third-party defendant or respondent, Buyer and Seller jointly and severally, agree to indemnify and hold Broker(s) harmless from and against any and all liability, loss, cost, damages or expenses (including filing fees, court costs, service of process fees, transcript fees and attorneys' fees) incurred by Broker(s) in such action or proceeding, providing that such action or proceeding does not result in a judgment against Broker(s).

As used herein, the term "Broker(s)" shall mean (a) the two (2) Brokers as identified at the top of Page 1 of this Contract; (b) the two (2) named Sales Associates as identified at the top of Page 1 of the Contract; and, (c) any agent, subagent, salesperson, independent contractor and/or employees of Broker(s). The term "Broker(s)" shall also mean, in the singular, any or either of the named Broker(s) and/or Sales Associate(s) as identified or, in the plural, both of the named Brokers and/or Sales Associates as identified.

Maryland Association of REALTORS® Residential Sales Contract (continued)

Residential Contract of Sale

This Paragraph 28 shall apply to any and all such action(s) or proceeding(s) against Broker(s) including those action(s) or proceeding(s) based, in whole or in part, upon any alleged act(s) or omission(s) by Broker(s), including, but not limited to, any alleged act of misrepresentation, fraud, non-disclosure, negligence, violation of any statutory or common law duty, or breach of fiduciary duty by Broker(s). The provision of this Paragraph 28 shall survive closing and shall not be deemed to have been extinguished by merger with the deed.

29. NON-ASSIGNABILITY: This Contract may not be assigned without the written consent of Buyer and Seller. If Buyer and Seller agree in writing to an assignment of this Contract, the original parties to this Contract remain obligated hereunder until settlement.

30. LEASES: Seller may neither negotiate new leases nor renew existing leases for the Property which extend beyond settlement or possession date without Buyer's written consent.

31. PROPERTY INSURANCE:

A. RISK OF LOSS: The Property is to be held at the risk of Seller until legal title has passed or possession has been given to Buyer. If, prior to the time legal title has passed or possession has been given to Buyer, whichever shall occur first, all or a substantial part of the Property is destroyed or damaged, without fault of Buyer, then this Contract, at the option of Buyer, upon written notice to Seller, shall be null and void and of no further effect, and

B. INSURABILITY: An informational brochure published by the Maryland Association of REALTORS®, Inc. titled "The New Reality of Property Insurance – What You Should Know" is available to explain current issues relative to obtaining insurance coverage for the Property to be purchased.

32. NOTICE TO THE PARTIES: BROKERS, THEIR AGENTS, SUBAGENTS AND EMPLOYEES, MAKE NO REPRESENTATIONS WITH RESPECT TO THE FOLLOWING:

A. Water quantity, quality, color, or taste or operating conditions of public and/or private water systems.

B. Location, size or operating condition of on-site sewage disposal systems.

C. The extensions of public utilities by local municipal authorities, existence or availability of public utilities, and any assessments, fees or costs for public utilities which might be imposed by local municipal authorities, should public utilities be extended or available to the subject Property. (Buyer should consult the Department of Public Works to determine the availability of proposed future extensions of utilities.)

D. Lot size and exact location: If the subject Property is part of a recorded subdivision, Buyer can review the plat upon request at the Record Office. If the subject Property is not part of a recorded subdivision, Buyer may verify exact size and location through a survey by a licensed engineer or land surveyor, at Buyer's expense.

E. Existing zoning or permitted uses of the Property: Buyer should contact the Zoning Office and/or a licensed engineer to verify zoning and permitted uses.

F. Brokers/agents are not advising the parties as to certain other issues, including without limitation: soil conditions; flood hazard areas; possible restrictions of the use of property due to restrictive covenants, subdivision, environmental laws, easements or other documents; airport or aircraft noise; planned land use, roads or highways; and construction materials and/or hazardous materials, including without limitation flame retardant treated plywood (FRT), radon, radium, mold spores, urea formaldehyde foam insulation (UFFI), synthetic stucco (EIFS), asbestos, polybutylene piping and lead-based paint. Information relating to these issues may be available from appropriate governmental authorities. This disclosure is not intended to provide an inspection contingency.

G. Buyer and Seller each assume full responsibility for selecting and compensating their respective vendors.

33. SINGLE FAMILY RESIDENTIAL REAL PROPERTY DISCLOSURE NOTICE: BUYER IS ADVISED OF THE RIGHT TO RECEIVE A "DISCLOSURE AND DISCLAIMER STATEMENT" FROM SELLER (SECTION 10-702 REAL PROPERTY ARTICLE, ANNOTATED CODE OF MARYLAND).

34. NOTICE TO BUYER CONCERNING THE CHESAPEAKE AND ATLANTIC COASTAL BAYS CRITICAL AREA: Buyer is advised that all or a portion of the property may be located in the "Critical Area" of the Chesapeake and Atlantic Coastal Bays, and that additional zoning, land use, and resource protection regulations apply in this area. The "Critical Area" generally consists of all land and water areas within 1,000 feet beyond the landward boundaries of state or private wetlands, the Chesapeake Bay, the Atlantic Coastal Bays, and all of their tidal tributaries. The "Critical Area" also includes the waters of and lands under the Chesapeake Bay, the Atlantic Coastal Bays and all of their tidal tributaries to the head of tide. For information as to whether the property is located within the Critical Area, Buyer may contact the local Department of Planning and Zoning, which maintains maps showing the extent of the Critical Area in the jurisdiction. Allegany, Carroll, Frederick, Garrett, Howard, Montgomery and Washington Counties do not include land located in the Critical Area.

35. DEED AND TITLE: Upon payment of the purchase price, a deed for the Property containing covenants of special warranty and further assurances, shall be executed by Seller and shall convey the Property to Buyer. Title to the Property, including all chattels included in the purchase, shall be good and merchantable, free of liens and

Buyer _____/_____   Page 6 of 10   Revision #9   10/04   Seller _____/_____

Maryland Association of REALTORS® Residential Sales Contract (continued)

Residential Contract of Sale

encumbrances except as specified herein; except for use and occupancy restrictions of public record which are generally applicable to properties in the immediate neighborhood or the subdivision in which the Property is located and publicly recorded easements for public utilities and any other easements which may be observed by an inspection of the Property. Buyer expressly assumes the risk that restrictive covenants, zoning laws or other recorded documents may restrict or prohibit the use of the Property for the purpose(s) intended by Buyer. In the event Seller is unable to give good and merchantable title or such as can be insured by a Maryland licensed title insurer, with Buyer paying not more than the standard rate as filed with the Maryland Insurance Commissioner, Seller, at Seller's expense, shall have the option of curing any defect so as to enable Seller to give good and merchantable title or, if Buyer is willing to accept title without said defect being cured, paying any special premium on behalf of Buyer to obtain title insurance on the Property to the benefit of Buyer. In the event Seller elects to cure any defects in title, this Contract shall continue to remain in full force and effect; and the date of settlement shall be extended for a period not to exceed fourteen (14) additional days. If Seller is unable to cure such title defect(s) and is unable to obtain a policy of title insurance on the Property to the benefit of Buyer from a Maryland licensed title insurer, Buyer shall have the option of taking such title as Seller can give, or terminating this Contract and being reimbursed by Seller for cost of searching title as may have been incurred not to exceed 1/2 of 1% of the purchase price. In the latter event, there shall be no further liability or obligation on either of the parties hereto; and this Contract shall become null and void; and all Deposit(s) shall be disbursed in accordance with the Deposit(s) paragraph of this Contract. In no event shall Broker(s) or their agent(s) have any liability for any defect in Seller's title.

36. WETLANDS NOTICE: Buyer is advised that if all or a portion of the Property being purchased is wetlands, the approval of the U.S. Army Corps of Engineers will be necessary before a building permit can be issued for the Property. Additionally, the future use of existing dwellings may be restricted due to wetlands. The Corps has adopted a broad definition of wetlands which encompasses a large portion of the Chesapeake Bay Region. Other portions of the State may also be considered wetlands. For information as to whether the Property includes wetlands, Buyer may contact the Baltimore District of the U.S. Army Corps of Engineers. Buyer may also elect, at Buyer's expense, to engage the services of a qualified specialist to inspect the Property for the presence of wetlands prior to submitting a written offer to purchase the Property; or Buyer may include in Buyer's written offer a clause making Buyer's purchase of the Property contingent upon a satisfactory wetlands inspection.

37. HOMEOWNER'S ASSOCIATION: The Property is not part of a development subject to the imposition of mandatory fees as defined by the Maryland Homeowner's Association Act, unless acknowledged by attached addendum.

38. FOREIGN INVESTMENT TAXES-FIRPTA: Section 1445 of the United States Internal Revenue Code of 1986 provides that a Buyer of residential real property located in the United States must withhold federal income taxes from the payment of the purchase price if (a) the purchase price exceeds Three Hundred Thousand Dollars ($300,000.00) and (b) the seller is a foreign person. Unless otherwise stated in an addendum attached hereto, if the purchase price is in excess of Three Hundred Thousand Dollars ($300,000.00), Seller represents that Seller is not a non-resident alien, foreign corporation, foreign partnership, foreign trust or foreign estate (as those terms are defined by the Internal Revenue Code and applicable regulations) and agrees to execute an affidavit to this effect at the time of settlement.

39. AGRICULTURALLY ASSESSED PROPERTY: The Property, or any portion thereof, may be subject to an "Agricultural Land Transfer Tax" as imposed by Section 13-301 et seq. of the Tax-Property Article, Annotated Code of Maryland, by reason of the Property's having been assessed on the basis of agricultural use. Agricultural taxes assessed as a result of this transfer shall be paid by _____.

40. INTERNAL REVENUE SERVICE FILING: Buyer and Seller each agree to cooperate with the person responsible for settlement by providing all necessary information so that a report can be filed with the Internal Revenue Service, as required by Section 6045 of the IRS Code. To the extent permitted by law, any fees incurred as a result of such filing will be paid by the Seller.

41. MARYLAND NON-RESIDENT SELLER: If the Property is not the Seller's principal residence and the Seller is a non-resident individual of the State of Maryland or is a non-resident entity which is not formed under the laws of the State of Maryland or qualified to do business in the State of Maryland, a withholding tax from the proceeds of sale may be withheld at the time of settlement except as otherwise provided by Maryland law. (See Maryland Non-Resident Seller Transfer Withholding Tax Addendum.)

42. GUARANTY FUND: NOTICE TO BUYER: BUYER IS PROTECTED BY THE REAL ESTATE GUARANTY FUND OF THE MARYLAND REAL ESTATE COMMISSION FOR LOSSES COVERED BY SECTION 17-404 OF THE BUSINESS OCCUPATIONS AND PROFESSIONS ARTICLE OF THE MARYLAND CODE, IN AN AMOUNT NOT EXCEEDING $25,000 FOR ANY CLAIM.

FIGURE 9.1

Maryland Association of REALTORS® Residential Sales Contract (continued)

Residential Contract of Sale

43. HOME AND/OR ENVIRONMENTAL INSPECTION, LIMITED WARRANTY: Buyer acknowledges, subject to Seller acceptance, that Buyer is afforded the opportunity, at Buyer's sole cost and expense, to condition Buyer's purchase of the Property upon a Home Inspection and/or Environmental Inspection in order to ascertain the physical condition of the Property or the existence of environmental hazards. If Buyer desires a Home Inspection and/or Environmental Inspection contingency, such contingency must be included in an Addendum to this Contract. Buyer and Seller acknowledge that Brokers, agents or subagents are not responsible for the existence or discovery of property defects. NOTICE TO BUYER: IF A WARRANTY PLAN IS BEING OFFERED WITH THE PURCHASE OF THE PROPERTY, IT MAY BE A LIMITED WARRANTY. SINCE SUCH WARRANTY PLANS DO NOT COVER STRUCTURAL DEFECTS AND MAY NOT COVER PRE-EXISTING DEFECTS, BUYER SHOULD REQUEST THE REAL ESTATE AGENT TO PROVIDE BUYER WITH ANY BROCHURE WHICH DESCRIBES THE PLAN IN ORDER TO DETERMINE THE EXTENT OF COVERAGE PROVIDED BY THE WARRANTY.

Inspection(s) Addenda Attached _____ _____ Inspection(s) Declined _____ _____
               BUYER   **BUYER**   **BUYER**   **BUYER**

44. LEAD-BASED PAINT HAZARDS:

A. FEDERAL LEAD-BASED PAINT LAW: Title X, Section 1018, the Residential Lead-Based Paint Hazard Reduction Act of 1992 (the Act), requires the disclosure of certain information regarding lead-based paint and lead-based paint hazards in connection with the sale of residential real property. Unless otherwise exempt, the Act applies only to housing constructed prior to 1978. A Seller of pre-1978 housing is required to disclose to Buyer, based upon Seller's actual knowledge, all known lead-based paint hazards in the Property and provide Buyer with any available reports in the Seller's possession relating to lead-based paint or lead-based paint hazards applicable to the Property. Seller, however, is not required to conduct or pay for any lead-based paint risk assessment or inspection. At the time that the offer to purchase is entered into by Buyer, Seller is required to provide Buyer with the EPA pamphlet entitled "Protect Your Family From Lead In Your Home" and a "Disclosure of Information on Lead- Based Paint and Lead-Based Paint Hazards" form. **Seller is required under the Act to provide Buyer with a ten (10) day time period (or other mutually agreeable time period) for Buyer, at Buyer's expense, to conduct a risk assessment or inspection for the presence of lead-based paint and/or lead-based paint hazards unless Buyer waives such assessment or inspection by indicating such waiver on the Lead-Based Paint Disclosure form. Notwithstanding the right of the Buyer under the Act to conduct a risk assessment inspection for presence of lead-based paint and/or lead-based paint hazards, Seller is not required by the Act to permit Buyer, and Buyer shall have no right, to rescind this Contract based upon the results of such inspection, even if the inspection reveals the presence of lead-based paint and/or lead-based paint hazards within the Property, unless otherwise provided in a written addendum to this Contract. (If applicable, see Lead-Based Paint Hazard Inspection Addendum.) Seller and any agent involved in the transaction are required to retain a copy of the completed Lead-Based Paint Disclosure form for a period of three (3) years following the date of settlement. A SELLER WHO FAILS TO GIVE THE REQUIRED LEAD-BASED PAINT DISCLOSURE FORM AND EPA PAMPHLET MAY BE LIABLE UNDER THE ACT FOR THREE TIMES THE AMOUNT OF DAMAGES AND MAY BE SUBJECT TO BOTH CIVIL AND CRIMINAL PENALTIES.** Seller represents and warrants to Buyer, Broker(s), Broker(s)' agents and subagents, intending that they rely upon such warranty and representation, that the property: **(Seller to initial applicable line):** _____was constructed prior to 1978 OR _____was not constructed prior to 1978 OR _____ the date of construction is uncertain. If the Property was constructed prior to 1978 or if the date of construction is uncertain, as indicated by Seller's initial above, Buyer and Seller mutually agree that the requirements of the Act shall apply to the sale of the Property. Buyer and Seller acknowledge that the real estate brokers and salespersons involved in the sale of the Property have no duty to ascertain or verify the date of construction and assume no such duty or responsibility. Buyer and Seller agree, represent and warrant, each unto the other, that no binding and enforceable contract shall be deemed to exist or to have been formed unless the requirements of the Act have been complied with prior to the execution of this Contract by Buyer and Seller. Buyer and Seller represent and warrant that each intended, as a material term of the offer and acceptance, that the requirements of the Act be complied with as an express condition of the formation of a binding and enforceable contract by and between the parties. Buyer and Seller acknowledge by their respective initials below that they have read and understand the provisions of this Paragraph.

_____**(BUYER)** _____**(BUYER)**   _____**(SELLER)** _____**(SELLER)**

B. MARYLAND LEAD POISONING PREVENTION PROGRAM: If the Property was constructed prior to 1950 and Buyer intends to lease the Property effective immediately following settlement or in the future, Buyer acknowledges that Buyer shall be required to register the Property with the Maryland Department of the Environment within thirty (30) days following the date of settlement or within thirty (30) days following the conversion of the Property to

Buyer _____/_____   Page 8 of 10   Revision #9 10/04   Seller _____/_____

FIGURE 9.1

Maryland Association of REALTORS® Residential Sales Contract (continued)

Residential Contract of Sale

rental property as required by the Maryland Lead Poisoning Prevention Program (the "Maryland Program"). Buyer shall be responsible for full compliance under the Maryland Program, including but not limited to, registration; inspections; lead-paint risk reduction and abatement procedures; payment of all fees, costs and expenses; and the notice requirements to tenants as well as the requirements of qualified offers.

_____(BUYER) _____(BUYER)

C. REGISTERED PROPERTY **(Applicable only in the event the Property is already registered under the Maryland Program):** Under the Maryland Lead Poison Prevention Program (the "Maryland Program"), any residential dwelling constructed prior to 1950 is required to be registered in the Maryland Program. Any residential dwelling constructed between 1950 and 1978 may be registered in the Maryland Program at the election of the owner. If the Property is required to be registered or has been registered under the Maryland Program at the election of the owner, the Property is deemed to be "Affected Property" under the Maryland Program. Seller hereby advises Buyer that the Property is an Affected Property as defined under the Maryland Program. Seller further discloses to Buyer that an event *(initial applicable line)* _____ has; or _____ has not occurred which obligates Seller to perform either the modified or full risk reduction treatment of the Property as required under the Maryland Program. If an event has occurred which obligates Seller to perform either the modified or full risk reduction treatment of the Property, Seller hereby discloses the scope of such treatment as follows:_____

_____

If such event has occurred, Seller *(initial applicable line)* _____ will; or _____ will not perform the required treatment prior to transfer of title of the Property to Buyer.

_____(BUYER) _____(BUYER)

45. FOREST CONSERVATION AND MANAGEMENT PROGRAM: Buyer is hereby notified that this transfer may be subject to the Forest Conservation and Management Program imposed by Section 8-211 et seq. of the Tax-Property Article, Annotated Code of Maryland. Forest Conservation/Management program taxes assessed as a result of this transfer shall be paid by the _____.

46. FOREST CONSERVATION ACT NOTICE: If the Property is a tract of land 40,000 square feet or more in size, Buyer is notified that, unless exempted by applicable law, as a prerequisite to any subdivision plan or grading or sediment control permit for the Property, Buyer will be required to comply with the provisions of the Maryland Forest Conservation Act imposed by Section 5-1601 et seq. of the Natural Resources Article, Annotated Code of Maryland, including, among other things, the submission and acceptance of a Forest Stand Delineation and a Forest Conservation Plan for the Property in accordance with applicable laws and regulations. Unless otherwise expressly set forth in an addendum to this Contract, Seller represents and warrants that the Property is not currently subject to a Forest Conservation Plan, Management Agreement or any other pending obligation binding the owner of the Property under said Act; further, Seller represents and warrants that no activities have been undertaken on the Property by Seller in violation of the Forest Conservation Act.

47. ADDENDA: The Addenda marked below, which are hereby attached, are made a part of this Contract:

☐ Affiliated Business Disclosure Notice
☐ Cash/Conventional Financing Appraisal
   Contingency Addendum
☐ Condominium Resale
☐ Disclosure of Licensee Status
☐ First-Time Maryland Home Buyer Transfer &
   Recordation Tax Addendum
☐ Homeowners Association Notice
☐ Kickout Addendum
☐ Lead-Based Paint Hazard Inspection
☐ Lead-Based Paint and Lead-Based Hazards
   Disclosure of Information
☐ Local City/County Certifications/Registrations
☐ Local City/County Notices/Disclosure

☐ Maryland Non-Resident Seller Transfer
   Withholding Tax
☐ Mold Inspection
☐ Notice to Buyer – Maryland Residential Real
   Property Disclosure/Disclaimer Act
☐ On-Site Sewage Disposal System Inspection
☐ Property Inspections
☐ Purchase Price Escalation
☐ Sale, Financing, Settlement or Lease of Other
   Real Estate
☐ Seller's Purchase of Another Property
☐ Third Party Approval
☐ Water Quality Addendum

☐ Other Addenda/Special Conditions: _____

Buyer _____/_____   Page 9 of 10   Revision #9   10/04   Seller _____/_____

FIGURE 9.1

Maryland Association of REALTORS® Residential Sales Contract (continued)

Residential Contract of Sale

48. PARAGRAPH HEADINGS: The Paragraph headings of this Contract are for convenience and reference only, and in no way define or limit the intent, rights or obligations of the parties.

49. ENTIRE AGREEMENT: This Contract and any Addenda thereto contain the final and entire agreement between the parties, and neither they nor their agents shall be bound by any terms, conditions, statements, warranties or representations, oral or written, not herein contained. The parties to this Contract mutually agree that it is binding upon them, their heirs, executors, administrators, personal representatives, successors and, if permitted as herein provided, assigns. Once signed, the terms of this Contract can only be changed by a document executed by all parties. This Contract shall be interpreted and construed in accordance with the laws of the State of Maryland. It is further agreed that this Contract may be executed in counterparts, each of which when considered together shall constitute the original Contract.

50. ELECTRONIC DELIVERY: The parties agree that this Contract offer shall be deemed validly executed and delivered by a party if a party executes this Contract and delivers a copy of the executed Contract to the other party by telefax or telecopier transmittal.

_____   _____   _____   _____
Buyer's Signature   Date   **Seller's Signature**   Date

_____   _____   _____   _____
Buyer's Signature   Date   **Seller's Signature**   Date

DATE OF CONTRACT ACCEPTANCE: _____

When they are themselves either the sellers or purchasers of real estate, licensees must notify the other party of their licensee status. This notification must be in writing and is typically within the contract itself.

A real estate sales contract must disclose *any ground rent or leasehold interest* involved in the sale. If the ground rent is irredeemable, this fact must be indicated. If the ground rent is to be redeemed at the time of settlement, responsibility for notice, costs of redemption, and so forth should be fixed as part of the written agreement. A contract for the sale of real property subject to a ground rent must contain a notice of the existence of the ground rent and notice that if ground rent is not timely paid, the reversionary owner of the ground rent may bring an action for possession against the ground rent tenant and, as a result of the action, may come to own the property in fee.

The Brokers Act requires that every contract for use in the sale of residential property used as a dwelling place for one or two single-family units must contain the following statement in conspicuous type or handwritten:

> Section 14-104 of the *Real Property* Article of the Annotated Code of Maryland provides that, unless otherwise negotiated in the contract or provided by local law, the cost of any recordation tax or any state or local transfer tax shall be shared equally between the buyer and seller.

Notwithstanding this statement, the *First-Time Home Buyers Closing Cost Reduction Act* of 1995 reduces 0.5 percent to 0.25 percent the State transfer tax in transactions involving first-time homebuyers, with that entire amount to be paid by the seller. In such a transaction, the seller must also pay the entire amount of recordation and local transfer tax, unless there is an express agreement between the parties to the contrary. Other details on this matter appear in Chapter 8 of this book.

If the property is subject to a *homeowners' association* (HOA) and *to the imposition of mandatory HOA fees*, this must be disclosed to purchasers, preferably by reference, within the purchase agreement. Similar reference should be included about a residential property within a condominium regime.

Contracts for the sale of real estate must contain a *notice of purchaser protection* by the Real Estate Guaranty Fund for actual losses in an amount not to exceed $25,000 for any one transaction.

A real estate broker must promptly place all earnest (deposit) monies in a special non-interest-bearing account unless directed to do otherwise by both buyer and seller. Contracts in which a licensee holds an earnest deposit should also authorize that broker to disperse the deposit according to the rules now contained in Section 505 of the Brokers Act (Title 17).

The Brokers Act mandates that contracts reveal that buyers of single-family dwellings may not be required to employ specific title insurance, settlement, or escrow companies, or title attorneys, but may choose their own. (See Chapter 1.)

Every seller is also required to notify the purchaser when land being transferred may be *subject to agricultural land transfer tax*. The statewide MAR Residential Contract of Sale provides that sellers who fail to notify buyers in accordance with this requirement are liable to those buyers for the agricultural land transfer tax that the buyers will have to pay. This provision can, of course, be removed from the contract language by negotiation before it is signed.

Contract Notice about "Critical Areas"

All contracts for sale of property suitable for one or two single-family units entered into after October 1, 2004, must contain the following notice:

> ### Notice to Buyer Concerning the Chesapeake and Atlantic Coastal Bays Critical Area
>
> Buyer is advised that all or a portion of the property may be located in the "Critical Area" of the Chesapeake and Atlantic Coastal Bays, and that additional zoning, land use, and resource protection regulations apply in this area. The "Critical Area": generally consists of all land and water areas within 1,000 feet beyond the landward boundaries of state or private wetlands, the Chesapeake Bay, the Atlantic Coastal Bays, and all of their tidal tributaries. The "Critical Area" also includes the waters of and lands under the Chesapeake Bay, the Atlantic Coastal Bays, and all of their tidal tributaries to the head of tide. For information as to whether the property is located within the Critical Area, Buyer may contact the local Department of Planning and Zoning, which maintains maps showing the extent of the Critical Area in the jurisdiction. Allegany, Carroll, Frederick, Garrett, Howard, Montgomery, and Washington Counties do not include land located in the Critical Area.

Other Required Clauses

The *Real Property* Article requires that contracts of sale must also include the following notices and disclosures, where applicable:

- Notice pertaining to sale of real property in Prince George's County creating subdivision
- Notice pertaining to resale of condominium unit
- Notice pertaining to initial sale of lot in development containing more than 12 lots
- Notice pertaining to resale of any lot or initial sale of lot in development containing 12 or fewer lots
- Notice pertaining to initial sale of lot not intended to be occupied or rented for residential purposes
- Notice pertaining to initial sale of cooperative interests
- Notice of liability for agricultural land transfer tax
- Notice to purchaser pertaining to sale of certain land in Prince George's County, that the land being sold is subject to a development impact fee, and the unpaid amount of that fee
- Notice pertaining to sale of certain agriculturally assessed land in St. Mary's and Charles Counties

Baltimore City and most counties have various additional contract requirements unique to their jurisdictions. Information about these requirements is available from local boards or associations for use by their members. For example, contracts for the sale of multiple-dwelling property in Baltimore City must contain a clause whereby the seller guarantees that the property being purchased complies with the Baltimore City Multiple-Dwelling Code and that the license will be delivered to the buyer at the time of settlement.

Property in Maryland not served by public sewerage and water systems is subject to the State Department of Health and Mental Hygiene laws and regulations pertaining to individual sewerage disposal systems and wells. The licensee must provide the buyer of unimproved land with a notice that if the property being purchased is to be used for residential purposes, the buyer, before signing the contract, should ascertain the status of sewerage and water facilities and, if required, whether the property will be approved for installation of a well and/or private sewerage system.

The Department of Veterans Affairs (VA), the Federal Housing Administration (FHA), and many private lenders require an evaluation by the local health department of the sewerage system and the water supply on residential property prior to settlement. When this is required, a bacteriologic sample must be collected from the well and analyzed by the health department. Consequently, licensees involved in such a transaction must allow sufficient time for these procedures when estimating a settlement date. Assistance and information are available from the Department of Health and Mental Hygiene, O'Connor Building, 201 West Preston Street, Baltimore, MD 21201, or from local health boards.

Contingency and Other Clauses

To express the exact agreements of the parties to a contract and to protect the best interests of their clients, licensees often employ contingency and other addenda. They should avoid drafting the language of such clauses but rather make use of clauses with wording drafted by competent legal counsel. Additional disclosure clauses and contingency language often address such matters as the following:

- Details of financing
- Impact of appraisal
- Buyer's prompt loan application and receipt of lender's commitment
- Lenders' fees and charges and who will receive the benefit of any favorable changes due to market conditions
- Home inspections and their impact
- Sale of purchasers' home and any release (kickout) clause
- Existence and extent of any leasehold interests
- Disposition of any agricultural crops
- Party to pay fees for IRS filing

Release from Contract of Sale

When one party is unable or unwilling to consummate a contract of sale and the other party agrees to release that party, the broker should provide a competently drafted release form for signatures of both parties. If, on the other hand, the parties do not agree on how the deposit is to be distributed, the broker is free to follow the procedure described in Chapter 3.

■ OPTION AGREEMENTS

In Maryland a **lease option agreement** is defined as any lease agreement containing a clause that gives the tenant some power to purchase the landlord's interest in real property. No lease option purchase of improved residential property is valid in Maryland unless it contains the statement in capital letters "THIS IS NOT A CONTRACT TO BUY" and a clear statement of the option agreement's purpose and effect with respect to the purchase of the property that is the subject of the option.

Even though details of times, prices, dates, financing, prorations, settlement expenses, and so forth—everything needed for a contract of sale—are clearly set forth in the option, it still "IS NOT A CONTRACT TO BUY." It is, rather, a unilateral contract that would become bilateral and binding on both parties only if option rights are exercised by the optionee.

■ CONSTRUCTION CONTRACTS

Prior to the signing of a contract for the construction of a single-family dwelling using alternating current (AC) electrical service and a public water system, a builder must, under certain conditions, offer prospective buyers the option of having a sprinkler system installed. Some jurisdictions in the state already require that such systems be installed in new homes in addition to smoke detectors.

■ NEW HOME WARRANTIES AND DEPOSITS

Before entering into contracts for sale or construction of new homes, builders must disclose to purchasers on a State-mandated form whether they participate in a **new home warranty** security plan and the extent of that plan. If builders do not participate in a new home warranty plan, they must disclose, among other things, that without a new home warranty, the purchaser may be afforded only certain limited (statutory) warranties.

The disclosure must also state that builders of new homes are not required to be licensed by the state and are not licensed in most local jurisdictions. Purchasers who acknowledge by their signature that they have been so informed then have five working days to rescind their contract and recover all money paid for their purchases. Contracts for purchase or construction of new homes that do not contain this notice are voidable by the buyers. Builders are, however, required to register with the Maryland Attorney General, thus bringing some oversight of that industry under State Government influence. If builders' registrations are revoked they are no longer allowed to sell homes they have built.

Any person knowingly misrepresenting the existence of a new home warranty is subject to a fine not exceeding $50,000, imprisonment for not more than two years, or both, in addition to other penalties provided by the *Real Property* Article.

In connection with the sale and purchase of new, single-family residential units, including condominiums that are not completed at the time of contracting the sale, if the vendor or builder obligates purchasers to pay any sum of money before units have been completed and the realty has been granted to the purchaser, the builder or vendor is required to

■ deposit or hold the sums in an escrow account to ensure their return to purchasers who are entitled to them, or
■ obtain and maintain a corporate surety bond to provide return of deposits to purchasers who are entitled to them.

The *Maryland Custom Home Protection Act,* found in the *Real Property* Article, provides protection for buyers of newly constructed homes. This law sets standards for contract payments, surety bonds, contract requirements, mortgage loans, and sales by licensed real estate brokers. Detailed provisions govern brokers' handling of deposit monies.

■ INSTALLMENT CONTRACTS

Maryland statutes provide protections for purchasers of residential property under **installment contracts,** which are stronger than protections provided by common law. Some Maryland requirements for sale of residential property by installment contract are presented in Chapter 12. The principal text presents general information on installment contracts in its chapters on contracts and on finance.

■ DISCLOSURE REQUIREMENTS OF INITIAL SALES OF CONDOMINIUMS

A contract for the initial sale or resale of a condominium unit requires the disclosure of certain information to the purchaser before the execution of the contract. The buyer of a condominium unit has 15 days (for initial sale) or 7 days (for resale) from the signing of such a contract within which to rescind the agreement. Looking at it from another perspective, the developer must deliver all required papers to condominium purchasers 15 days prior to settlement. Purchasers cannot waive this requirement in a sales contract. However, they are permitted to proceed to settlement without having received the required papers. If they do this, they still retain the right to rescind the transaction for up to one year. A contract for the initial sale of a residential condominium unit to a member of the public must also contain notice of the developer's warranties.

■ RESIDENTIAL PROPERTY DISCLOSURE AND DISCLAIMER STATEMENT

The required use of the Residential Property Disclosure and Disclaimer Statement is presented in Chapter 4 of this book. Failure to present the Statement to purchasers in a timely fashion may enable them to rescind the contract as late as the day when settlement is to take place—or at least until they apply for the loan required for the purchase.

Use of the Disclosure and Disclaimer Statement is *not* required in

- the initial sale of a single-family residential real property that has never been occupied or for which a certificate of occupancy has been issued within one year before the seller and buyer enter into a contract;
- the transfer of properties exempt from transfer tax under the *Tax-Property Article* (land installment contracts and certain options to purchase require the use of the statement);
- sale by a lender, an affiliate, or a subsidiary of a lender of property acquired by foreclosure or by deed in lieu of foreclosure;
- a sheriff's sale, tax sale, or sale by fore-closure, partition, or by court-appointed trustee;
- a transfer by a fiduciary in the course of the administration of a decedent's estate, guardianship, conservatorship, or trust;
- the transfer of a single-family residential real property to be converted by the buyer into use other than residential use or to be demolished; or
- the sale of unimproved real property.

POWERS OF ATTORNEY

Attorneys-in-fact are *persons* granted authority in *documents* called *powers of attorney* to sell or grant property in a Maryland real estate transaction on behalf of the owner who granted the power. When a deed or other instrument is signed by an attorney-in-fact who is acting under such a document—properly signed and acknowledged—that document must be recorded either *before or on the day* the deed or mortgage is placed in the public record. It may even be recorded after the deed has been recorded if

- the power of attorney was both dated and acknowledged on or before the effective date of the deed;
- the power of attorney had not been revoked up to the time of the recording of the deed; and
- the deed that was recorded contained or was accompanied by an affidavit from the attorney-in-fact (agent) stating he or she had no actual knowledge that the person who granted the power of attorney had either revoked it, had become legally disabled, or had been incompetent at the time of the agent's signing the deed.

It is prudent, in all cases, for licensees, in preparing for settlement, to check with settlement officers before the scheduled closing to make sure such powers of attorney are in a form acceptable to them and to the lending institutions involved.

DUTIES AND OBLIGATIONS OF LICENSEES

The Regulations of the Commission set forth a number of duties and obligations that the real estate licensee has toward clients, the public, and fellow licensees with respect to contracts. These include

- prompt presentation of all written offers and counteroffers,
- reduction of all agreements to a written form that sets forth all the obligations of the parties,
- seeking proper signatures on all forms, and
- giving and retaining copies of all signed agreements.

■ EQUITABLE TITLE AND RISK OF LOSS

When a contract of sale has been signed by all parties, the buyers receive **equitable title.** This is called the *doctrine of equitable conversion.* Under Maryland common law, possession of equitable title places the risk of loss due to accidental damage to the premises on the buyers who hold an **executory contract**—one that exists between contract signing and closing. This is true unless the sellers cause the damage or the buyers have taken presettlement, physical possession of the premises. To offset this possibility, most contracts in Maryland include a provision that the sellers will maintain until settlement or occupancy—whichever occurs first—full insurance on the property and bear the risk of loss due to damage of the property. Licensees should see that this issue is addressed in any contract they negotiate.

■ RESIDENTIAL SALES CONTRACT PROVIDED FOR MARYLAND REALTORS®

The residential sales contract form that appears as Figure 9.1, beginning on page 107, is provided to members of the Maryland Association of REALTORS® for their exclusive use. The Association also provides a wide variety of addenda for specific situations and to meet certain legal requirements. Examples are the Lead-Based Paint Hazard Inspection Addendum, required by federal law in residential sales of structures built before 1978, and the First-Time Maryland Home Buyer Transfer and Recordation Tax Addendum.

An industry form is also provided that warns sellers that providing the buyers with the Commission's Residential Property Condition Disclosure and Disclaimer Statement form does not relieve them from affirmative disclosure of material facts relating to the property.

QUESTIONS

1. In Maryland, contracts for the sale of real estate must be
   1. in writing to be enforceable.
   2. on a standard printed form.
   3. signed by the seller only.
   4. signed by the buyer only.

2. Oral contracts for the sale of real estate are
   1. valid.
   2. called parol agreements.
   3. enforceable in a court of law.
   4. illegal.

3. Licensees buying or selling real property must
   1. advise the other party of their licensee status.
   2. advise lending institutions of their status.
   3. write to the Real Estate Commission.
   4. advise the Attorney General.

4. Which of the following disclosures will *NOT* be necessary in a Maryland real estate sales contract?
   1. That a leasehold interest is involved in the sale
   2. That the owner/seller is a real estate licensee
   3. The existence of possible tax charges for agricultural land development
   4. The title insurance company name

5. Use of the Critical Areas notice is required
   1. in all counties with major waterways.
   2. only in counties bordering on Atlantic or Chesapeake waterways.
   3. in all counties, regardless of whether they are affected by such regulation.
   4. throughout the State, except in Allegany, Carroll, Frederick, Garrett, Howard, Montgomery, and Washington Counties.

10

TRANSFER OF TITLE

■ OVERVIEW

Title to land in Maryland, as elsewhere, can pass by descent, devise, adverse possession, gift, escheat, eminent domain, erosion, foreclosure, and tax and sheriff's sales. This chapter deals with six of the more prevalent ways a title can change hands.

■ TRANSFER OF TITLE BY DESCENT

Surviving spouses are provided for by the Maryland Law of Descent and Distribution that abolished dower and curtesy. This statute also names other classes of heirs who inherit property owned by decedents who die **intestate** (without a valid will). Some of the particular situations the law addresses are those in which there is a surviving spouse

- and a minor child: each gets half;
- and no minor children, but there are **surviving issue** (adult children and perhaps their children): spouse gets $15,000 and half of the **residue** (rest);
- and no **issue** (children) but there are parents of the decedent: spouse gets $15,000 and half of the remainder;
- and no surviving issue and no parents of the decedent: spouse takes all.

When the decedent is not intestate but leaves a will that gives the spouse less than the amount provided in the situations above—or even nothing—the spouse may renounce the will and elect (choose) to claim the intestate share granted by the statute governing descent. This is called the survivor's **elective share.**

Title to real property of decedents passes immediately to their *personal representatives* (formerly called *administrators* in situations without a valid will). These individuals pay decedents' debts and estate taxes and then distribute the remainder of the estate according to the statute.

Persons who receive property by descent are called **heirs.** Persons who receive property through a will are called **beneficiaries.** Beneficiaries are of two types:

devisees, who receive real property (a **devise**), and **legatees,** who receive personal property (a **legacy**).

If the decedent was both intestate and entirely without heirs, the estate is converted to cash and that cash paid to the Maryland Medical Assistance Program if the decedent received long-term care benefits from that program. If that is not the case, the cash is paid to the board of education in the county in which the personal representative was granted authority to administer the estate.

■ TRANSFER OF TITLE BY ACTION OF LAW

To obtain title to real estate through **adverse possession,** an adverse user must be in actual possession of the property, and that possession, alone or combined with that of previous adverse owners, must have been continuous for 20 years. The possession also must be or have been open, **notorious** (known to others), exclusive, **hostile** (without permission), and—because Maryland law does not recognize "squatters' rights"—under claim of right or color of title. Each of those terms has a very specific legal meaning. Situations involving adverse possession can be very technical and should always be handled with guidance from legal counsel.

■ TRANSFER OF TITLE BY WILL

There are statutory requirements for a valid will. Persons age 18 or over, who are of sound mind and are legally competent, may make a will. Wills should be prepared carefully by testators' attorneys and signed and witnessed as required by law. While surviving spouses can contest wills that grant them less than what would have been their intestate share, other heirs, such as testators' children, may not do so.

Omitted Children

Children born after a testator's will is signed and before the testator's death are said to be **pretermitted** (omitted). This category also includes children of the decedent who had not yet been born at the time of the decedent's death. Under common law, pretermitted children do not have a share in the decedent's estate. However, Maryland statute has set aside this aspect of common law and treats pretermitted children as if they were born before the will was signed.

Nuncupative (oral) **wills** are not recognized in Maryland. **Holographic wills** (those in the handwriting of the testator) are recognized if they are properly **attested** (witnessed).

■ TRANSFER OF TITLE BY DEED

Maryland statutes also set forth requirements for a valid deed. A **deed** must be prepared by an attorney or by one of the parties, in writing, executed by a competent grantor 18 years of age or older, state the actual consideration or be accompanied by an affidavit that does, and give a legally sufficient property description.

Deeds must be typewritten and in English to be recorded, although an accompanying official consular translation into English satisfies this requirement for a deed written in another language.

A deed signed only by the **grantor** (the one granting the property) is effective if delivered and accepted by the grantee. It is called a *deed poll*. In contrast, transfers of property belonging to a minor and of properties involving corporate sellers or purchasers are situations in which both grantees and the grantors are required to sign the deed.

Recordation of Deeds and Mortgages

Maryland law specifies that the transfer of any fee or freehold estate, any declaration or limitation of use, and any estate extending beyond seven years (such as a deed or a long-term lease) shall be effective only if the deed is executed and recorded. Chapter 13 of this book also points out that leases for more than seven years must be recorded. Title to property passes, as between the parties, on delivery and acceptance of a valid deed. Consequently, unrecorded deeds are valid between grantors and grantees and also against third persons, but only those with actual notice. The grantees under unrecorded deeds are subject to having their equitable title interests extinguished if their grantor subsequently grants the property to others. The law requires that deeds be recorded to alert potential purchasers of land to the possible interests of others. Recording deeds can also protect grantees against third persons without actual notice. The recording of a deed constitutes constructive notice as of date of recording. Deeds are recorded in the county where the land lies. For land lying in more than one county, the deed must be recorded in each of the counties.

Recordation requires acknowledgment before a notary or other authorized public officer and payment of all required transfer taxes, ad valorem taxes, and special assessments. The deed is considered made (done) on the date it is signed, sealed, and delivered, even though it be acknowledged at a later date and recorded still later.

Mortgages or deeds of trust are exempt from the recordation tax if they secure home loans made for the initial purchase or for renovation of the mortgagor's (borrower's) principal residence.

■ TAXES ON CONVEYANCES

The **documentary stamp tax** (so-called because its payment until several decades ago was indicated by attaching actual revenue stamps to the deed) is a Maryland state tax levied at the rate of $0.55 per $500 or fraction thereof on the full sales price of the property. Several cities and counties have added their own stamp tax.

Another state tax is the Maryland **transfer tax.** It is one-half of one percent of the full consideration except for transfers to a first-time Maryland homebuyer, as explained in Chapter 8. Cities and counties collect additional transfer taxes.

Transfers Between Relatives Not Taxed

Transfers between relatives, including in-laws and former spouses, are exempt from recordation and transfer taxes only on the mortgage or deed of trust indebtedness assumed by the transferee.

■ AGRICULTURAL TRANSFER TAX

The agricultural transfer tax is calculated by the Assessments Office and is payable at the time of property transfer. It is imposed when land subject to agricultural ad valorem tax assessment is sold with nonagricultural use in view. The student is referred to the full discussion and resources given in Chapter 8 of this book.

■ MARYLAND UNIFORM TRANSFERS (GIFTS) TO MINORS ACT

This law authorizes a **donor** (one who gives a gift) to **nominate** (propose the name of) a custodian to act on behalf of the minor **beneficiary** (the one receiving the gift). The designation, powers, and responsibilities of a custodian and procedures for transfers of custodial property and claims against such property are set forth in the statute. Use of legal counsel is important in such a transfer.

QUESTIONS

1. One requirement for obtaining title to the property of another by adverse possession is that the claimant *MUST*
   1. post a sign on the subject property.
   2. notify the original owner in writing.
   3. have been in possession of the property for 20 years.
   4. own the adjoining land.

2. The Maryland Law of Descent and Distribution
   1. can affect estates of those not leaving a valid will.
   2. assures surviving spouses part of any estate.
   3. can affect the estates of both those leaving a valid will and those dying intestate.
   4. does all of the above.

3. To be valid between the parties, a deed to Maryland real property must meet all the following requirements *EXCEPT* that it be
   1. voluntarily delivered during the lifetime of the grantor.
   2. in writing and signed.
   3. signed by a grantor who is competent.
   4. recorded.

4. To be eligible for recordation, a deed conveying Maryland real estate
   1. need only show a nominal consideration.
   2. must be in the handwriting of the grantee.
   3. must have been prepared by an attorney or by one of the parties.
   4. must be witnessed by two persons not mentioned in the deed.

5. In Maryland, a valid will
   1. must be delivered during the lifetime of the testator/testatrix.
   2. must be signed by at least one of the beneficiaries.
   3. must be acknowledged before an officer of the court (notary public).
   4. requires a minimum of two witnesses.

CHAPTER ELEVEN

TITLE RECORDS

■ OVERVIEW

According to Maryland State law, deeds, mortgages, ground leases, and other instruments creating an estate in real estate for longer than seven years must be recorded. This practice is for the benefit of owners, prospective purchasers, and lenders. Recording benefits buyers who need to know who claims to own the property they are considering. It protects grantees by giving constructive notice to the world of their claim of interest in a property. It also enables lenders to know if a mortgage loan applicant is the "owner of record" of the property being mortgaged.

■ DETAILS OF RECORDATION

Deeds and Mortgages

To be eligible for recordation, a deed must state the full, actual consideration paid for the property. If the information is not in the deed, it must be stated in an affidavit attached to the deed. Only deeds acknowledged before a notary public or similar official may be recorded.

Deeds and mortgages on real estate are recorded by the circuit court clerk of each county and Baltimore City. Recording must take place *in the county or city where the land is located.* If property is located in two counties, *it must be recorded in both,* with each county receiving a recording fee proportional to the amount of land located in the county, as shown by the tax assessment. Occasionally recordings are made in a county other than that in which the property is located.

It should be noted that Maryland has only one system of recording. The Torrens system, described in the main text, is not used in Maryland.

Real estate records are gathered in two indexes: one organized by the names of grantors and one by those of grantees. Because Maryland regards mortgages as conveying legal title, mortgagors are in the grantor index; mortgagees, in the grantee. All references to a previously recorded conveyance should give not only the **liber** (book) and **folio** (page) numbers where the conveyance is found but also the name of the grantor and the grantee who were parties to that conveyance.

Purchasers who finance a property purchased with a purchase-money mortgage or deed of trust given to a financial institution are the grantees named in their own deed. They will then be regarded as grantors in the deed of trust (or mortgagors in the mortgage) they give to a financial institution. In the first instance, their names will be recorded in the grantee index; in the second, in the grantor index.

No deed conveying real estate may be recorded in any county of Maryland until all taxes and other public assessments or charges on the property have been paid and the record of ownership has been transferred on the tax assessment books to the grantee who is named in the deed to be recorded. If the deed transfers all of the real estate owned by the grantor in the county, then, in many counties, all of the grantor's personal property tax must also be paid prior to recording.

In Baltimore City, a deed conveying real estate may not be recorded if there is an outstanding unpaid water bill over $50. In Harford County, no deed conveying real estate may be recorded unless *any* water bill is paid. Licensees preparing for settlement should check requirements in the county or municipality where the property that is the subject of the transaction is located.

Other than the recording and transfer taxes, fees are charged for the recording of deeds and other documents. These fees are set by the counties. In many counties, it costs $3 per page, or portion thereof, plus $1 for each name to be recorded in the grantor-grantee index. In addition, there is a $20 surcharge per instrument imposed by statute until 2006 for recording all land records and financing statement records. This surcharge funds the repair, replacement, improvement, modernization, and updating of office equipment and equipment-related services in the land records office of the clerk of the circuit court of that county.

One who records a document takes it to the office of the clerk of court, pays the proper amount of documentary stamps and transfer tax stamps, pays the recording fee, and leaves the document with the clerk. The clerk's staff then reproduces the document in the public record, stamps the original to indicate where the information has been recorded, and returns it to the person designated to receive it.

Leases

Recording of leases that are for periods longer than seven years serves to protect lessees if mortgage lenders foreclose on their lessor. It also provides protection against certain judgment creditors of the lessor. Lease recordation costs are often as great as the costs of recording deeds. However, most leases of seven years or less are not subject to the recordation tax.

Plats of Subdivision

The law requires that subdividers get plats of subdivision approved by state and local authorities as a prerequisite to recording those plats. Documents such as listings, sales contracts, and deeds typically refer to recorded plats by *liber and folio* (book and page). Such reference to the properly recorded plat in a later document can satisfy the need for exact property description. No lot within a subdivision can be offered for sale until the plat of subdivision has been recorded.

Recordation and development of individual lots in a subdivision are regulated on a local level by the county in which the property is located. Licensees should always be sure that the deeds to the individual lots for sale in a subdivision have been properly recorded and that all local laws regarding recordation have been met before advertising the lots for sale. Failure to do so could result in a **judicial injunction,** which would halt the marketing of the property. In addition, depending on the situation, the licensees may also be in violation of the state license law and thus subject to suspension or revocation of their real estate licenses.

■ TITLE EVIDENCE

In Maryland, it is customary for buyers in a real estate transaction to obtain and pay for title evidence, although this, like so many other things, is negotiable. Generally, buyers will hire attorneys who will do one of two things:

1. Have an abstract of title prepared and, based on that abstract, prepare a **report** (opinion) **of title** indicating their professional view of the present condition of the title as contained in the public record, or
2. Acting as licensed representatives of a title insurance company, personally issue a title insurance policy binder based on examination of the abstract.

The attorneys will either deliver this abstract to the purchaser or forward it to the title insurance company so that the company may issue a title policy. The person performing settlement is required by statute to explain owner's title insurance and make it available to residential purchasers. A policy of title insurance is the most frequently used form of title evidence in Maryland.

Note that Maryland law requires that the following notice be given to buyers, printed in bold type in the body of each sales contract presented by licensees: **YOU ARE ENTITLED TO SELECT YOUR OWN TITLE INSURANCE COMPANY, SETTLEMENT COMPANY, ESCROW COMPANY, OR TITLE ATTORNEY.**

■ PREREQUISITES TO RECORDING

No fee simple deed, mortgage, or deed of trust may be recorded unless it bears a certification that the instrument has been prepared by attorneys admitted to practice before the Maryland Court of Appeals, under the supervision of such attorneys, or by one of the parties to the instrument. There are other requirements imposed by various localities.

■ UNIFORM COMMERCIAL CODE

The Uniform Commercial Code (UCC) is in effect in Maryland. Two provisions of this code may affect real estate practices.

1. The use of chattel mortgages on fixtures or contents has been replaced by use of security agreements and financing statements.
2. The bulk sales provision applies when a person sells all of the stock in trade when selling a business. The main text contains more information about the UCC.

QUESTIONS

1. Buyers purchased a parcel of real estate that is located in two counties. They should record in
   1. the county with the larger portion.
   2. the county with the smaller portion.
   3. the State capital.
   4. both counties.

2. When a parcel of Maryland real estate is sold, title search is usually ordered on behalf of the
   1. seller.
   2. buyer.
   3. broker.
   4. seller and broker together.

3. Deeds and mortgages may be recorded in each county with the
   1. clerk of circuit court.
   2. Torrens system office.
   3. personal property tax office.
   4. municipal office of planning and zoning.

4. In Maryland counties, deeds conveying real estate are NOT
   1. indexed under the name of the grantor.
   2. indexed under the name of the grantee.
   3. indexed under the name of the selling broker.
   4. referenced to previously recorded conveyances.

5. Which of the following is NOT true concerning requirements for recording a deed?
   1. It may be drafted (prepared) by one of the parties.
   2. It may be witnessed rather than notarized.
   3. It may be drafted (prepared) by an attorney.
   4. It must be notarized.

12

REAL ESTATE FINANCING

■ OVERVIEW

Most real estate is purchased using borrowed funds. Both the traditional mortgage and the deed of trust are common in Maryland and are used in both third-party and in owner financing. The State allows, but stringently regulates, another form of owner financing—the installment land contract.

■ NOTE TO STUDENT

The deed OF trust—also called a *trust deed*—is different from a **deed IN trust**, which is used to place property into a trust. Both are different from a **trustee's deed** by which property is transferred out of a trust by the trustee. The student should review the discussion of these terms in the principal text.

■ MORTGAGE AND DEED OF TRUST LOANS

Maryland is considered a **title theory** state, as defined in the main text. A lender who records a properly signed and delivered mortgage or deed of trust holds legal title to the real estate pledged. Maryland's mortgage and deed of trust foreclosure and sale laws, however, are similar to those of a lien theory state, except that lenders, rather than delinquent landlords, *are allowed to collect rents on investment properties being foreclosed.*

Deeds of trust are widely used throughout the state as financing instruments for real estate. **Deed of trust financing** is a three-party arrangement involving borrower (the trustor), trustee, and lender (beneficiary). This arrangement is so popular in Maryland that it is sometimes called a *Potomac Mortgage.*

The deed of trust forms used in Maryland have a **power-of-sale clause** that gives the trustee authority to sell pledged property in the event of borrower's default. In such a case, there is no court action. After giving adequate public notice, the trustee has the property sold at a **trustee sale**—a public auction.

The money the trustee obtains from the sale is then applied to the principal of the mortgage debt plus the accrued interest and legal costs caused by the sale. Any money left, over and above what is due any lienholder, is returned to the defaulted borrower.

In Maryland, only a natural person and not a corporation or partnership may serve as trustee under a deed of trust and sell the property in case of default under the provisions of the document's power-of-sale clause. In some other jurisdictions any person, including corporations and partnerships, may serve.

■ DEFAULT, FORECLOSURE, AND DEFICIENCY

The parties to a mortgage are the **mortgagor** (borrower) and the **mortgagee** (lender). If the borrower defaults, the lender who wishes to foreclose seeks a court order to sell the mortgaged property at public auction, unless there is a power-of-sale clause in the mortgage. When the funds from a **judicial** (court-ordered) **mortgage foreclosure** sale are insufficient to satisfy the debt, a judgment may be issued against the borrower for the deficiency. However, when a deficiency occurs after a nonjudicial foreclosure, either by a trustee or by the mortgagee under a power-of-sale clause, no such judgment is entered. Deficiency actions are not allowed in Federal Housing Administration (FHA) loans, and the Department of Veterans Affairs (VA) is reluctant to allow them.

■ MORTGAGE INTEREST RATE LIMITS AND PREPAYMENT

In Maryland, there is no limit on the rate of interest lenders may charge in first mortgage loans. The state interest ceiling on second mortgage loans and land installment contracts is 24 percent. The written agreement between mortgagor and mortgagee must specify the rate of interest.

A mortgage debt can be prepaid at any time without penalty, if the agreement between mortgagor and mortgagee did not expressly limit prepayment and/or impose a penalty for it. When such a penalty has been agreed to, it may not exceed two month's advance interest on the total of all amounts prepaid within a 12-month period, inexcess of one-third of the original loan. Moreover, prepayment charges may only be imposed on prepayments made during the first three years of the loan term.

A lender who violates the usury ceiling for second mortgages, except for a bona fide error of computation, may collect only the principal amount of the loan and may not collect any interest, costs, or other charges with respect to the loan. In addition, a lender who *knowingly* violates any provision of this subtitle shall forfeit to the borrower three times the amount of interest and charges already collected in excess of that authorized by law, or $500, whichever is greater.

■ MORTGAGE EXPENSE ACCOUNTS

Maryland savings institutions that require a **tax and insurance expense account**—also called an *escrow* or *impound account*—for mortgage and deed of trust loans must pay interest on these funds at passbook rate, but not less than 3 percent. The interest is computed on the average monthly balance in the escrow account and paid annually by crediting the borrower's account with the amount of interest due. This payment is reported to the IRS on a Form 1099. Loans sold to agencies in the secondary mortgage market are exempt from this requirement.

■ DISCRIMINATION

Under Maryland law, a lender may not refuse loans to any person based solely on geographic area, neighborhood, race, creed, color, age, sex, disability, marital status, familial status, or national origin. However, a lender may refuse to make a loan based on higher-than-normal risks connected with the loan.

■ GROUND RENT—FHA/VA LOANS

The Department of Veterans Affairs will guarantee loans only on properties subject to ground rent that are located in Anne Arundel County, Baltimore City, Baltimore County, and the Joppatowne subdivision in Harford County. If a veteran purchases leasehold property located in another part of the state using such financing—formerly called a *GI loan*—the ground rent must be redeemed on or prior to the date of closing.

For Federal Housing Administration (FHA) loans on Maryland property held subject to a ground rent, the residential mortgage limit must be reduced by the capitalization value of the annual ground rent. Ground rents are discussed in Chapter 13 of this book.

■ RELEASE OF MORTGAGE LIEN

When a mortgage note has been fully repaid by the borrower, the lender must prepare and provide to the borrower a release of lien document. This may be either a **satisfaction of mortgage** or a **deed of release.** Although the lender will often record this instrument, it is the borrower's responsibility to see that the document does get recorded.

In some instances, a mortgagee simply enters the statement of release directly in the margin of the recorded mortgage instrument; then that document is rerecorded so that the public record will indicate the release. Recording the release provides public notice that the original mortgage lien has been canceled.

■ MORTGAGE PRESUMED PAID

A mortgage or deed of trust will be presumed to have been paid and the lien created by that document removed if a period of 12 years has elapsed since the last payment date called for in the instrument (its **maturity date**). Alternatively, if the maturity date cannot be ascertained and 40 years have elapsed since the date of the document's recording, the mortgage will be presumed paid and the lien extinguished.

■ FORECLOSURES AND TRUSTEE SALES

The mortgage or deed of trust—but not the note—must be recorded before a lender may start foreclosure proceedings in case of borrower default. State law requires that to record a residential mortgage or deed of trust, a lender must execute and attach an affidavit to each mortgage stating

■ that the mortgage document accurately sets forth the amount of the loan, and
■ that the entire amount was disbursed when the mortgage was executed or delivered to the lender by the borrower.

When a mortgage does not contain a provision giving the mortgagee the power of sale, a foreclosure sale ordered and supervised by the court is the lender's final remedy for default by the borrower.

Because there is no statutory right of redemption in Maryland, a defaulted borrower has to make redemption by paying the necessary funds to the mortgagee *before* the sale has been completed—that is, before the court officer delivers the sale deed to the purchaser.

Mortgagees or trustees are permitted to personally purchase properties in default at the sale rather than sell them to satisfy debts, provided they have diligently attempted to obtain the best possible price for each property on the market.

Holders of subordinate interests in real property may record a request for a **notice of sale,** requiring holders of superior interests in property to give notice of an impending foreclosure sale. They must file a **surplus money action** to receive any of the proceeds of a scheduled foreclosure sale that are not used to satisfy superior liens. If holders of such junior liens fail to do these things, their liens will be extinguished, no matter how large the proceeds from the sale.

Note that foreclosure sale under a deed of trust or mortgage in default may terminate any leaseholds on the property that began after the deed of trust was executed and recorded. Leaseholds entered into before the date of the mortgage may survive if they meet requirements for recordation of leases longer than seven years. Tenants whose leases contain subordination agreements or who have later granted such agreements will not be protected. Strict foreclosure, as described in the principal text, is not recognized in Maryland.

■ LAND INSTALLMENT CONTRACTS

The state law regarding land installment contract sales of real estate is found in the Annotated Code of Maryland in Title 10 of the *Real Property* Article. Note that this law applies only to the sale of improved properties, occupied or to be occupied by the purchaser for a dwelling, or of an unimproved, subdivided lot or lots intended to be improved for residential purposes. In other cases, common-law rules apply with fewer protections for **vendees** (purchasers).

Land installment contracts should be prepared and processed by attorneys. The purchaser may rescind the contract and demand that all sums paid be returned if the vendor does not record the contract within 15 days of its being signed by all parties. Land installment contract financing also requires cumbersome ongoing reporting by the vendor, which is designed to protect the purchaser.

■ JUNIOR FINANCING

The maximum interest rate a lender may charge in Maryland for a **secondary mortgage** (one that is not a first mortgage) is 24 percent; the maximum loan origination fee that may be charged is $250 or 10 percent of the proceeds of the loan, whichever is less. Only an actual cost such as a recording fee or title insurance may be charged in addition to the origination fee. A lender may refinance a junior loan not more than once in any 12-month period and not more than twice during any five-year period. The *Commercial Law* Article of the Maryland Annotated Code sets forth the details.

Maryland law permits all fees, discounts, and points allowed or required under federally related second mortgage purchase programs. However, the points and interest rate computed together may not exceed an annual percentage rate (APR) of 24 percent.

Prohibited Practices

Junior (secondary loan) **lenders** in Maryland are prohibited from certain practices, including the following:

- Attempting to have the debtor waive his or her legal rights
- Requiring accelerated payments for any reason other than default
- Having the debtor execute an assignment of wages for payment of the loan
- Charging a fee to execute a release after the loan is paid

Balloon Payments

Maryland Secondary Mortgage Law requires that lenders, including private sellers, who take back a second mortgage containing a **balloon clause** (a clause that makes the final payment significantly larger than previous payments) grant—on the borrower's request—an automatic, one-time, six-month extension beyond the maturity date. This provision applies to second mortgage loans made for buying residential property for owner occupancy.

■ RESIDENTIAL PROPERTY LOAN NOTICES

Lenders who make loans on residential property are required to provide prospective borrowers with a written notice informing them of their right to choose an attorney or a title insurance company. This notice must be provided within three days of their application for the loan. Lenders are also required to notify applicants that by completing their loan applications, they are terminating any right they might have had to rescind the contract for lack of a Property Disclosure and Disclaimer statement. The text of the Secondary Mortgage Loan Law, Title 12 of the *Commercial Law* Article, is found at

WWWeb.Link

http://198.187.128.12/maryland/lpext.dll?f=templates&fn=fs-main.htm&2.0

In the law, as seen on this Web link and in bound hardcopy volumes, each subsection has a title in *italic* print. These titles are called *catchlines*. They are not part of the law but just a convenience for the reader. Lexis Publishing™ holds the copyright to all these catchlines.

QUESTIONS

1. Mortgages on Maryland real property
   1. must be recorded to be valid between lender and borrower.
   2. may not be refused to any persons because of their religion.
   3. by law must be for a minimum ten-year term.
   4. may be foreclosed by strict foreclosure if in default.

2. The VA will guarantee a loan on real property in Maryland that is held subject to a ground rent
   1. only in certain areas of the State.
   2. and the loan limit must be reduced by the capitalized value of the annual rent.
   3. only to the in-fee value of the property.
   4. only in Baltimore City.

3. When Paul Jennings obtained a loan to purchase a new home from BNN Savings Bank, BNN failed to record the mortgage document. The mortgage does not give BNN the power of sale in case of default. Which of the following is *TRUE?*
   1. As things stand, BNN Savings Bank will be able to enforce the mortgage in a court of law if Jennings defaults on his loan.
   2. If Jennings defaults on the loan, BNN cannot foreclose on the mortgage in court until the instrument is recorded.
   3. As mortgagor, it is Jennings' obligation to record the mortgage for his own protection.
   4. If Jennings defaults on the loan, BNN could sell the property without foreclosure action.

4. Bonita Harrison needs $165,000 to purchase a new home, and she borrows it from First Maryland Savings Bank. Which of the following security arrangements may First Maryland Savings Bank use?
   1. Mortgage or deed of trust
   2. Real estate trust
   3. Installment contract
   4. Deed of release

5. Clint Hayward obtains a 30-year loan from Liberty Savings Association to purchase a Baltimore condominium unit. Along with monthly payments of principal and interest, the lender requires that Hayward deposit funds in an escrow account for the payment of taxes and property insurance. Which of the following is *TRUE?*
   1. Liberty Savings must pay Hayward interest on these escrow deposits when the loan is paid off.
   2. Hayward may require the lender to maintain his escrow account in an interest-bearing depository.
   3. Liberty Savings must credit Hayward's account for passbook rate interest on his escrow deposits annually.
   4. Hayward must pay the lender a minimum of 3 percent interest for maintaining such an account for him.

CHAPTER THIRTEEN

13

LEASES

■ OVERVIEW

Leaseholds in Maryland are the four familiar **common-law estates:** (1) leases for a specified time period ("for years"), (2) leases from period to period ("from year to year"), (3) tenancies at will, and (4) tenancies at sufferance. Long-term ground leases, an example of the first type, are common in certain areas.

■ MARYLAND GROUND RENTS

Ground leases exist in many areas in the State. Some of them may be **redeemed** (freed from ground rent) after specified time periods, while others are irredeemable. The **ground lease** tenant typically owns the improvements located on the rented ground. One reason developer might establish a ground rent would be to keep the selling price of his or her houses within the financial reach of more purchasers. The purchaser of a house under ground rent does not have to purchase the lot, just rent it.

Ground rental is money paid to the landowner (landlord) by a tenant who possesses the landlord's land by virtue of a lease. Such leases usually give tenants possession of land for specific time periods not to exceed 99 years. Possession of the land **reverts** (goes back) to the fee simple landowner when the lease finally expires, if it is terminated by the tenant's default, or if it is not renewed. Many such agreements have options for renewal for additional time periods either at predetermined graduated rentals or at rentals to be based on reappraisal of the land and improvements at the time of renewal.

Creation of a Ground Rent

Anyone who owns unencumbered fee simple property can subject the property to ground rent, thus creating a *leasehold estate*. The **worth of the reversion** (the price to redeem) is based on the capitalized value of the ground rent. Although any amount of ground rental can be charged for a property, the rent typically is kept reasonable to make the property marketable. Ground rent amounts are usually based on rents charged for comparable lots (competitive rents) in the neighborhood or simply "what the market will bear." The student should be aware that capitalization of the annual ground rent amount does not necessarily represent the true value of the piece of land.

Ground Rent Disclosure

When property subject to ground rent is sold, the contract of sale must inform the buyer that nonpayment of the ground rental may result in

- reversion of the entire property, in fee, to the ground landlord, and
- termination of the buyer's leasehold.

Owners, or licensees representing them, when posting signs announcing property for sale that is already subject to ground rent, are required to show on the sign *the amount of annual ground rental and cost of capitalization* in numbers as large and clear as the numbers showing the price of the property.

Land subject to ground rent is not held in fee simple. The ground landlord has a **leased fee** and the tenant/occupant has a **leasehold.** Therefore, if a contract of sale for property subject to ground rent does not disclose existence of the ground rent and yet the agreement calls for delivery of fee simple title to the purchaser, the seller must redeem the property before settlement. If the property is irredeemable, the seller cannot deliver fee simple title and will be in breach of contract.

■ MARYLAND RESIDENTIAL LEASES

In the *Real Property* Article, the Maryland Statute of Frauds provides that to be enforceable, leases for a year or less need not be in writing. Those whose term is more than one year must be written. The time periods are measured from **the inception of a lease**—the date the lease agreement is made, not the date of permitted occupancy—until the end of its term.

Leases longer than seven years must be **recorded.** Recordation of a document requires acknowledgment before a notary public or similar official. Note, however, that even when such leases have not been properly recorded, they are still valid and binding between the original parties, against their creditors, and against their successors and assignees who have actual notice of the lease or who acquire the property when a tenant is in actual occupancy. **Possession** (occupancy) of property by a tenant under a lease for seven years or less gives **constructive notice** of the tenant's rights. Occupancy at any time under an unrecorded lease that is for longer than seven years does not give such notice. It is clear that recording the longer lease serves to protect the tenant. Mere occupancy under a shorter (seven years or less) lease would be enough to protect the tenant. Although the law requires that any lease for a term longer than seven years be recorded, a recorded **memorandum of lease** satisfies this requirement.

An **application for a lease** must contain a statement explaining the liabilities incurred by the tenant on signing the application, including the tenant's obligation to take possession if the application is accepted. If the landlord requires any fees other than a security deposit—perhaps a credit check to verify information in the application—and these fees exceed $25, the landlord is required to return the fees in excess of the amount actually spent. This applies to landlords who offer five or more rental units on one parcel of property but not to seasonal rentals or condominiums.

Postsettlement Occupancy Excepted

No portions of the Landlord and Tenant statute dealing with residential leases apply when, after the sale of an owner-occupied residence, the sellers and purchasers enter into an agreement that sellers may remain in possession for a period of 60 days or less.

Disclosure of Representation

Licensees must provide written disclosure of agency representation to both lessors and lessees when negotiating any residential lease for *longer than 125 days*. This disclosure must be made no later than the first scheduled face-to-face meeting between the licensees and any prospective tenant or landlord. Please review the discussion on disclosure of representation in Chapter 2.

Security Deposits

On all residential leases landlords may not require **security deposits** of more than two months' rent or $50, whichever is more. The landlords must give tenants a receipt for such deposits. Failure to do so makes the landlord liable to the tenant for the sum of $25. Moreover, landlords are liable to tenants for up to three times any security deposit taken in excess of this limit, plus reasonable attorney fees.

Within 30 days of their receipt, deposit monies must be placed and maintained by landlords or their agents in accounts opened for this sole purpose in a branch of a federally insured bank or a savings institution licensed to do business in Maryland.

In lieu of such accounts, a landlord may hold security deposits in insured certificates of deposit issued by banks, described above, or in securities issued by the federal government or the State of Maryland. The total of all these deposit accounts, certificates, and securities must be sufficient in amount to equal all the security deposits for which a landlord or landlord's broker is liable. Broker licensees' records of these funds must be available for inspection by members of the Commission or its agents during normal business hours.

At the time leases are written, landlords must give tenants written notice of various **tenant rights.** One example is the right to demand from the landlord at the beginning of the lease a written property condition inspection and report. The tenant must request this property-condition inspection by certified mail within 15 days of taking occupancy. A landlord who fails to provide this report to tenants who make the proper request becomes liable to the tenants for as much as three times the amount of any security deposit taken. This amount could be offset (reduced) by amounts due in unpaid rent and tenant damages to the premises.

The tenant also has the right to request by certified mail—sent at least 15 days before intended move-out—to be present at the final inspection. The landlord must set a date between five days before and five days after intended move-out and notify the tenant in writing of this date.

When a lease is terminated, the landlord must return the tenant's security deposit within 45 days, including simple interest at the statutory rate—presently 3 percent per annum. Interest accrues at six-month intervals from the day the tenant gives the security deposit and does not compound.

Security deposits may be withheld by the landlord to cover

- unpaid rent;
- losses due to breach or violation of lease terms (the landlord is entitled only to the actual financial loss—**damages**—caused by the breach); and
- cost of repairs to leased premises because of damage to the leased premises by the tenants or their families, guests, agents, invitees, or employees in excess of ordinary wear and tear.

Landlords who wish to withhold deposits to cover damages must present to their tenants, within 45 days of the termination of the tenancy, a written statement of damages including a written list of repair costs *actually incurred*. Failure to comply with this could make landlords liable to a tenant for three times the amount of the security deposit wrongfully withheld, plus reasonable attorneys' fees. The landlords' right to recover from the security deposit any unpaid rent or rental income lost due to breach of lease can also be forfeited. A legal action concerning security deposits may be brought by tenants any time during tenancy or within two years after its termination. A tenant may not waive any of these protections. Any provision purporting to do so in a lease agreement would be of no force and effect.

State law requires that every landlord maintain a records system showing the dates and amounts of rent paid by tenants and showing that receipts of some form were given to each tenant for each cash rent payment.

■ MISCELLANEOUS REQUIREMENTS

Note that Baltimore County and City landlords must give tenants of multi-family dwellings notice when they are located in *floodplain areas*.

Owners of residential rental units in Baltimore City must file an *annual registration statement* with the Baltimore City Commissioner of Housing and Community Development, whether the units are occupied or not, and pay a registration fee. Other jurisdictions also may have registration requirements and conduct periodic inspections.

Owners of multifamily residential rental property are required by State law to post in a conspicuous place a sign listing the name, address, and telephone number of the property owner or managing agent. The information may instead be included in the lease or the rent receipt.

■ SALE OF LEASED PREMISES

Unless specified to the contrary in the lease, the purchaser of a property occupied by a tenant under a lease is bound by the conditions and terms of that lease, just as the original landlord was. A purchaser not wishing to become a landlord should include a clause in the property purchase contract requiring that the premises be delivered unoccupied and vacant at the time of settlement. Baltimore City and several other jurisdictions require that a landlord give the tenant the *right of first refusal* before leased premises can be sold to someone else.

■ TERMINATION OF PERIODIC TENANCIES

The requirements to terminate **periodic tenancies** differ throughout the State. In all counties except Montgomery County and Baltimore City, the landlord must give the tenant written notice to terminate, as follows:

- One week for a week-to-week tenancy
- One month for a month-to-month tenancy
- Three months for a year-to-year tenancy

By contrast, a tenant's **parol** (oral) **notice** is sufficient to terminate such tenancies. If landlords can prove that the tenants gave such notice, they do not need to give their own notice to those tenants.

In Montgomery County, the parties may agree in writing to longer or shorter notice periods. The local laws of Baltimore City generally require that a landlord give the following written notices to terminate:

- 60 days for a tenancy of less than one year, or at sufferance
- 90 days for a periodic tenancy
- 30 days in all other cases

A tenant may terminate any of these tenancies by giving the landlord 30 days' notice.

When a landlord consents to a tenant's **holding over** (remaining on the premises), the tenant becomes a week-to-week tenant if the lease status was week-to-week prior to the holding over. In all other cases, the tenant becomes a month-to-month tenant unless the lease provides otherwise and this lease provision (stating otherwise) is initialed by the tenant.

A tenant under a lease who unlawfully holds over beyond the termination of the lease is liable to the landlord for actual damages that may be caused by the holding over.

Landlords' Rights to Summary Dispossession

Landlords who give the required notice or have court orders for termination of tenancy may **dispossess** tenants and repossess property by simple court suit before a district court judge. The length of notice landlords must give tenants before beginning **dispossession proceedings** is generally one month in renewable monthly tenancies or in tenancies with a fixed term and no provision for renewal. For automatically renewable yearly tenancies, this notice (with certain exceptions) is three months; for renewable monthly or weekly tenancies, it is one month or one week.

Tenant Refusal to Comply

If the tenant or person in possession refuses to comply with the written request to remove from the property, the landlord may make a complaint in writing to the district court of the county where the property is located. The court issues a summons, served by the sheriff to the tenant, to appear before the court, and an attested copy is affixed to the property in a conspicuous place. This is considered sufficient notice.

Back Rent on Renewal of Lease

Tenants or assignees who apply to their landlords for renewal under a covenant in their leases giving them the right to renew must produce vouchers or evidence showing payment of rent accrued for three years preceding this demand and application. If tenants do not provide such proof, landlords, before executing the renewal of the lease, are entitled to demand and recover not more than three years' back rent, in addition to any renewal fine that may be provided for in the lease. This commonly occurs in situations involving ground rent.

Failure to Demand Rent

If there is no demand or payment of rent for more than 20 consecutive years, landlords lose not only the unpaid rental but also the reversion of the property. Landlords under any legal disability when the 20-year period expires have two years after the removal of the disability to assert their rights. Therefore, a landlord's failure to demand rent for 20 years could result in the tenant's receiving fee simple title.

Receipts for Tenants' Rental

In Anne Arundel County, unless the tenant makes payment by check or rents the property for commercial or business purposes, the landlord is required to give the tenant a receipt showing the amount of payment and the time it covers. If convicted of violating this section of the law, any person or agent forfeits the rent for the period in question.

In other counties, when the tenant makes payment other than by check, the landlord or the landlord's agent must give the tenant a receipt.

Surrender of Premises

When a lease contains a covenant or promise by the tenant to leave, restore, surrender, or yield the leased premises in good repair, this does not bind the tenant to erect any similar building or pay for any building destroyed by fire or otherwise if the damage was not due to the negligence or fault of the tenant.

Landlords may ask the district court to seize and sell tenants' personal property for unpaid rent by filing a petition. Landlords may do this only if tenancy has continued for longer than three months (by written lease or periodic tenancy) or was *at will*. **Distraint** is the term used for a landlord's right to both seize and sell such property and for the court's action in awarding this right.

A rental agreement must clearly state information such as when tenancy expires, when rent accrues, or whether rent is to be paid in advance or in arrears. If it does not, a court may find the agreement's terms too vague and deny the landlord's request for distraint.

■ PROHIBITED RESIDENTIAL LEASE PROVISIONS

In Maryland, the following provisions are prohibited in residential leases:

- A provision (**cognovit clause**) that authorizes an attorney for the landlord to plead the tenant guilty (**confess judgment clause**) on a claim arising from the lease, especially failure to pay rental
- A provision under which the tenant agrees to waive or forgo any rights or remedies against the landlord as provided by law
- A provision allowing the landlord to charge a penalty for late payment of rent that is more than 5 percent of the amount of rent due for the period in which the rent is delinquent (In weekly rentals, this late charge may not exceed $3 per week or $12 per month.)
- Any provision under which the tenant waives his or her right to a jury trial
- Any provision under which the tenant agrees to a period for the landlord's notice to quit (in the event that the tenant breaches the lease terms) that is less than the period prescribed by law (Both parties, however, are free to agree to a period that is *longer* than that prescribed by law.)
- Any provision authorizing the landlord to take possession of the leased premises or any of the tenant's personal property unless the lease has been terminated by operation of law and such personal property has been abandoned by the tenant
- Any **exculpatory clause** (language in the lease intended to exempt or hold the landlord harmless from liability to the tenant or any other person for any injury, loss, damage, or liability arising from the landlord's omission, fault, negligence, or other misconduct on or about the leased premises in areas that are not under the tenant's control; such areas include stairways, elevators, hallways, and so forth) is contrary to public policy and void
- A provision (not specifically signed or initialed by the tenant) allowing the automatic renewal of the lease term for more than one month
- A requirement that the tenant give the landlord a longer period of notice to terminate the tenancy than the period granted the landlord to similarly notify the tenant

All of the preceding provisions, if included in a Maryland lease, are considered *unenforceable*. Landlords who threaten or attempt to enforce one or more of these provisions may be liable to a tenant for actual damages and attorney's fees incurred as a result. Unfortunately for tenants, there is no penalty for a landlord's merely including these clauses in a lease.

■ WITHHOLDING RENT

Maryland law requires that a landlord provide and maintain premises for tenants that are free of defects and do not present substantial and serious threats of danger to the life, health, and safety of the tenants. Where hazardous conditions exist on leased property, a tenant may give the landlord written notice by certified mail of the conditions and then wait as long as 30 days. If the hazardous conditions are not corrected within that period, a tenant may withhold rent from the landlord or pay it into an escrow account for necessary repairs. Such conditions include fire or health hazards or other defects that may threaten the safety or occupancy of renters, such as

- lack of adequate sewage disposal facilities;
- infestation of rodents in two or more dwelling units; or
- failure to meet the standards set in the *Environment* Article at §6-815 or §6-819 for dealing with lead-based paint hazards. (See Table 13.1 and Chapter 14 in this book.)

The Baltimore City Code holds that there is an implied **warranty of habitability** by a landlord that the premises are fit for human habitation. It also provides for remedies for tenants if the premises are unsafe and dirty to the extent that tenants' health is threatened. The warranty of habitability differs from *rent escrow laws* in that tenants already have the use of their rent money to make those repairs the landlord has failed to complete. Under the rent escrow law, rent must be paid into an account where it is held until the repairs are made.

The district court can order tenants to pay rents into a *rent escrow account* of the court or administrative agency of the county. If the tenant fails to pay rent accrued or as it becomes due, the court, on certification of the account, can give judgment in favor of the landlord and issue a warrant for possession. On final disposition of the action, the rent escrow account is distributed in accordance with a judgment or hearing.

Note that minor, not dangerous, defects or housing code violations that go uncorrected are not considered just cause for nonpayment of rent.

■ LEASE AGREEMENT FORMS

A number of lease forms are available from local realty boards or associations, property owner associations, and tenant organizations. Any landlord who offers more than four dwelling units for rent on one parcel of property or at one location and who rents by means of written leases substantially increases the requirements concerning the form of written lease.

■ RETALIATORY EVICTIONS

A landlord may not evict tenants, increase rent, or decrease any services to which they are entitled for their doing any of the following things:

- Filing written complaints with the landlord or with a public agency against the landlord
- Filing a lawsuit against the landlord
- Joining a tenants' organization

■ PEACEABLE AND QUIET ENTRY

Landlords are required by law to ensure that tenants may peaceably and quietly enter the leased premises at the beginning of the lease. Failure to do so allows the tenant, on written notice to the landlord before possession is delivered, to rescission of the lease, abatement of rent, or actual damages.

■ SAFETY REQUIREMENTS

Tenant safety is an ongoing concern of landlords and their agents and property managers.

Compliance with Risk Reduction Laws

Licensees helping rent older properties must be prepared to protect their clients and their customers by meeting the lead-based paint hazards disclosure requirements outlined in Table 13.1. See Chapter 14 for more details on lead-based paint hazards.

Sprinkler Systems

Sprinkler systems must be installed in every newly constructed dormitory, hotel, lodging or rooming house, town house, and multifamily residential dwelling. Sprinkler systems are not required, however, if a dwelling unit is not serviced by a public water supply system.

Smoke Detectors

Smoke detectors must be installed in all multifamily buildings and hotels constructed before 1975 and having four to nine units, but in *all* buildings—*regardless of when they were built*—having more than nine units. The landlord is responsible for the installation, repair, or replacement of the detectors. The occupant of a one-family, two-family, or three-family residential

T A B L E   13.1

Lead-Based Paint Disclosure and Registration Requirements

Dates	Federal Compliance Requirements
Built Before 1/1/1978 "Targeted Property"	Both of the following must be given to all lessees at the beginning of every tenancy and again every two years. Tenants' receipt of these is to be verified by their signature. 1. EPA Booklet, *Protect Your Family from Lead in Your Home,* to be given to all lessees at the beginning and renewal of every lease. 2. Lead Based Paint (Rental) Disclosure Form (Form to be given, signed, and copies kept).
	Maryland Compliance Requirements
Built before 1/1/1950 "Affected Property"	1. The property must be registered with the Maryland Department of the Environment and then reregistered annually. 2. Before a property is rented, it must be inspected by state-approved inspectors and any necessary abatement performed. 3. Maryland Department of the Environment Pamphlet *Notice of Tenants' Rights* and the EPA Booklet, *Protect Your Family from Lead in Your Home*, are to be given to tenants at the beginning of every tenancy, every two years thereafter, and whenever the rental changes.

dwelling constructed before July 1975 is required to equip the apartment with at least one approved smoke detector and to maintain it. A smoke detector operated both by battery and by alternating current (AC) must be installed in every newly constructed residential dwelling unit. At least one smoke detector must be installed on each level, including basements but not attics.

■ LEASE OPTION AGREEMENTS

A **lease option agreement** includes any lease that contains a clause giving the tenant the option to purchase the landlord's interest in the property until some specified date. No lease option on improved residential property in Maryland, with or without a ground rent interest, is valid unless it contains the statement "THIS IS NOT A CONTRACT TO BUY" in capital letters. It must also contain a clear statement of the option's purpose and effect with respect to the ultimate purchase of the property.

■ MOBILE HOME PARKS

Title 8A of the *Real Property* Article sets forth the rights and responsibilities of mobile home park tenants and owners. It addresses such matters as park rules, maintenance, and tenancy.

■ SOURCES OF ASSISTANCE

Baltimore Neighborhoods, Inc., a private nonprofit civil rights agency working in behalf of fair housing and tenants' rights in the Baltimore area, publishes guides to laws covering tenant/landlord relations in Baltimore City, the counties, and the State. These guides, revised annually to incorporate new laws, may be purchased from the organization at 2217 St. Paul St., Baltimore, MD 21218. The organization's Web address is

WWWeb.Link

http://www.bni-maryland.org/

Find the text of the Landlord and Tenant Law, Title 8 of the *Real Property* Article, at

WWWeb.Link

www.michie.com/resources1.html

Once there, click "Maryland"; then "Maryland Code"; then "Next Doc"; then "Real Property."

QUESTIONS

1. Sampson sold a house he owned that was occupied by Rawlins under a one-year lease having six months to run. Therefore
   1. Rawlins must vacate at the closing of the sale.
   2. Rawlins's lease continues until its expiration.
   3. the lease terminates at closing.
   4. the lease is not binding on the new owner.

2. A landlord holding a tenant's security deposit of $500 is required to
   1. credit the deposit account $15 interest per year.
   2. allow the tenant 5 percent simple interest per year.
   3. return the deposit within 30 days after termination of the lease.
   4. give the tenant a receipt or be liable to the tenant for a sum of $250.

3. In Maryland, which of the following leases does *NOT* need to be acknowledged, recorded, and in writing?
   1. Seven-year apartment lease
   2. Eight-year residential lease
   3. Nine-year commercial lease
   4. Ten-year residential lease

4. John Builder has just completed a new house, which he is offering for sale at $68,000 with fee simple title. If, to satisfy an immediate buyer, he creates a ground lease requiring $240 a year ground rent at an 8 percent redemption rate, then
   1. the property may not be redeemed for at least 50 years.
   2. he can reduce the price to $65,000.
   3. he can reduce the price to $56,000.
   4. the in-fee price would be $71,000.

5. Arthur Buyer is interested in buying a residence for $40,000 with a ground rent of $180. Arthur will receive
   1. a deed conveying to him a fee simple interest.
   2. a leasehold estate subject to an annual ground rent of $180.
   3. no deed until such time as he redeems the ground rent.
   4. a fee simple deed after paying ground rent for five years.

6. A man who owns and occupies his home and pays a semiannual ground rent owns an estate in real estate that is called a(n)
   1. fee simple estate.
   2. leasehold estate.
   3. estate at will.
   4. estate at sufferance.

7. Ground rents are sometimes originated to
   1. reduce the amount of cash required to purchase a property.
   2. force the tenant to keep the property in good repair.
   3. provide further assurances to the mortgagee.
   4. prevent the lender from foreclosing.

8. The ground rent on a residence is $180 a year, and the lease has been in effect for more than five years. A redemption at
   1. 5 percent will require $3,200.
   2. 6 percent will require $3,000.
   3. 10 percent will require $6,400.
   4. 12 percent will require $6,000.

9. The right of a landlord to have a court seize and sell a tenant's personal property for unpaid rent is called
    1. ejectment.
    2. abandonment.
    3. dispossession.
    4. distraint.

10. Which of the following provisions, if included in residential leases in Maryland, is enforceable?
    1. Tenants agree to pay the landlord a 5 percent penalty for late rent payments.
    2. Tenants agree to let landlords use their passkeys to take possession of tenants' property if tenants fall more than one month behind in rent payments.
    3. Tenants agree to waive or forgo any rights or remedies against landlords provided by law.
    4. Tenants waive their rights to jury trial.

14

ENVIRONMENTAL ISSUES AND REAL ESTATE TRANSACTIONS

■ OVERVIEW

The State of Maryland, like most states, faces complex environmental challenges. Almost all of them call for balancing economic growth with human safety and quality of life for present and future generations. These tensions can pit the rights of property owners against the wishes of others for preservation or restoration of natural resources. Literally hundreds of statutes, ordinances, and regulations are written statewide each year to address these matters.

Various resources are available on Maryland environmental concerns and programs at the Web site of the Maryland Department of the Environment (MDE):

WWWeb.Link

http://www.mde.state.md.us/

■ MULTIPLE CHALLENGES

Some of the greatest areas of environmental concern are loss of woodlands, farmlands, tidal wetlands, and nontidal wetlands. These overlap such ecological issues as endangered species, clean air, clean water, fisheries, and other wildlife. Recreation and camping needs are also part of the puzzle.

A variety of hazards to human health are created by auto emissions and other air and/or water pollution; for example, by ozone, asbestos, radon, radium, lead-based paint, wastewater sewage, industrial waste, leakage from underground storage tanks, and acid rain.

■ MEETING THE CHALLENGES

The Maryland Smart Growth Initiative is designed to motivate local jurisdictions in the State to plan more effectively for growth without sprawl—the wasteful use of space. In the words of the *Maryland Manual Online*, "Maryland is committed to limiting sprawl development by revitalizing older neighborhoods and redirecting growth to already developed areas, thereby saving the State's farmland, open spaces, and natural resources." For a better understanding of smart growth in this State, consult "The Maryland Office of Smart Growth," at

WWWeb.Link   http://www.smartgrowth.state.md.us/sginmd.htm

■ MULTILEVEL APPROACHES

The State reaches upward, outward, and inward in its efforts: upward toward federal agencies, outward toward neighboring states, and inward to subdivisions and municipalities. To this last group, the State typically grants enabling powers to authorize their participation through zoning and other environmentally related activities. The various subdivisions are authorized to set standards even more rigorous than those set by the State. If they are less strict than the State's, the more rigorous State law will prevail.

**Cooperative
Approaches**

It is rare that an environmental issue can be handled effectively by the Maryland State Government acting alone. Its activities and interests overlap and interact with those of the federal government, neighboring states, Maryland subdivisions and municipalities, and private and corporate citizens.

■ ENFORCEMENT

Enforcement of standards, set forth in statutes, regulations, and ordinances, is carried out by the MDE, except in cases where county enforcement capabilities and resources are comparable to those of the Department. The Secretary of MDE may delegate enforcement powers to such counties for a two-year period.

■ THE CHESAPEAKE BAY

The Chesapeake Bay, nearly 200 miles long and fed by 48 major rivers, 100 smaller rivers, and thousands of other tributaries, is the largest and most productive estuary in the United States. It covers 64,000 square miles and provides habitat for myriad species of plants and animals. Its 15-million-person population is expected to swell to 18 million by 2020.

**Chesapeake Bay
Critical Area Act**

This law identifies the "Critical Area" as all land within 1,000 feet of the average high-water line of tidal waters or the landward edge of tidal wetlands and all waters of and lands under the Chesapeake Bay and its tributaries.

The Buffer

The act designates as the "Buffer," a 100-foot, natural vegetation, forested zone from the mean high-water line, landward from tidal waters and from the edge of tidal wetlands. The Buffer's trees filter runoff water returning to streams and reduce sediments, fertilizers, and toxic substances. Human activities in the area are sharply reduced because of their adverse impact on the nearby waterways and wildlife. No disturbance of the Buffer may be permitted by local jurisdictions unless an applicant can meet strict provisions for a variance.

A wealth of interesting and useful information on this matter is found at the Web site of the Critical Area Commission for the Chesapeake and Atlantic Coastal Bays.

WWWeb.Link

http://www.dnr.state.md.us/critical area

FILLING OF WETLANDS RESISTED

Filling wetlands, for whatever purpose, is regarded as one of the most environmentally pernicious of actions. It may be permitted only when no alternative course of action is available or when new areas of wetland will be created to compensate for those being filled by the person seeking a permit. The replacement area ratios range from *one-new-for-each-one-lost* to *4.5-new-for-each-one-lost*.

IMPACT ON RESIDENTIAL REAL ESTATE

Many of these environmental issues directly and indirectly affect availability of residential housing. As a consequence of efforts to preserve agricultural space and wetlands, various levels of government reduce the amount of land available for development. For instance, the present policy of Maryland is not just to maintain but to *increase* the number of wetland areas.

In seeking to achieve environmental and public safety goals, the State and its subdivisions impose regulatory and impact fees and increasingly require costly safety measures and techniques that protect both people and the environment. By slowing development and imposing fees on developers—which are then passed along to consumers—governments make it more costly for people to buy homes in less-developed areas. This is intended to guide renewal of older, developed areas and more intense use of that land, rather than "sprawling" into rural and semirural areas.

One statutory requirement that affects every licensee is that all contracts for sale of property suitable for one or two single-family units entered into since October 1, 2004, have had to contain the "Notice to Buyer Concerning the Chesapeake and Atlantic Coastal Bays Critical Area," quoted in full in Chapter 9.

MARYLAND DEPARTMENT OF THE ENVIRONMENT

Targeting Asbestos

Within the MDE, the Air and Radiation Management Administration, among its other duties, sets and enforces standards for **asbestos** removal and encapsulation projects and licenses people who work in that field. Much attention of the Department is directed toward asbestos identification and its containment in or removal from public buildings such as public schools, colleges, and universities.

However, asbestos is found in varying amounts in single-family homes, with older homes often having greater amounts. Until the 1970s, asbestos, because of its insulation properties, was a popular component of siding, kitchen floor tiles, and heating and cooling insulation. Licensees should not attempt to answer questions about asbestos and should neither minimize nor exaggerate its effects. Refer questions to companies that are licensed to deal with asbestos.

Waste Management Administration

Also within the MDE is the Waste Management Administration, which deals with environmental restoration and land redevelopment, oil control, lead poisoning, solid waste, scrap tires, sewage sludge, and hazardous materials. It oversees aboveground **storage tanks** for oil and gas and underground tanks for storage of regulated substances. It seeks to identify, prioritize, and abate contaminated sites.

Owners of certain underground storage tanks containing petroleum products must remove or pay for the removal of tanks that leak. MDE regulations set standards for evidence of financial responsibility of owners for costs of cleanup, corrective action, and liability.

Of ongoing concern is the presence of **MTBE (methyl tertiary-butyl ether)** in the air and in groundwater. This substance has been increasingly used to replace tetraethyl lead in gasoline as an agent to reduce knocking in gasoline motors. As federal requirements for clean air get stricter, more MTBE is used. The increased use of such reformulated gasoline (RFG) produces less carbon monoxide (CO) from automobile operation, but, inevitably, some of the MTBE additive gets into the ground and the air; some from spills, some from leaking underground storage tanks (LUSTs), and some from simple evaporation.

MTBE is suspected of being **carcinogenic** (cancer-causing) although this has not yet been proven. Yet, even before MTBE reaches suspected unsafe levels, drinking water infiltrated by it has an unpleasant taste and odor. This problem is especially bothersome in areas where there is no public water supply and citizens use individual wells. Moreover, once MTBE is released into the environment, it breaks down into tertiary butyl alcohol (TBA), which cannot be detected by taste and odor at similar levels of concentration. Enforcement of remediation is most active in areas that do not have public water and where levels from 20 to 40 parts per billion have been detected. Where wells have been affected, property transfers by sale have often been halted. Proper filtration can abate the problem but imposes considerable cost on the party responsible for its installation.

Water Management Administration

Among the most important functions within the MDE are those given to the Water Management Administration, which seeks to protect *drinking water*. With its team of inspectors, it also oversees tidal and nontidal wetlands, floodplains, water appropriations, waterway and floodplain construction, sediment control, stormwater management, coal mining, and oil and gas exploration.

Mold

There are a great many varieties of **mold,** some toxic, some irritating, some mildly annoying, and some (such as penicillin) of great usefulness. Mold identification and removal—and the training of technicians to do those things—has become an industry in itself. It is a complex subject about which there is considerable interest, modest knowledge, and some fear. There are 50 Web sites offering legal help for people who have found mold in their houses for every one Web site giving information about the problem. The presence of mold has inspired litigation among some homeowners, some suing for millions of dollars in damages and medical costs.

It can be very costly to remove toxic mold from a home, once it is identified. Greater human and financial costs threaten persons who have physical reactions to the presence of mold. Licensees are urged not to disturb mold by, for example, pulling out bathroom drywall or wallpaper. Even dead mold creates severe allergic reactions in some persons. Licensees are never to assure buyers or tenants that a home is mold-free or even mold-safe. Give no reassurances, but do not generate unnecessary fears. Refer all questions to attorneys and certified, licensed experts.

Mold formation can be reduced by proper ventilation of areas where water may condense or drip. Household relative humidity greater than 40 percent encourages mold growth. It thrives on moisture, wood, paper, and darkness. A house with improperly installed roof "flashing" or poorly maintained soffits, drains, and downspouts will have water finding its way into wall spaces where it joins all the other factors that foster mold growth. Engineering inspections of houses will often reveal situations that can produce mold, even if they do not find the mold itself. Maryland is damp country year around, so proper home construction and maintenance are the leading methods of reducing mold infestation, related respiratory diseases, and possible consequent litigation.

■ REDUCTION OF LEAD RISK IN HOUSING ACT

The purpose of Maryland's *Reduction of Lead Risk in Housing Act* is "to reduce the incidence of childhood lead poisoning, while maintaining the stock of available affordable rental housing." This act, the environmental law that affects more existing Maryland residential properties than any other, undergirds Maryland's Lead Paint Poisoning Prevention Program.

To see the full text of the *Reduction of Lead Risk in Housing Act*, go to

WWWeb.Link

www.michie.com/resources1.html

Click "Maryland"; then "Maryland Code"; then "Environment"; then "Title 6"; then "6-801."

There is broad-based scientific agreement that exposure to lead-based paint can produce devastating results in young children, newborns, and fetuses. This law is an earnest attempt to reduce the exposure of children under age six and of pregnant women to the effects of lead-based paint in residential rental properties built before 1979.

**Lead Paint
Poisoning Abatement**

State and federal legislation concerning lead levels in certain rental properties impose substantial responsibilities and burdens on investor-owners of many income properties and on their agents. At the same time, these laws allow investors to limit their liability for lead poisoning by following certain procedures.

**Children and Mothers
Targeted for Protection**

Maryland's Lead Paint Poisoning Prevention Plan makes children under age six and pregnant women with elevated blood lead (EBL) levels eligible for specific financial relief for medical treatment ($7,500) and for relocation to lead-safe housing ($9,500). These amounts come from either landlords or their insurance companies. Investors wishing to limit their liability to their tenants for lead poisoning must bring their property into compliance with "lead-safe" standards and keep it that way.

**Plan Encourages
Modest Settlements**

The plan doesn't actually limit or "cap" the liability of landlords. Rather, it makes them eligible to present "qualified offers" of amounts up to $7,500 for medical expenses and up to $9,500 for relocation and rent supplement expenses to their tenants found to have EBL levels. If tenants with EBL levels accept the "qualified offer," they give up the right to sue the landlord for larger sums. They get their money as soon as needed and don't have to face the prolonged uncertainty of initiating a lawsuit that may be particularly difficult to win.

Companies insuring residential properties that are or have been made lead-free or lead-safe are required to provide liability coverage for lead-paint poisoning up to $17,000 (the total of $7,500 and $9,500).

Active Enforcement

The law is currently being vigorously enforced. Moreover, its requirements increase periodically. Note: **affected properties** are those constructed before 1950 that contain at least one rental dwelling unit; the term also refers to an individual unit within such a multiunit building, as well as residential rental properties built between 1950 and 1977, for which the owner has elected to comply with this law.

**Properties to
Be Registered**

This law divides residential rental properties into three groups, based on dates of their construction:

1. Before 1950
2. From 1950 through 1977
3. 1978 and after

Under this law, effective since October 1994, more than 50,000 rental dwelling properties have already been registered with the MDE. Owners must register every residential dwelling unit built *before* 1950 and pay an annual fee of $15. There is no annual fee for a rental dwelling unit built *after* 1949 that is not an affected property. All registrations must be renewed annually.

**Licensees'
Responsibilities**

Licensees acting as agents of landlords who have affected residential rental properties share their legal responsibilities. Consequently, they must become familiar with aspects of inspection, lead reduction procedures, property registration, periodic renewal of registration, insurance, and limitation of liability with respect to lead-paint issues. The State—through its leadership and agencies—is manifesting its determination to pursue the goal of a lead-safe rental environment for the children of Maryland.

■ FEDERAL LAW ALSO APPLIES

The requirements of Maryland law are in addition to and do not take the place of the requirements set forth in federal law concerning lead in residential properties built prior to 1978. The federal law requires distribution of information in the form of the booklet *Protect Your Family from Lead in Your Home* both to potential tenants and to purchasers of properties built before 1978. This 13-page booklet can be seen at and downloaded from

WWWeb.Link

http://www.epa.gov/lead/leadpdfe.pdf

Additional HUD/EPA requirements require giving *purchasers* a form, "Disclosure of Lead-Based Paint and Lead-Based Paint Hazards." The form becomes a part of the contract to purchase. It allows purchasers as much as a ten-day interval to secure a lead assessment inspection of the property and to rescind the contract if sellers will not correct any deficiencies that are found. The inspection or risk assessment period can be lengthened, shortened, or waived by mutual written consent between the purchaser and the seller.

The form also contains the sellers' disclosure of all known lead-paint hazards in the property and a lead warning statement. It requires the purchasers' signatures regarding receipt of this information, receipt of the EPA/HUD pamphlet, and their decision as to whether they will make use of the maximum ten-day contingency period.

Even owners who sell or rent their own property without the aid of brokerage services are required to provide the form and the pamphlet. *The rental form makes no provision for an inspection period*, but otherwise contains essentially the same information as the form for sales. It refers, of course, to *lessors* and *lessees* rather than to *purchaser's* and *seller's*. Figure 14.1 presents a typical form for sales. The student should remember that a different form is used for rental transactions and that it does not contain a ten-day period for lead inspection and subsequent cancellation.

The form contains many "blanks" that require a response—either an initial or a check mark. Licensees should make certain that there is such a response *in every blank*. When one or more blanks are not responded to, this is treated as *failure to meet the federal requirement*. Significant financial penalties are imposed on sellers, landlords, and their agents for such failure. Therefore, every form must be scrutinized for completeness before it is delivered to its recipient.

There is no official federal form, only the requirement that any form used have "substantially the same language" as that prescribed in HUD regulations. Many associations of brokers, therefore, use HUD's language word for word.

F I G U R E   14.1

Lead-Based Paint Disclosure Form

Disclosure of Information on Lead-Based Paint and/or Lead-Based Paint Hazards

Lead Warning Statement

Every purchaser of any interest in residential real property on which a residential dwelling was built prior to 1978 is notified that such property may present exposure to lead from lead-based paint that may place young children at risk of developing lead poisoning. Lead poisoning in young children may produce permanent neurological damage, including learning disabilities, reduced intelligence quotient, behavioral problems, and impaired memory. Lead poisoning also poses a particular risk to pregnant women. The seller of any interest in residential real property is required to provide the buyer with any information on lead-based paint hazards from risk assessments or inspections in the seller's possession and notify the buyer of any known lead-based paint hazards. A risk assessment or inspection for possible lead-based paint hazards is recommended prior to purchase.

Seller's Disclosure

(a) Presence of lead-based paint and/or lead-based paint hazards (check (i) or (ii) below):

    (i) _____   Known lead-based paint and/or lead-based paint hazards are present in the housing (explain).

    _____

    (ii) _____   Seller has no knowledge of lead-based paint and/or lead-based paint hazards in the housing.

(b) Records and reports available to the seller (check (i) or (ii) below):

    (i) _____   Seller has provided the purchaser with all available records and reports pertaining to lead-based paint and/or lead-based paint hazards in the housing (list documents below).

    _____

    (ii) _____   Seller has no reports or records pertaining to lead-based paint and/or lead-based paint hazards in the housing.

Purchaser's Acknowledgment (initial)

(c) _____   Purchaser has received copies of all information listed above.

(d) _____   Purchaser has received the pamphlet Protect Your Family from Lead in Your Home.

(e) Purchaser has (check (i) or (ii) below):

    (i) _____   received a 10-day opportunity (or mutually agreed upon period) to conduct a risk assessment or inspection for the presence of lead-based paint and/or lead-based paint hazards; or

    (ii) _____   waived the opportunity to conduct a risk assessment or inspection for the presence of lead-based paint and/or lead-based paint hazards.

Agent's Acknowledgment (initial)

(f) _____   Agent has informed the seller of the seller's obligations under 42 U.S.C. 4852(d) and is aware of his/her responsibility to ensure compliance.

Certification of Accuracy

The following parties have reviewed the information above and certify, to the best of their knowledge, that the information they have provided is true and accurate.

Seller	Date	Seller	Date
Purchaser	Date	Purchaser	Date
Agent	Date	Agent	Date

There is a substantial fine for failure to present the properly completed form. Giving the wrong form (a purchase form to a renter or a renter form to a purchaser), failing to respond to *every question* on the form, or failing to get required signatures of buyers, sellers, and agents has the same effect as not presenting the form at all. When a licensee agent makes any of these mistakes, both the licensee *and* the principal—whether home seller or landlord—are held responsible. Fines of up to $10,000 may be imposed, and an assessment of treble damages can be levied for deliberate failure. Fines are assessed **jointly and severally** (that is, not proportionately).

Unlike the federal law, Maryland statutes require inspection and, if necessary, remediation by owners of "affected residential rental property" [as defined in 6-801(b)] in addition to delivery of the MDE Notice to tenants every time such properties have change of occupancy or change in rental.

The requirements for distribution of lead-based paint literature by both the Federal Government and Maryland are presented in Table 14.1.

TABLE 14.1

Federal and Maryland Requirements for Residential Structure Lead-Paint Poisoning Disclosure Literature

Built Dates Are Inclusive	Lease	Sale	Federal Requirements	MD Requirements
1/1/1979 and forward (Fed) and 1/1/1978 and forward (MD)	Y	Y	n/a	n/a
1950–1978 (Fed) 1950–1977 (MD	Y	Y	EPA Booklet & Rental Disclosure Form	n/a
Before 1/1/1950	Y		EPA Booklet & Rental Disclosure Form	MD DOE Notice
Before 1/1/1950		Y	EPA Booklet & Sale Disclosure Form	n/a

QUESTIONS

1. All the following are sources of Maryland air pollution *EXCEPT*
   1. radon.
   2. leakage from underground storage tanks.
   3. asbestos.
   4. automobile emissions.

2. Preservation of open space and ecological challenges
   1. are concerns that must be addressed separately.
   2. are not appropriate issues for State government to address.
   3. overlap in many ways.
   4. can best be dealt with by local municipalities.

3. The Maryland Smart Growth Initiative, in addition to other things,
   1. is a disguised "no-growth" plan.
   2. seeks to develop new areas in a systematic and orderly fashion.
   3. seeks to revitalize older neighborhoods.
   4. encourages reduction in density of housing.

4. Environmental regulations imposed by local jurisdictions within the State
   1. must not be stricter than those imposed by the State itself.
   2. may be stricter than those imposed by the State.
   3. are authorized by federal mandate.
   4. do not require State enabling acts.

5. Most environmental issues
   1. can usually be handled by the State alone.
   2. require cooperation between the State and local municipalities.
   3. require cooperation among local municipalities, the State, and other states.
   4. involve local, state, and regional (interstate) as well as federal cooperation.

6. The Chesapeake Bay Critical Area Act
   1. does not clearly define what a Critical Area is.
   2. establishes "buffer zone" size at 1,000 feet.
   3. keeps local governments from approving virtually any disturbance of the land in a "buffer zone."
   4. defines Critical Area as all land within 100 feet of high-water line of tidal bodies and within 100 feet of the dry edge of tidal wetlands.

7. A *buffer zone*
   1. preserves and protects trees and other natural vegetation, mainly to help purify the air.
   2. extends 100 feet further inland than does a Critical Area.
   3. is meant to provide wildlife a safe habitat.
   4. provides a pleasant area for fishing and hunting.

8. Filling of wetlands is
   1. regarded as mildly hurtful to the environment.
   2. allowed only as a "last resort."
   3. subject to multiple levels of regulation.
   4. no longer allowed under any circumstance.

9. Environmental actions by state and local governments produce *ALL BUT WHICH* of the following effects?
   1. An increase in the amount of land available for real estate development
   2. An increase in the size of the State's wetland areas
   3. An increase in the cost of housing in less-developed areas
   4. An increase in the intensity of land use in older, developed areas

10. Inclusion of the "Notice to Buyer Concerning the Chesapeake and Atlantic Coastal Bays Critical Area"
    1. is required in all contracts for the sale of real property in the State.
    2. is required in all contracts for the sale of Maryland residential property.
    3. is not required in certain Maryland counties.
    4. informs purchasers whether the property they are purchasing is located in the Critical Area of the Chesapeake and Atlantic Coastal Bays.

CHAPTER FIFTEEN

FAIR HOUSING

■ OVERVIEW

Competent real estate licensees realize that fair housing compliance is very demanding. The licensee must have knowledge of applicable federal, state, and local laws, each of which often has its own list of protected groups and of prohibited and required activities. In this chapter, you may notice some similarities and some differences between state, federal, and local law regarding fair housing.

In this chapter, the term *Commission* refers to the State of Maryland Commission on Human Relations.

■ COMMISSION ON HUMAN RELATIONS

The Human Relations Commission comprises nine members who are appointed by the Governor for staggered six-year terms. Its chairman is chosen from among its members, and it is served by an Executive Director and a Deputy Director. The Executive selects an attorney to serve as the Commission's General Counsel. The body meets monthly with additional special meetings after five days' notice to the members.

In addition to its work with fair housing, the Commission works to reduce discrimination in employment and in public accommodations. It not only follows up on complaints from the public but may also take the initiative and generate complaints when at least three of its members agree to do so. The Commission is also subject to the very law from which it receives its authority: It must not show partiality or favoritism in its own staffing and personnel policies because all state agencies, departments, boards, and their employees are subject to Article 49b, the Human Relations Commission law.

Processing Complaints

Complaints *to the Commission* must be made within one year of the alleged discriminatory action or the end of such action, whichever is later. Complaints must be made in writing and under oath. When a complaint is received, the Executive Director considers it and refers it to staff for investigation. Copies of the written staff report submitted to the Executive Director are then sent both to the **complainant** (the aggrieved party making the complaint) and to the **respondent** (the party accused of discriminatory behavior). If the respondent is also a real estate licensee, a copy of the report is sent to the state Real Estate Commission.

If the report concludes that a discriminatory act has probably been committed, staff members seek to deal with the matter by conference, conciliation, and persuasion. If no agreement is reached between complainant and respondent, a report of that fact is sent to all parties.

If the initial conclusion of staff is that there is no probable cause, the report is considered a "final order" that can then be appealed by the complainant to a circuit court in the county where the alleged violation occurred.

When there is found to be probable cause and no agreement is reached, all findings are certified by staff. A written notice is then sent in the name of the Commission to the respondent requiring an answer to the charges at a public hearing before a hearing examiner, to be held in the county of the alleged violation.

If conciliation is productive, a **conciliation agreement** is written and signed by the parties. Its terms are made public unless the parties request they not be *and* the Commission determines such disclosure would not serve the purposes of the statute.

Up to this point, all proceedings are nonpublic and held in strict confidence. Indeed, a Commission member or one of its staff members who violates this confidentiality can be punished by a fine of not more than $1,000 and a term of not more than one year in prison.

At a public hearing, the General Counsel makes the case in support of the complaint. The respondent may give written answer, be heard in person, call and examine witnesses, and be represented by counsel.

If hearing examiners find (conclude) that respondents have engaged in a discriminatory practice, they may order the respondents to

■ cease and desist,
■ take positive action to remedy the situation,
■ reinstate or rehire (in an employment dispute), or
■ provide any other appropriate equitable relief.

If the finding is that there was no discriminatory practice, the examiner shall issue and file an order of dismissal. False and/or malicious complaints are punishable by a fine of not more than $500 and/or one year in prison.

If a respondent fails to do what is ordered, the Commission may sue to enforce compliance with any order within its authority.

Alternative
Complaint Procedure

Whereas complaints to the Human Relations Commission must be made within one year, the complainant may apply *to a court* for relief at any time up to two years from the time of the alleged discriminatory event or breach of a conciliation agreement.

During the early stages of, or instead of, the processing of a complaint by the Commission, a civil action (suit) may be initiated against the respondent in a circuit court in the appropriate county. If this happens, the administrative hearing process on the same alleged discriminatory practice must stop immediately. The complainant is required to notify all parties of initiating civil action.

■ FAIR HOUSING LAWS

Persons who believe they are being discriminated against in a Maryland property transaction—whether it involves real property or personal property—because of their race may petition a federal court to order an end to the discrimination, by virtue of the 1866 Federal Civil Rights Act. Alternatively, they may choose to file a complaint with the Maryland Human Relations Commission if they experience discrimination in a residential real estate–related transaction. Aspects of a real estate–related transaction that would be covered include not only selling and brokerage but also appraisal, insuring, and lending, either for purchase or improvement and repair of a home.

Because Maryland has laws and enforcement mechanisms that have been adjudged "substantially equivalent" to the federal *Fair Housing Act of 1968*, as amended, residential discrimination complaints are handled by State agencies and by State courts.

The federal Fair Housing Act of 1968 as amended in 1988 may be found at

 **WWWeb.Link**

http://www.usdoj.gov/crt/housing/title8.htm

Those seeking help under the Maryland law—Article 49b, §§19 and following—will find that the protected categories are similar to, but go beyond, those in the federal law. In addition to the federal categories of race, color, religion, sex, familial status, national origin, and disability, Maryland includes *marital status and sexual orientation*. The Act defines **sexual orientation** as "identification of an individual as to male or female homosexuality, heterosexuality, or bisexuality."

A Maryland statute passed in 2000 required replacement of the phrase *handicapped person* with the phrase *individual with a disability* throughout the Maryland Annotated Code.

Exceptions

The Maryland law has exceptions to its antidiscrimination requirements that parallel those in the 1968/1988 Fair Housing Act.

In both, an individual is permitted to discriminate in the sale or rental of a single-family dwelling if the property is sold or rented without the help of any broker, of any person in the business of selling or renting dwellings, or of any agent of either of these. The seller must use no discriminatory advertising in marketing the property. Unlike the federal law, Maryland's Article 49B makes no requirement about the number of properties such seller may own or how many may be sold within a specified time period.

The Maryland statute, as amended in 2001, allows an owner-occupant of a single-family principal residence to reject tenant applicants *for rooms* based on sex, marital status, and/or sexual orientation.

A building's owner *who occupies one of the units in a multifamily dwelling* may also reject applicants in the three categories above if the building has no more than five rental units. This contrasts with the federal law's standard of a *total* of four units.

Maryland's other exceptions closely follow those in the federal Fair Housing Act by permitting exclusion of certain protected groups under specific circumstances:

- Religious organizations (no protection for one gender or the other; no protection for nonmembers of the religious denomination)
- Private clubs (no protection for nonmembers seeking overnight accommodations)
- Persons convicted of manufacture or distribution of illegal drugs (excluding these persons)
- Housing for elderly—two kinds:
  1. All residents are required to be age 62 and above (no protection for families with young children)
  2. One person age 55 or above is required in 80 percent of the units (no protection for families with young children)
- Reasonable occupancy standards—based on space or number of rooms—set by local government units (no protection for families whose members outnumber the occupancy limit, possibly removing protection for families with young children)

Counties, municipalities, and other local governments are also empowered to enact ordinances and extend protection to additional groups.

Additional Protected Groups

All jurisdictions include the federal "core" of protected categories: race, color, religion, national origin, sex, handicap (*disability*, in Maryland), and familial status. The State and some counties and cities have added others. *Marital status* and *sexual orientation* are added by the State of Maryland and most of its jurisdictions; *occupation* and *personal appearance*, by Howard and Prince George's Counties; and *ancestry* and *source of income*, by Montgomery County.

Sources of law relating to enforcement include the *Civil Rights Act of 1866*; *The Civil Rights Act of 1964*; *The Fair Housing Act of 1968*, as amended; Article

49B of the Maryland Code; §16-526 of the Business Occupations and Professions Article of the Maryland Code; Chapter 27 of the Montgomery County Code; Title 12, Subtitle 2 of the Howard County Code; Division 12, Subdivision I of the Prince George's County Code; and Chapter 13 of the Laws of Rockville. Although not comprehensive, this list is suggestive of the number of laws governing and protecting the people of Maryland in the area of fair housing.

■ DISCRIMINATION IN HOUSING

Examples listed in the Maryland statute of unlawful discriminatory housing practices against protected groups include

- refusing to sell, rent, or negotiate after a bona fide offer;
- making unavailable or denying a dwelling, or representing that a property is not available for inspection, sale, or rent when it is in fact available;
- discriminating in terms, conditions, or privileges of sale or rental of a dwelling;
- discriminating in the provision of related services or facilities;
- making or ordering to be made any publication, notice, or statement concerning properties for sale or rent indicating any preference, limitation, or discrimination; and
- seeking, *for profit*, to induce any person to sell or rent a dwelling by making representations regarding the entry of a protected group into an area.

Special Provisions for Individuals with Disabilities

In addition to the protections in the previous list, the following prohibited acts are added on behalf of persons with disabilities:

- Discrimination against an applicant with a disability or a nondisabled applicant who will have a person with a disability residing in the dwelling after it is sold, rented, or made available
- Discrimination in sale, rental, or availability of a property
- Discrimination in terms, conditions, or privileges of sale or rental or in connection with the dwelling after sale or rental
- Refusal to permit reasonable modifications of existing premises occupied or to be occupied by individuals with disabilities (These modifications are those necessary to give the disabled person full enjoyment of the dwelling and are made at tenants' expense and with the tenants' agreement to restore the premises to their condition before the modification. This right also applies to unit owners or residents in condominiums.)
- Refusal to make reasonable accommodations in rules, policies, practices, or services when such accommodations are necessary to give persons with disabilities equal opportunity to use and enjoy a dwelling
- Failure to design or construct a multifamily dwelling for first occupancy so that the public use and common areas are readily accessible to and usable by persons with disabilities; all doors for passage into and within all premises within the dwelling are wide enough to accommodate wheelchairs; and all premises have suitable adaptive design features (for example, an accessible route into and through the dwelling; light switches,

electrical outlets, thermostats, and other environmental controls in accessible locations; reinforcements in bathroom walls to allow later installation of grab bars; and kitchens and bathrooms designed so that individuals in wheelchairs can maneuver about the space.)

Discrimination in Real Estate Services

The law forbids any person or business entity that engages in real estate–related transactions

- to discriminate against any person in making available a transaction or in the terms or conditions of a transaction because of membership in a protected group, or
- to deny access to, or membership in, or participation in a multiple-listing service, brokers' organization, or other service, organization, or facility relating to the business of selling or renting dwellings, or to discriminate in the terms or conditions of membership or of participation based on protected group status.

Maryland statute makes it unlawful to coerce, intimidate, threaten, interfere with, or retaliate against persons who seek to exercise the rights granted by this law or persons who encourage others to exercise such rights. Persons guilty of such actions may be fined not more than $1,000, or suffer imprisonment for not more than one year, or both. If the violation results in bodily injury, penalties may range up to $10,000 and ten years in prison; if it results in death, imprisonment for any term of years or for life.

Enforcement of Agreements

The Commission may sue to enforce an agreement that a respondent in the case of a complaint has breached.

At the time a complaint is first received, the Commission itself may also initiate a civil action in the circuit court of the county where the property is located for relief of the complaining party. Having done this, the Commission may still proceed with its administrative proceedings. But if an aggrieved party initiates a civil action under federal or State law seeking relief for a discriminatory housing practice, the Commission may review the complaint and refer the matter to the State Attorney General but may not continue further on the same charges.

Anyone who deliberately submits false information to the Commission as it investigates, who fails to make full disclosure, or who changes previous records, reports, or accounts shall be fined not more than $100,000 or imprisoned for not more than one year, or both.

Aggrieved persons may begin civil actions in an appropriate State court not later than two years after the discriminatory action. They may file no such civil actions, based on the same discrimination, after the Commission or a State or local agency has succeeded in producing a conciliation agreement that the aggrieved parties agreed to, except to enforce such agreement.

Relief granted in a civil action may not set aside any lease or sales contract to other bona fide purchasers or tenants who did not have actual notice of the filing of a complaint with the Commission or of the civil action.

Pattern of Discrimination

When the Commission believes there is a pattern of discrimination or resistance to the rights granted by this law, it may commence a civil action in circuit court. The court may award preventive relief or grant temporary or permanent injunctions and restraining orders against those responsible for violations. The court may also award—in addition to attorney's fees—monetary damages to aggrieved persons in amounts not to exceed $50,000 for a first violation and $100,000 for subsequent violations.

■ COMMERCIAL PROPERTY

Neither the owners or the operators of commercial property, their agents and employees, nor any persons licensed or regulated by the State may discriminate against an individual in the terms, conditions, or privileges of property leased for commercial usage, or in the provision of services or facilities in connection with the property, because of the individual's race, color, religion, sex, age [*sic*], physical disability, marital status, or national origin.

■ THE REAL ESTATE BROKERS ACT

The Brokers Act also addresses discrimination against protected groups.

Whether or not acting for monetary gain, a person may not knowingly induce or attempt to induce another person to sell or rent a dwelling or otherwise transfer real estate or knowingly discourage or attempt to discourage another person from purchasing real estate

■ by making representations regarding the entry or prospective entry into a neighborhood of individuals of a particular race, color, sex, religion, or national origin;

■ by making representations regarding the existing or potential proximity of real property owned or used by individuals of a particular race, color, sex, religion, or national origin; or

■ by representing that the existing or potential proximity of real property owned or used by individuals of a particular race, color, sex, religion, or national origin will or may result in the lowering of property values; a change in the racial, religious, or ethnic character of the block, neighborhood, or area; an increase in criminal or antisocial behavior in the area; or a decline in the quality of schools serving the area.

This contrasts with both Human Relations Commission Law and the federal Fair Housing Act, which require *the profit motive* for such blockbusting.

A person may not provide *financial assistance* by loan, gift, or otherwise to another person if the person has actual knowledge that the financial assistance will be used in a transaction that results from a violation of these prohibitions.

Solicitation of Residential Listings

If one of the purposes of the solicitation or attempted solicitation is to change the racial composition of a neighborhood, a person may not solicit or attempt to solicit the listing of residential properties for sale or lease by in-person, door-to-door solicitation, telephone solicitation, or mass distribution of circulars.

Baltimore City law prohibits the solicitation of residential properties for purchase or sale by general door-to-door solicitations, in person or by telephone, or by the mass distribution of circulars. *There are no exceptions to the law.* Solicitations as a result of personal referrals, general knowledge that a property is for sale, or offerings by an owner also constitute violations of the law. The court has added that any uninvited call or visit could constitute a violation of this ordinance.

Baltimore County law provides several methods of canvassing that are *not* considered solicitation. These include advertisements in bona fide newspapers of general circulation or on radio or television; literature distributed through the United States mail; legitimate personal referrals; contacts with property owners resulting from the owners' having personally advertised the property for sale; and solicitation for the purpose of obtaining information for appraisals or similar collection of general sales or market data.

Violation of either the Baltimore City or Baltimore County law is punishable as a misdemeanor, with penalties, on conviction, of a fine, imprisonment, or both.

Laws concerning solicitation vary from jurisdiction to jurisdiction. It is the responsibility of licensees to be familiar with the local laws where they perform acts of real estate brokerage.

Conservation Areas

The Brokers Act empowers the Real Estate Commission to identify and designate certain localities as *conservation areas*. In these areas and for limited time periods, all advertising of properties for sale and the use of "For Sale" signs is suspended. Brokerage firms may not solicit listings from owners of such properties but may list them when approached by their owners. This is done for the purpose of preserving racial stability in the affected locality in the event of a threatening volume of real estate transactions. Requirements for establishing such areas are presently so cumbersome that not one such area has been designated for more than a decade.

■ ENFORCEMENT

A person aggrieved by a fair housing violation may have to decide the avenue through which to seek redress—whether it will be a local, county, State, or federal agency.

Federal Laws

In the area of race, aggrieved persons may go directly to federal district court for injunctive relief. For race and other matters, they may sue in local courts for damages. If complaint of an alleged Maryland violation is reported to HUD, HUD will refer the matter to the Maryland Human Relations Commission, because Maryland laws are "substantially equivalent" to the federal fair housing laws.

State Enforcement

Complaints made or referred to the Maryland Human Relations Commission are investigated, mediated, and resolved by agreements enforceable in the courts.

Financial Penalties

If the Maryland Human Relations Commission, after proper investigation and hearing, concludes that a respondent—the person against whom the charge was brought—has engaged in any of the unlawful practices listed above, it may seek an order assessing a civil penalty against the respondent not exceeding $500 for a first offense. If it is the second offense within five years, the penalty can be in an amount not more than $1,000. If there were two prior offenses within the last seven years, the maximum penalty would be $2,500.

If the respondent is a **natural person**—an individual rather than a firm or organization—the penalty may be imposed without regard to the time periods between previous violations.

Fair housing provisions of the Brokers Act may be enforced administratively by the State Real Estate Commission or judicially by the Office of the Attorney General. Courts and other government agencies finding licensees guilty of discrimination are required to report their findings to the Commission.

Local Laws and Their Enforcement

Chartered counties are empowered to enforce fair housing law violations with fines or penalties not to exceed those provided in the federal Fair Housing Act Amendments of 1988 and 1993. Many counties have Human Rights or Human Relations Commissions instead of, or in addition to, possible court enforcement.

■ DISCRIMINATION IN FINANCING

It is unlawful for any bank, savings association, credit union, insurance company, or other creditor to deny a housing loan or credit to persons who apply, or to discriminate against them in the fixing of the down payment, interest rate, duration, or other terms or conditions of a loan, because of the race, color, religion, creed, marital status, familial status, sex, national origin; the physical or mental disability of such person or of any member, stockholder, director, officer, or employee of such person; or of the prospective occupants, lessees, or tenants of the dwelling for which the loan application is made.

■ HUD FAIR HOUSING ADVERTISING GUIDELINES

Section 804(c) of the federal Fair Housing Act makes it unlawful,

> To make, print, or publish, or cause to be made, printed, or published any notice, statement, or advertisement, with respect to the sale or rental of a dwelling that indicates any preference, limitation, or discrimination based on race, color, religion, sex, handicap, familial status, or national origin, or an intention to make any such preference, limitation, or discrimination.

TABLE 15.1

Fair Housing Advertising Guidelines

Issue	Typical Phrases That Will Create Liability	Phrases That Will Not Create Liability
Race, Color, and National Origin	White family home No Irish Pakistanis welcome	Master bedroom Rare find Desirable neighborhood
Religion	No Jews Jews welcome Christian home Near Lutheran nursing home Any particular clearly religious graphic* No Muslims Muslims welcome	Merry Christmas Happy Easter Images of Santa Claus or Easter Bunny Valentine's Day graphic Kosher kitchen in building Chapel on site
Sex	Males only Females only	Mother-in-law suite Bachelor apartment
Handicap	No wheelchairs	Great view Walk-up apartment Walk-in closets Jogging trails Walking distance to bus stop Wheelchair ramps
Familial Status†	No children Adults only Couples only Singles welcome	Two-bedroom Cozy family room No bicycles allowed Quiet streets

* If a property refers to a religion in its name (Lutheran home, Beth Torah home) or a Cross or the Star of David appears, the ad should contain such words as, "This home does not discriminate on the basis of race, color, religion, national origin, sex, handicap, or familial status."
† Certain exceptions exist for age-qualified communities limited to 55- and 62-year-old+ adults.

Table 15.1 summarizes current HUD guidelines as to certain phrases that will and will not create liability under this Section.

Ads should focus on the property advertised rather than on potential tenants or purchasers. It is better to say "swimming pool on site," than "great place for swimmers." Care should be taken not to advertise in media that are directed solely toward a racially or religiously segmented geographic or economic market. If more than one local publication or electronic medium is used, the same phraseology should be used in all of them.

Advertisements may describe the behavior expected of prospective residents, for example, "non-smoking," "sober."

■ THE MARYLAND STATUTE

Maryland's fair housing law, Article 49B, Sections 19 to 39, has been found to be "substantially equivalent" to the federal Fair Housing Act of 1968 as amended. It is of central importance and is the source of much of the material in this chapter. The entire text may be found at

WWWeb.Link

www.michie.com/resources1.html

Click on "Maryland," then on "Maryland Code," then on "More," until "Article 49B Human Relations Commission" is visible. Click on "49B," then on "Discrimination in Housing." Sections 19 to 39 deal with housing discrimination.

■ EDUCATION REQUIREMENTS

Real Estate Commission General Regulations 11, 14, and 17 require that all license applicants as a part of their educational requirements be instructed in the human relations aspects of the practice of real estate, including study of fair housing laws and the effects of such undesirable practices as exploitation, steering, block-busting, prejudicial solicitation, discriminatory practices, misleading advertising, and other related activities.

QUESTIONS

1. James and Frances Wong, who are of Chinese descent, tell their real estate salesperson that they need a three-bedroom house in the $320,000 to $330,000 price range that is within walking distance of an elementary school. The salesperson, after identifying the Wongs as genuine prospects, finds a house on Judson Street that meets all the Wongs' requirements, but the salesperson knows that the residents of the neighborhood are unhappy about Asians moving into the area. The agent should
   1. refrain from telling the Wongs about this particular house.
   2. tell them about the house but suggest that they would be happier in another neighborhood.
   3. file a complaint with the Human Relations Commission.
   4. inform the Wongs about the availability of the house and arrange to show them the listing.

2. With respect to fair housing, all persons engaged in real estate transactions
   1. must be familiar with all applicable federal, state, and local antidiscrimination statutes and ordinances.
   2. carry E&O insurance to be protected.
   3. may refuse to be held liable.
   4. have the right to decide what is best for their customers and clients.

3. Two salespersons are trying to sell a residential property listed in a neighborhood that is predominantly Caucasian. They
   1. are acting properly by not showing this listing to white prospects.
   2. violate Maryland and federal laws when they decide whether to show a listing based on a prospect's race.
   3. need not introduce into the neighborhood anyone not of the predominant race of the neighborhood.
   4. should have a salesperson of the same race as the prospect show the property.

4. A broker approaches homeowners seeking to list their property for sale. They had not been thinking of selling, but the broker tells them, "The time to sell is now," because the neighborhood is experiencing a large minority group influx and that the value of their property, ". . . is sure to drop," if they wait any longer. This broker's behavior is
   1. blockbusting.
   2. steering.
   3. blind advertising.
   4. redlining.

5. A private club, by limiting the rental or occupancy of its lodgings to club members, as long as the club is not operated as a commercial hotel, is violating
   1. the federal Fair Housing Act of 1968.
   2. the Maryland Fair Housing Law.
   3. the Real Estate License Law.
   4. no state or federal laws.

16

CLOSING THE REAL ESTATE TRANSACTION

■ OVERVIEW

Whether it is called *settlement, closing, going to escrow,* or some other name, this event is the culmination of real estate brokerage activities. At this event, legal title to property passes from sellers to purchasers and then, usually, to the lender. As a result of the closing, purchasers take on long-term debt and sellers get equity funds from the sale of their property. From these funds, sellers typically pay commissions to their listing broker and satisfy outstanding mortgages or other liens against the property sold.

Listing brokers may divide their commissions with in-house affiliates who *assisted purchasers,* intracompany agents who represented *buyers and sellers,* or other brokers who either assisted buyers *as subagents* or represented them *as buyers' agents.*

■ EVIDENCE OF TITLE

In Maryland, it is customary for buyers to order a **title search** and a **binder** (interim commitment) for mortgagee **title insurance** at the time of entering into a purchase contract. In most cases, the title (settlement) company orders the title search and preparation of an abstract of title. If the information in the abstract indicates marketable title, a settlement company that is authorized to do so by a title insurance company will issue a binder—a commitment from the title insurance company to issue a permanent policy at the time of settlement. Some attorneys issue their own certificates of title. Others simply indicate their opinion of title based on the abstract, without any insurance. The issuance of title insurance is dependent upon a favorable interpretation of the abstract of title.

Lenders almost always require **mortgagee** (lender's) title insurance for the protection of their position. In addition, State law requires that purchasers be offered **homeowner** (buyer) title insurance by the settlement officer at every residential closing. Buyers who decline homeowner title insurance are asked to confirm their refusal in writing. For the different characteristics and functions of each of their policies, the student should consult the principal text.

■ SETTLEMENTS

Most purchase contracts and sale agreements are closed in the office of a title insurance company, the buyer's or seller's attorney, the mortgage lender, or the real estate broker. Closing in Maryland is usually performed at a meeting involving buyers, sellers, agents, and a settlement officer. Closing in escrow, as described in the principal text, is generally not practiced in Maryland.

Real estate brokers or their salespersons normally are present at settlement, although the interaction is—and should be—principally among the officer conducting the settlement, the parties to the agreement, and any attorneys present. Licensees are present for whatever nonlegal services they may be asked to render, to provide personal support for their clients, and, of course, to receive the commission for their companies.

■ CLOSING AND TAX STATEMENTS

The buyers' or sellers' attorney or a settlement company officer will prepare the necessary *closing statement*. Licensees should know how these statements are calculated in order to estimate accurately sellers' expenses of sale and net proceeds from the transaction. They should also be able to estimate for purchasers the amount of additional cash needed at closing to complete the purchase. They should be able to understand and explain to customers and clients every entry on the typical settlement sheet, HUD Form #1.

Closing costs are apportioned according to statute, where applicable, and/or by contractual agreement. Typically, the seller is responsible for such property charges for the day of closing as ad valorem taxes, special assessments, and utilities.

By federal law, all owner/sellers must provide the closing agent with their forwarding addresses and Social Security numbers. Corporate sellers must provide their corporate tax identification numbers.

If the Maryland property is being sold by an out-of-state owner, Maryland statute requires that 4.75 percent of the total payment to the seller be withheld. **Total payment** is defined as the consideration for the property reduced by mortgages paid and other costs of the sale; essentially it means the seller's bottom line: "cash to seller." This is prepaid income tax on any possible capital gain or other income tax liability the seller may owe to the State. If the seller is not a natural person, but a corporation or trust located in another state, the percentage to be set aside is 7 percent. A seller claiming to be a resident of Maryland is required to sign an affidavit to that effect at closing. Obviously, it is easier to collect taxes from an owner who lives within the State. Sellers who had their permanent residence within the State at the time of closing will not have these amounts withheld at settlement.

Buyers and sellers must sign an affidavit as to the accuracy of information they have given that will be reported to the IRS. Typically, the person conducting settlement will request photo IDs of the principals. Copies of these IDs are maintained in the title company's records. Licensees should make sure that their sellers are prepared to provide all the required information at the time of settlement. The closing agent or title company can answer any questions that may arise.

■ EVIDENCE OF RELEASE

Within 30 days after closing, settlement (title) company officers, who are responsible for disbursement of funds, must mail or deliver to the sellers evidence of having recorded the *release of mortgage*. If the recording of release is delayed beyond the 30-day period for causes beyond their control, settlement officers must mail or deliver to the sellers a letter explaining the delay. They must send another letter for each additional delay of 30 days. Failure to follow these rules may subject them to audit of all their accounts by the court.

However, if persons conducting closing properly disburse all funds entrusted to them in the closing procedure within five days, no such evidence is required unless specifically requested by purchasers or vendors. Vendors and purchasers are to be informed in writing of these requirements before the deed is delivered at closing.

Settlements in Maryland must be performed by, or under the supervision of, an attorney. This does not mean that an attorney is present or has even seen the paperwork. It does mean that there must be an attorney responsible for the preparation and execution of closing and the proper disbursement of funds. To be recorded, deeds on Maryland realty, as mentioned in Chapter 10, must be prepared by an attorney or by either the deed's grantor or grantee. "Prepared by an attorney" may well mean "prepared by personnel trained and supervised" by the attorney who is responsible for their performance at closing. Supervision does not always have to be done in person. The student is reminded of the "evidences of reasonable and adequate supervision" required of real estate brokers listed in Chapter 3.

Representation

Whom do settlement officers represent? They usually owe certain fiduciary duties to several parties, but exclusive loyalty to none. When they order and evaluate the abstract of title, they owe the purchaser due care. When they issue title insurance, they are acting as agents of the title insurance company. In collecting taxes for the state and tax information for the Internal Revenue Service, they have responsibility to gather and handle those funds and that information with due care. They owe the sellers the duty of paying off old liens and recording releases of liens on behalf of the old mortgagee, and buyers er16   Closing the Real Estate Transaction   **179**

the duty of recording their new deed. They must also record any mortgages that were given to lenders at settlement. In addition to their duties to all these parties, settlement officers represent themselves and their title company.

QUESTIONS

1. Residential closings in Maryland
   1. are usually performed by an escrowee.
   2. are always performed by real estate brokers.
   3. are always performed by title company clerks.
   4. are always performed under an attorney's supervision.

2. Proof of release of debt on a property after a closing must be
   1. sent to the county courthouse within 30 days of closing.
   2. sent to purchaser within 5 days of closing.
   3. sent to seller within 30 days of closing.
   4. sent to the former mortgagee within 5 days.

3. An attorney who personally conducts settlement
   1. owes all parties due care in execution of closing duties.
   2. represents the seller.
   3. represents the buyer.
   4. may represent both the buyer and the seller.

4. In Maryland, title search is usually ordered
   1. at the direction and expense of the seller.
   2. at the direction and expense of the purchaser.
   3. by the salesperson who prepares the contract.
   4. by the broker of the listing client.

5. When the property being closed is sold by an out-of-state corporate owner,
   1. the buyer is no longer protected by the Maryland Guaranty Fund.
   2. the buyer must set aside 4.75 percent of the consideration.
   3. the closing officer must withhold 7 percent of the seller's proceeds of sale.
   4. the closing officer must withhold 4.75 percent of the consideration.

MARYLAND REAL ESTATE LICENSE EXAMINATIONS

■ OVERVIEW

Passing the state licensing examination is a major challenge for persons seeking a real estate license. Every applicant would like to pass the exam on the first try, not only to speed up the licensing process but also to reduce the cost of taking it over, minimize inconvenience, and avoid embarrassment.

Since 1998, the salesperson license examination can be taken only after 60 hours' prelicense instruction. A total of 135 hours is required before the broker examination. These requirements must be met *before* taking the examinations.

■ THE REAL ESTATE LICENSE EXAMINATION

PSI Examination Services, Inc. (PSI), Las Vegas, Nevada, an independent testing service under contract with the Commission, prepares and administers the licensing examinations. PSI's testing program is adapted to each state's real estate license laws and practices and to the priorities of its licensing agency.

Candidates receive two scores for their examination: the state score and the national score. The passing grade set by the Commission is currently 70 percent for each section. This means the salesperson candidate must answer at least 56 out of 80 questions on the national portion correctly and 21 out of 30 on the state portion. Broker candidates must correctly answer 56 out of 80 on the national and 28 out of 40 questions on the state portion. Broker and salesperson candidates each have 120 minutes to complete the entire exam.

Candidates receive two scores for their examination: the state score and the national score. The passing grade set by the Commission is currently 70 percent for each section. This means the salesperson candidate must answer at least 56 out of 80 questions on the national portion and 21 out of 30 on the state portion correctly. Broker candidates must correctly answer 56 out of 80 questions on the national portion and 28 out of 40 questions on the state portion. Broker and salesperson candidates each have 120 minutes to complete the entire exam. (Statewide, between 60 and 65 percent of all candidates taking the salesperson exam for the first time pass both portions.)

The *national* section of the examinations for both broker and salesperson contains questions based on general real estate information. Subjects include Property Ownership, Land Use Controls and Regulations, Valuation and Market Analysis, Financing, Laws of Agency, Mandated Disclosures, Contracts, Transfer of Property, Practice of Real Estate, Mathematics, and Specialty Areas.

The *Maryland (State) section* contains questions based on Title 17 of the *Maryland Annotated Code* (the Brokers Act) as well as questions relating to the General *Regulations* and the *Code of Ethics* established by the Maryland Real Estate Commission. Test questions deal with duties and powers of the Commission, licensing requirements, and business conduct. Questions relating to Environmental Issues, Water Rights, Listing and Buyer Agreements, and Common Interest Ownership Properties will also be found in the State portion.

Because tests are not preprinted, they can be generated daily from a computer database. Thus they can be continually updated, revised, and the order of items rearranged.

■ APPLICATION PROCEDURES

Students obtain the *Application Bulletin*, containing instructions and application forms for the examinations, from the school where they take their class. They can also be downloaded from the PSI Web site:

www.psiexams.com

Those who are ready to take the examination should mail the application form, together with evidence of passing the prelicense course, as well as the testing fee and any other required documents, to

> PSI Examination Services
> ATTN: Examination Registration MD RE
> 3210 East Tropicana
> Las Vegas, NV 89121

Failure to follow exactly the instructions on the registration form may result in students' not being scheduled promptly for the examinations they request.

The registration fee for taking a Maryland Real Estate Licensing Examination (either broker or salesperson) is $60. Payment can be made to PSI by personal check, money order, company check, or cashier's check.

Candidates who have previously provided complete certification of eligibility to PSI may register by mail or through *Express Registration* on the telephone, by fax, or on the Internet. These applicants may be persons who failed all or part of a previous exam or those whose initial application form was incomplete but was accompanied by proper proof of their completion of the education requirement. A $10 fee is charged for Express Registration in addition to the basic $60 for the examination. A valid VISA card or MasterCard is needed.

First-time applicants are to send their Registration Forms, other necessary documents, and the registration fee directly to PSI. In return, PSI will mail them (usually within two weeks) a Registration Confirmation Notice. This notice explains how to make an examination appointment. Once this appointment, including place, date, and time for examination, has been made, applicants may still request changes. They may do this by calling 1-800-733-9267, two or more days before their scheduled testing date. All examinations—even if delayed—must still be completed within 90 days of original registration, or the candidates must reapply and pay another registration fee. The expiration date is shown on each student's Confirmation Notice.

The Registration Form asks for information that will be relayed to the Commission so it can process the license applications when candidates pass their tests. It also asks for certification that the candidate has successfully completed the mandatory educational hours. In addition, it contains a statement of *irrevocable consent*, which is required from applicants who live outside Maryland.

Applicants must answer the Registration Form questions to the best of their ability. The form is then signed as an affidavit, subject to the penalties of perjury.

■ TESTING PROCEDURES

Candidates may take an examination at any of the several testing centers located in Maryland. All candidates must bring positive identification to the testing site. This identification must include at least one government-issued picture ID with your signature on it—such as a driver's license, state ID, or passport. The second (additional) form of ID could be a credit card that has your signature and preprinted legal name. But all IDs must have exactly the same name as the document certifying completion of the required prelicense education and the Registration Form, including the same middle initial and same use of generation (Jr., Sr., II, III, etc.).

PSI uses a computerized testing system approved by the Commission. On conclusion of the testing session, the computer will show candidates whether they passed or failed; official notification of examination results, however, will be mailed to candidates. The computerized real estate examinations are administered every business day during the week at most locations. There is no "walk in" testing.

Candidates take their examinations seated at specially designed, semiprivate computer work stations. On-screen instructions provide a 15-minute tutorial in the use of the keyboard. About as many keys are used as are found on a touch-tone telephone. Taking the test requires no computer skills. Instructions appear on the screen to guide the candidate through each step of the test. The testing period is 120 minutes. There is an on-screen clock for the candidate to watch.

No notes, books, cell phones, pagers, or children are allowed in the examination center. Silent, nonprinting, nonprogrammable, battery-operated calculators are permitted, but they must not have alphabet keys. There is no smoking, eating, or drinking at the center. A candidate who tries to copy a question or an answer or to communicate examination content to another person may be disqualified and possibly subject to legal action for violation of copyright laws.

When candidates first take the real estate exam, they take the state section first, then the national. Candidates who have already taken the exam but passed only one of its two sections are permitted to reregister and retake the group of questions—state or general—that they still need to pass. Candidates must pass both sets of questions to be eligible for a Maryland real estate license.

■ TYPES OF QUESTIONS ON EXAM

The tests use multiple-choice answer format. An incomplete statement or a question is presented and is followed by four possible choices. Applicants are sometimes asked to *find the one correct answer*. At other times they must find the *one wrong answer*. Here are examples of each:

■ EXAMPLE 1

Which one of the following cities is the capital of the state it is located in?

1. New York City, NY
2. New Orleans, LA
3. Lincoln, NE
4. Scranton, PA

■ EXAMPLE 2

All the following are even numbers *EXCEPT:*

1. 118
2. 230
3. 734
4. 437

The PSI testing approach is designed to test reasoning processes as well as factual real estate knowledge. These questions are not representative of those on the examination. Examples of more difficult questions and problems have been included in the chapters of this book so that you will become familiar with them and be better prepared for the examination.

In answering examination-type questions, consider all answers carefully and eliminate the least likely ones instead of randomly selecting an answer. However, it is better to guess than to give no answer at all. The purpose of the examination is to provide a measure of your knowledge of real estate and thereby allow you to demonstrate your qualification for licensure. You should try to answer all questions without spending too much time on any one question. The fourth answer choice for each math test item is often *None of the above*. Do not be surprised by it.

Here are the answers to the model questions:

1. 1   2   3   4
    [ ] [ ] [x] [ ]

2. 1   2   3   4
    [ ] [ ] [ ] [x]

■ MORE HELP IN PREPARING FOR THE LICENSE EXAMINATION

The author has tried to prepare you for the Maryland Real Estate License Examination by including in this book the kinds of items usually found on the test. Familiarity with the test items, however, will not in itself ensure a passing score. Your most important preparation for this examination involves thoughtfully studying real estate principles and practices and brokerage laws and regulations.

Concentrate on learning the material by studying the principal text and this book. When using the tests and exercises in these books, be sure that you find *and understand* the correct solutions for any questions you miss. Use the answer keys in these books thoughtfully.

Dearborn™ Real Estate Education® publishes other instructional materials in addition to *Modern Real Estate Practice* and *Maryland Real Estate: Practice & Law* that are especially designed to aid you in passing the licensing exam: *Mastering Real Estate Math*, Seventh Edition, *Study Guide for Modern Real Estate Practice, Guide to Passing the PSI Real Estate Exam*, Fifth Edition, and *Maryland Real Estate Exam Prep*. If copies of these books are not available through your local bookseller, you may purchase them online, directly from the publisher at

 **WWWeb.Link**   http://www.dearborn.com/recampus/Home.asp

Practice with the *interactive software, Real Estate Exam Prep–North Atlantic,* which includes Maryland, will give you the experience of answering on-screen questions similar to state exam questions while seated at a computer keyboard, the way you will take your test.

■ TYPICAL MARYLAND-SPECIFIC TEST ITEMS

The Maryland-related questions throughout this volume are in the format found on the real estate licensing exam. Use them to identify strengths and weaknesses in your knowledge.

List the items you miss and use that list as a guide for further intensive study of the text. Sometimes you may want to test yourself on an entire list of questions. Other times you may wish to attempt the items one by one, checking your answers as you go. Decide why every correct answer *IS* correct. In items that ask you to find the *WRONG* answer, do so; but then try to learn all you can from the three CORRECT answers to the same questions. Make intelligent use of all practice questions and the answer keys.

TABLE A.1

Summary of Facts about Examinations

Exam	Portion	Number of Questions	Total Time Allowed	Minimum Number Correct Required To Pass	Fee Regular	Fee Express
Salesperson	National	80		56		
	State	30		21		
	Both	110	120 minutes		$60	$70
Broker	National	80		56		
	State	40		28		
	Both	120	120 minutes		$60	$70

PRACTICE EXAM

1. When a salesperson whose license was not renewed negotiates a sale of real property, the commission is payable to
    1. the broker only.
    2. no one.
    3. the salesperson only.
    4. the broker and the salesperson according to prior agreement.

2. If a salesperson license is issued on 20 September 2005, it will expire on
    1. 20 September 2007.
    2. 20 September 2009.
    3. 30 April 2007.
    4. 1 March 2007.

3. When prospective purchasers first arrive at a brokerage office to inquire about real estate assistance, the Brokers Act requires that they be treated as
    1. customers.   3. agents.
    2. clients.   4. factors.

4. Salespersons' licenses must be
    1. kept in a safe place by the salespersons.
    2. carried by the salespersons.
    3. displayed in their brokers' offices.
    4. maintained in their personnel files by their brokers.

5. The maximum amount that a claimant may collect per transaction from the Guaranty Fund is
    1. unlimited.   3. $25,000.
    2. $250,000.   4. $10,000.

6. When the license of a broker is suspended or revoked, the broker's salespeople must
    1. find a new broker-employer.
    2. continue listing and selling.
    3. stop listing and selling with that broker.
    4. obtain a broker's license.

7. Membership on the State Real Estate Commission includes
    1. only licensed salespersons.
    2. only licensed brokers.
    3. unlicensed persons and licensed brokers and salespersons.
    4. those persons appointed by the Attorney General.

8. Maryland real estate salesperson and broker licenses are issued
    1. by the Board of REALTORS®.
    2. to all applicants who have successfully passed required educational courses.
    3. by the Maryland Association of REALTORS®.
    4. by the Real Estate Commission.

9. Ethical standards that must be observed by all Maryland real estate licensees are set by the
    1. National Association of REALTORS®.
    2. State Real Estate Commission.
    3. Maryland Association of REALTORS®.
    4. local Boards and Associations.

10. When a broker provides brokerage services through a partnership, which of the following statements is FALSE?
    1. The broker is responsible for the real estate brokerage activities of the partnership.
    2. The broker must have a contractual or employment agreement with the partnership.
    3. The broker must be one of the partners.
    4. The broker must be designated by the partnership as its broker of record.

11. When builders sell houses they have built and own, which of the following is *TRUE*?
    1. They need not hold real estate licenses. ✓
    2. They must be licensed if they sell more than six per calendar year.
    3. They must be licensed brokers.
    4. They may be licensed as salespersons but not affiliated with brokers.

12. A developer desiring to convert a building that is more than five years old into a time-share project in Maryland must
    1. give each tenant 180 days' notice.
    2. give each tenant 120 days' notice.
    3. not give tenants any prior notice.
    4. notify each tenant within 10 days after filing the Public Offering Statement.

13. The responsibilities of real estate licensees do *NOT* include
    1. fair treatment of third parties.
    2. competence in performance of duties.
    3. duty to give legal interpretations.
    4. loyalty to their principal.

14. In what kind of states do lenders receive defeasible fee interests in mortgaged land?
    1. Title theory states
    2. Lien theory states
    3. Modified lien theory states
    4. Trust theory states

15. Under the Maryland Real Estate Brokers Act, the Commission may impose a penalty per violation. The penalty is not more than
    1. $500 and/or one year in jail.
    2. $5,000.
    3. $2,000.
    4. $1,000 and/or one year in jail.

16. The amount of commission set in a listing agreement is determined by
    1. Maryland statute.
    2. the local Board or Association of REALTORS®.
    3. mutual agreement between the parties to the agency agreement.
    4. the Real Estate Commission sitting in executive session.

17. Earnest money received by salespersons must be
    1. deposited in their trust accounts.
    2. given to the sellers of the property.
    3. placed in their broker's safe.
    4. given to their broker for prompt deposit in the firm's trust account.

18. Which of the following is *NOT* true about tenancy by the entirety?
    1. If husband and wife divorce, it is terminated.
    2. Both spouses' signatures are required to sell such property if both are living.
    3. Upon death of either spouse, the form of ownership converts to tenancy in common.
    4. In Maryland, only a legally married husband and wife can own property under it.

19. When a broker receives a less-than-full-price offer from a prospect and at the same time a full-price offer through a cooperating firm, the broker should present
    1. only the full price offer.
    2. only the offer from the broker's customer.
    3. both offers.
    4. the first offer received and if it is rejected, present the other offer.

20. The law requiring certain contracts for the transfer of an interest in realty to be in writing in order to be enforceable is the Maryland
    1. written instrument law.
    2. parol evidence law.
    3. statute of limitations.
    4. statute of frauds.

21. In Maryland, a land installment contract need *NOT*
    1. be recorded by the vendor within 15 days after it has been signed.
    2. include all terms of the transaction.
    3. be signed by the vendor and vendee.
    4. be filed with the Real Estate Commission.

22. The Commission's form, "Understanding Whom Agents Represent," can
    1. inform prospective purchasers and lessees of the various ways they can be served by real estate brokerage firms.
    2. create a representation agreement between the agent who presents the form and the prospect to whom it is presented.
    3. give a licensee the prospect's permission to engage in a transaction involving dual agency.
    4. end a licensee's presumed buyer representation of a prospect.

23. Material facts learned from a client remain confidential until
    1. the client dies and the estate is probated.
    2. the agency relationship (either presumed or contractual) is terminated.
    3. the Statute of Limitations has expired.
    4. the fact becomes common knowledge from other sources.

24. When does Title 17 require the Commission's form, "Understanding Whom Agents Represent," to be presented?
    1. At first contact with a prospective purchaser or lessee
    2. At the first fact-to-face contact between a licensee and the prospect
    3. Not later than the moment a prospect expresses the desire to look at a property listed with the licensee's company
    4. Not later than the first scheduled face-to-face meeting between the licensee and the prospect

25. Agency relationships can be created by
    1. ministerial actions of a licensee.
    2. magisterial guidance from a licensee.
    3. payment or promise of payment to a licensee.
    4. a prospect's expectations of a licensee.

26. Which of the following statements is *NOT* true about rental security deposits?
    1. The landlord must pay the tenant 4 percent per annum simple interest on these funds at the end of the lease.
    2. The interest is computed in six-month intervals and is compounded.
    3. The portion of the deposit not withheld must be returned to the tenant within 45 days of end of occupancy together with an accounting of how any withheld portion was used.
    4. Tenants may recover three times the amount of security deposit improperly withheld by the landlord, plus reasonable attorney fees.

27. Licensees may have their licenses suspended or revoked and/or be subject to fines by the Commission for *ALL BUT WHICH* of the following?
    1. Drunken driving convictions
    2. Accepting a net listing
    3. Performing acts of brokerage on an expired license
    4. Failure to be current in their court-ordered child-support payments

28. A licensee representing a buyer
    1. owes certain statutory duties to the seller.
    2. cannot be compensated by the seller.
    3. is regarded as a cooperating agent and is the sub-agent of the seller.
    4. does not need a written representation agreement to qualify for compensation.

29. In purchasing a condominium, the most important document to the buyer is the declaration, which in most cases
    1. authorizes a board of directors to administer the condominium affairs pursuant to the bylaws and to assess the owners so as to adequately maintain the condominium.
    2. describes the condominium units and the common areas and any restrictions on their use.
    3. establishes the undivided interest percentages.
    4. does all of the above.

30. The condominium declaration
    1. must be recorded to place the property under a condominium regime.
    2. cannot be rescinded once it is recorded.
    3. can be changed only with the unanimous approval of the council of unit owners.
    4. must be printed in a daily newspaper before changes may be made.

31. In which of the following situations is deficiency judgment possible when a property sells at foreclosure for less than the mortgage debt?
    1. Judicial foreclosure
    2. Nonjudicial foreclosure
    3. FHA loans
    4. All of the above

32. A broker's choices of how to handle a contested earnest money deposit do NOT include
    1. putting his or her client's interests ahead of the other party's because of fiduciary duties.
    2. deciding to let the money remain in the brokerage's trust account.
    3. notifying both buyers and sellers how he or she intends to distribute the contested funds.
    4. not distributing the money as he or she intended if one of the parties gives proper notice of protest.

33. Rental security deposits may
    1. not be withheld by the landlord for unpaid rent.
    2. be kept during the lease in the landlord's personal savings account to earn interest.
    3. be withheld by the landlord to cover estimated damages at the end of the lease.
    4. be withheld by a landlord for the actual cost expended to repair damages caused by tenants.

34. According to Title 17, all the following could be considered "evidences" of reasonable and adequate supervision by a broker EXCEPT
    1. a proven pattern of the broker's physical presence in the broker's office, 9 to 5, seven days per week.
    2. availability of company policy and procedure manual in each office containing, among other things, rules for handling funds of others and the requirements of fair housing laws.
    3. existing records of every-other-month training meetings for all the broker's affiliates together with the roll of those attending and a list of topics presented.
    4. a paper trail showing that all contracts are approved by an experienced supervisor before being presented.

35. An agency agreement listing a Maryland property for sale
    1. may contain a provision for the broker to keep all the sale proceeds above a certain amount as the brokerage commission.
    2. is proper if it is signed by the owner of the largest share in a property owned by several owners.
    3. may indicate that the amount of brokerage to be paid will depend upon negotiations entered into after an offer is presented.
    4. may not require notice from either party to activate its termination date.

36. Which of the following statements about usury in Maryland loans is TRUE?
    1. There is no interest limit on first mortgages involving Maryland real estate.
    2. There is no interest limit on second mortgages involving Maryland real estate.
    3. There is no interest limit on land (installment) contracts involving Maryland real estate.
    4. Interest limits imposed on mortgages are not imposed on deeds of trust.

37. A pair of prospects who enter a Maryland brokerage office and ask help in finding a house to rent
    1. are considered by Maryland statute to be represented by that brokerage firm.
    2. are considered customers by Maryland statute.
    3. will owe a "reasonable and customary" brokerage fee if the firm finds them a property that they lease.
    4. must be given the Commission's form "Understanding Whom Agents Represent" immediately upon their arrival.

38. When real estate licensees with less than ten years' active license history in Maryland renew their licenses, they must attest to having completed
    1. at least three hours of continuing education in fair housing.
    2. at least one and one-half hours of continuing education in ethics.
    3. a total of at least 15 hours of approved continuing education courses.
    4. at least six hours of continuing education on changes in federal, state, and local laws.

39. Maryland's requirements for a broker licensee's office include all the following EXCEPT that
    1. it be a place where the firm regularly conducts insurance sales.
    2. it have a sign visible to the public that includes the words *Real Estate*, REALTORS®, or *Realtist*, as applicable.
    3. records of all trust funds in a secured area be available to Commission's inspectors on demand.
    4. it have on display the license of the broker and every affiliate that works out of that office.

40. Associate Broker John Buonasera, known as "Mr. B," has published a flier to attract business. Below is the entire ad.

    Come to Mr. B for all your real estate needs: Buying, Selling, or Renting.
    Use my services and you will be pleased. Results guaranteed!
    I charge 2% less than most other REALTORS® for my excellent service.
    My personal assistants and I are available to you at all hours to answer your real estate questions and meet your brokerage needs.
    Call my personal cell phone, toll free: 1-888-555-5555.

    Which of the following statements about his advertisement is NOT correct?

    1. The designated name of Mr. B's brokerage company should have been shown in his ad.
    2. As a Maryland licensee, Mr. B is not permitted to work for a below-average brokerage fee.
    3. If Mr. B gives his own phone number, he does not need to show the number of the office out of which he works.
    4. Since Mr. B has his nickname registered with the Commission and shown on his license and pocket card, he does not have to show his full, legal name in the ad.

COMPLAINT PROCEDURE

Possible Steps in Handling Complaints Against a Licensee

1.	Complaint is received by Commission (REC).
2.	Complaint is reviewed by REC designee, usually the Executive Director.
2.1.a	OR: If complaint is deficient in form, i.e., unsigned or not made under oath, it is returned to complainant as rejected with explanation for the rejection.
2.1.b	OR: If complaint lacks facts alleging prima facie case, it is returned to Complainant as rejected with that reason given.
3.	Complaint is adjudged by REC designee to be in good form and contain facts that suggest that a violation of Brokers Act or REC Regulations has taken place.
4.	REC designee refers complaint to a hearing panel of the REC.
4.1	REC informs Complainant that the complaint is being processed.
5.	Hearing panel examines the complaint and if they find it is worthy of action, refers the matter to Investigative Services for investigation.
5.1	OR: Panel concludes that the facts do not warrant further pursuit of the complaint. Complainant is notified of this finding of insufficient grounds and that the complaint is rejected. There is no right to appeal this finding.
6.	Licensee who is being complained about (the Respondent) and Respondent's broker are informed of the complaint and asked by the panel for written comment.
7.	Investigative Services investigates and reports its findings to the hearing panel.
8.	Hearing panel examines the report from Investigative Services and the responses from the Respondent and Respondent's broker. Panel concludes that Respondent has violated law or regulation they **set the matter in for** (schedule) a hearing.
8.1	OR: Panel concludes that the facts do not warrant further pursuit of the complaint and that the complaint is rejected. Complainant is notified of this decision. There is no right to appeal this finding.
9.	Panel notifies Respondent and Respondent's broker of the scheduled hearing and informs them of their rights to be present, to respond, to be represented by counsel, and to have witnesses subpoenaed (at Respondent's expense). They are also informed what the charges are and the possible penalties that could be imposed. Respondent must have 10 days' notice prior to the hearing. Complainant is also notified.

Possible Steps in Handling Complaints Against a Licensee (continued)

10.	In almost every case, the hearing is held before an Administrative Law Judge (ALJ). It is open to the public. Written and/or oral testimony is given. An Assistant Attorney General (AAG) presents the Commission's case. Respondent has opportunity to be heard in defense or mitigation. ALJs base their conclusion on **preponderance of evidence. Hearsay evidence** is admitted but weighed with discretion. The AAG and the respondent's attorney may both rebut testimony and give summations. No decision is announced at the hearing. Hearing is conducted according to the Rules of Procedure of the Maryland Office of Administrative Hearings. [COMAR 28, Subtitle 02.01—Ca 16-page document.] Some days after the conclusion of the hearing, the **proposed decision** of the ALJ is sent to the REC.
11.	A *new* hearing panel is given the proposed decision to review along with the case record. Panel adopts (or modifies) the proposed decision and sends it to the Respondent and the Complainant, giving each one notice of the right to file an exception within ten days.
12.	If either Complainant or Respondent takes exception within ten days, the panel sets a date for a hearing at which the parties can present arguments against the decision and rebut each other's argument. Parties must have 14 days advance notice of this hearing.
13.	The panel that sent out the proposed decision hears the arguments taking exception to the decision. The panel reaches a decision.
14.	Some days later the panel notifies parties of its decision rejecting the exception and issues a **final written order.**
15.	Parties submit to the decision contained in the final written order.
15.1	OR: A party **appeals** to the **circuit court** (The appeal alone does not create a **stay** of the decision for a licensee.)
15.1.a	AND: Appellant (one who is appealing), if a licensee, petitions the circuit court for a stay of the decision (perhaps delaying the suspension or revocation of appellant's license). Court usually grants this request and seeks a bond not exceeding $50,000.
15.1.b	AND: Circuit court denies the appeal and lets final order stand.
15.2	BUT: Appellant carries appeal to Court of Special Appeals
15.2.a	AND: Court of Special Appeals affirms the final order.
15.3	BUT: Appellant carries appeal to Court of Appeals
15.3.a	AND: Court of Appeals sustains the final order.
15.1.2. or 3	OR: Any of the three courts could have granted the appeal and set aside the final order.
16	Appeals are exhausted; final order will be executed by the REC.
	End of Case
	Note: This case addresses a violation of the statute or the regulations in which no financial damages were experienced and no reimbursement sought from the Guaranty Fund.

MARYLAND REAL ESTATE-RELATED WEB SITES

■ KEEPING UP-TO-DATE

Print materials like this volume are up-to-date when written and printed. Changes in laws, regulations, and the business environment are constant. In various chapters of this book Web sites (URLs) been given for specific topics. Here, in Appendix D, the author lists several "master" Web sites of great value. They can aid students in meeting their responsibility to remain current on all real estate matters. These sites are veritable "springboards" into a wealth of information for the student of Maryland Real Estate Brokerage. Most are listed according to the entity that maintains them. A discussion follows each Web link.

The Maryland General Assembly

www.mlis.state.md.us

This is the main source of information for everything that happens in the Legislative Branch of Maryland Government. It gives the dates for the annual sessions, and the number of Senators, Delegates, and Districts. It enables its readers to identify their Legislators by giving their own zip codes and to contact any State Legislator by e-mail.

The site lists all bills that have been introduced in the State legislature from 1996 to present. It gives the status of current bills and the ultimate disposition of all bills from previous sessions. Bills are indexed by Subject, Statute affected, Sponsor, and Bill Number. When asked to choose, select a topic such as "Agents and Brokers," "Real Estate Brokers," or "Real Property."

The site also sets forth the Order of Business for both the Senate and House, their current agendas and hearing schedules. It lists all the bills either signed or vetoed in the most recent session. In the case of a veto, a link is given to the letter in which the State Governor explains the veto.

In every instance above, the actual texts of bills can be brought to the screen and then printed out or saved to disk.

State of Maryland Homepage

www.maryland.gov

At this site, click *Online Services* near the top right corner; next, click *Alphabetical Index.* Here are over 100 live links to Maryland business, geographic, economic, and legal information. The *Homepage* also gives links that connect the student with the Executive Branch, the Maryland Judiciary, the Maryland State Law Library, Maryland State Departments, Agencies, Boards and Commissions, and important links to the Federal Government. It links to each Maryland county for local government information and business developments.

Office of the Secretary of State Division of State Documents

www.dsd.state.md.us

This Web site provides links to: COMAR—the Code of Maryland Regulations, which offers the entire text of every State Agency Regulation together with tips on how to search; *The Maryland Register*—the official publication for the State Government where changes to COMAR are published; the *Annotated Code of Maryland* where the Brokers Act can be found in the *Business Occupations and Professions Article*, at Title 17. Any of this information can easily be downloaded and saved.

The Maryland Real Estate Commission

www.dllr.state.md.us/license/occprof/recomm.html

Here the student will find the names of Commission members, their terms, and the area of the state that the licensee members represent. At this site the Commission makes available forms for complaints against licensees and forms for license renewal. It provides a means of inquiring about licensees by name. It contains information about licensing requirements, examinations required, license reciprocity, continuing education, and requirements for reinstatement of expired licenses. It also gives direct access to the current year's new laws and administrative changes that impact real estate licensees. It also links to COMAR and to the *Annotated Code.*

Maryland Statutes Text

www.michie.com/resources.html

This site gives immediate access to the text of every Maryland Statute and those of nine other jurisdictions, including Delaware and the District of Columbia. It does not, however, give the *catchlines*—the section and paragraph titles that appear in the bound volumes. Nor does it provide the commentary and explanations found in the *Maryland Annotated Code.* It is not indexed, but it has an internal searching device. Parts of any statute can be downloaded, but only one section at a time.

The State Department of Assessments and Taxation

www.dat.state.md.us/

Billed as "Maryland's Largest Source of Real Estate Data," this site not only gives information about Homeowners' Tax Credit, Homestead Tax Credit, and Renters' Tax Credit but also the assessment of every parcel of real estate in Maryland. It also explains the new full-value assessment with its consequent lower tax rates, as well as the semiannual payment schedule.

The site provides average sale prices of residential properties sold by county and by quarter for the last several years. Rates for Transfer Tax, Recordation Tax, and Tax Stamps are also provided county by county.

The Maryland State Archives

www.mdsa.net

At this site portions of nearly 700 volumes of the State Archives can be viewed by the student by clicking *Archives of Maryland Online*. Or click *Maryland Manual On-Line* for a complete guide to Maryland government. This *Manual* contains links to the three branches of Maryland State Government as well as to county and federally related agencies. It is updated daily.

PSI Examination Services Information and Tutorial

www.psiexams.com

At this site, click *Guide* (near the left side of the screen) to see a tutorial about taking a licensing examination at a PSI computer terminal. It pictures the keyboard used and the function of the most important command keys. It is a preview of the tutorial given to the applicant, on screen, at the time of taking the examination. The site also has a link to the locations of all the testing centers used for taking Maryland real estate licensing exams. Under *Testing Centers, Maryland, Real Estate*, the student can download the Candidate Information booklet that contains the application to take an exam.

DOCUMENTATION REQUIRED IN MARYLAND RESIDENTIAL REAL ESTATE SALES TRANSACTIONS

When prospects seek assistance in locating property to purchase or lease	No document is in play at this point, but the law presumes that licensee represents prospects and owes them such **fiduciary** duties as confidentiality and loyalty.
While marketing (or locating) property	Commission's agency relationship information form, **Understanding Whom Agents Represent,** to be presented at first scheduled face-to-face meeting with buyer (or lessee) and seller (or lessor). This is a disclosure form, not a contract to represent any party.
First written agreement	Written Agency Agreement, to represent either buyer (or lessee) or seller (or lessor). This may require an amended (new) **Understanding Whom Agents Represent** form in situations where buyer representation and/or dual agency are undertaken and were not checked in the original form. No such form is necessary when dealing with prospect at the customer level, because licensee is acting as cooperating agent of seller.
When brokerage firm represents opposing parties, i.e., is performing dual agency	Commission's Form: **Consent for Dual Agency** signed by buyers (or lessees) and sellers (or lessors). An additional **Consent for Dual Agency** form is required for each property to be shown under dual agency, because the forms are both property-specific and owner-specific.
Prior to submitting a written offer	Purchasers are to be given the following before the offer to purchase is signed: 1. The **Property Condition Disclosure/Disclaimer** form properly completed and signed by sellers. This is a duty of all sellers, which must be assured by licensee representing the seller, by a cooperating agent assisting the buyer, or by the licensee representing the buyer. A buyer not receiving this form prior to ratification of contract may rescind the contract at any time prior to applying for financing. 2. The **_Lead-Based Paint Disclosure Statement_** and the booklet **_Protecting your Family from Lead-Based Paint Hazards_** are to be given to purchasers of residential property built before 1978. This form is to _accompany_ the contract of sale from this point forward.
At time of contract	Copies of, or receipts for, disclosures given to all parties are to accompany the signed contract. These include **Understanding Whom Agents Represent, Consent for Dual Agency, Property Condition Disclosure-Disclaimer,** and, if applicable, the federally mandated **_Lead-Based Paint Disclosure Statement_** and information booklet **_Protecting Your Family from Lead-Based Paint Hazards._**

ANSWER KEY

CHAPTER 1

Maryland Real Estate License Law and Related Regulations

1. (3)   Salespersons are not employed by owners but by brokers. They must not only work for brokers who are duly licensed but for brokers *under whom they themselves* are licensed.

2. (2)   An affiliate's license certificate must be displayed in the office out of which the affiliate works. Affiliates' licenses are rarely if ever in their own possession. Affiliates carry their pocket cards, not their licenses.

3. (4)   Changes in office location, company names, or employment of an affiliate must be communicated to the Commission. Sharing of a commission, whether between broker and affiliates or among brokers, is not the domain of the Commission.

4. (1)   Salespersons must not "split" or otherwise divide their commissions with anyone. Brokers pay commissions, but never—in whole or in part—to a nonlicensee.

5. (2)   Freedom from broker control is not an IRS requirement to be an IRS-recognized "qualified agent." Moreover, broker control is vital for reasonable and adequate supervision required by law.

6. (3)   Only license renewal fees are paid every two years (biennially).

7. (3)   It is a misdemeanor for which the penalty is not more than a $5,000 fine and imprisonment for not more than one year. It is unethical; not a felony; and an illegitimate listing technique.

8. (2)   The Commission has this authority over nonlicensees who perform acts of real estate brokerage. The same violation may also result in a fine and imprisonment imposed by a court of law.

9. (3)   Unlicensed practice of real estate brokerage is a misdemeanor.

10. (3)   Puffery, intemperance, and slander of competitors are ill-advised, but Title 17 does not mention them. It does, however, forbid acts of bad faith.

11. (4)   Title 17 regards a deliberately false statement to the Commission in a matter involving a Guaranty Fund claim, a misdemeanor with up to $5,000 fine, and/or not more than one year's imprisonment as penalties.

12. (4)   While out-of-state businesses such as corporations, LLCs, and partnerships may be licensed under special conditions to perform commercial brokerage, only individuals may be licensed to do residential brokerage.

13. (2)   Neither the Executive Director nor the House of Delegates is involved. The Senate is involved to "advise and consent" to the appointment of a member of the Commission, but the actual appointment is made by the Governor.

14. (2)   Salesperson licenses expire two years from their date of issue. Previously they had expired on April 30 of the next even-numbered year. Broker licenses had expired on March 1 of the next even-numbered year.

15. (2) The Brokers Act is an exercise of the police power of the State that protects the public interest. The "public" includes both consumers of brokerage service and its providers.

16. (3) The Executive Director is chosen by the Secretary of Labor, Licensing, and Regulation from a list of three nominees submitted by the Commission. The Governor, the Senate, and the classified system are not involved.

17. (3) Ads placed by affiliates for the sale of listed property must all clearly reveal the designated (official) name of the brokerage firm. Showing the affiliates' names, phone numbers, e-mail addresses, and/or Web site URLs, is permitted if the phone number of the brokerage is also meaningfully and conspicuously displayed.

18. (1) The Guaranty Fund must be maintained at not less than a $250,000. If it falls below that amount, an assessment for all new licenses and renewals is authorized.

19. (2) The three parts of the Code of Ethics refer to licensees' relations with the public, the client, and fellow licensees.

20. (2) The Commission has five licensee members and four consumer (nonlicensee) members.

21. (1) When the Commission is hesitant to issue a license to an applicant, they deny the request and offer the applicant a chance to be heard. Depending on the outcome of the hearing, the Commission either maintains its original position or grants the license.

22. (4) License and other fees charged by the Commission have been set by the General Assembly in the statute, Title 17.

23. (2) In return for a fee, helping someone buy or sell Maryland real estate is an act of brokerage that requires licensure.

24. (1) The Commission retains no funds paid for license fees. They are passed through to the General Fund.

25. (1) The other alternatives are all excluded from such positions.

26. (1) It is the broker's responsibility to return such certificates to the Commission.

27. (2) Maximum recovery from the Fund is $25,000 per transaction. Only actual losses are covered.

28. (4) Not *every* person because there are a number of categories exempt from the requirement.

29. (2) Sales associates may deliver brokerage services only through and under a broker under whom they are licensed.

30. (3) A single power-of-attorney document can authorize only the sale of one specific property by a nonlicensed attorney-in-fact. The developers and trustees mentioned in other choices are exempt.

CHAPTER **2**
Real Estate Agency

1. (2)   Real estate brokers are engaged by clients to act as agents on their behalf. These clients are also called *principals*.

2. (3)   Such "dual agency" can be performed in Maryland real estate only when a broker appoints two such intra-company agents.

3. (4)   The players are properly identified; Marie is not a "single agency" broker because she is performing "dual agency" here through her company.

4. (2)   A broker who represents a client-buyer must disclose that fact to any seller or the agent of any seller he encounters.

5. (4)   "Presumed representation" ends when a buyer asks to make a contract offer on a property.

6. (4)   The only way a broker may represent both buyer and seller in the same transaction is to appoint two intra-company agents—one to represent the buyer and the other the seller.

7. (4)   All these are expressions of the five fiduciary duties: Disclosure, Obedience, Care, Accounting, and Loyalty.

8. (3)   Title 17, the Brokers Act, requires disclosure as early as possible but not later than the first scheduled face-to-face meeting with buyers.

9. (3)   Obedience is required for clients, not customers.

10. (2)   Only firms with three or more licensees may engage in dual agency under Maryland law because there must be two intra-company agents appointed by a broker. The broker may not appoint himself or herself.

CHAPTER **3**
Real Estate Brokerage

1. (2)   If price is shown, so must be the amount of the annual ground rent and the cost to redeem the lot.

2. (1)   An ad may show the name of the listing salesperson but must show the broker's designated name.

3. (4)   Statute calls for the office to be at a definite (fixed) location. A van or RV is presumed to be mobile and so has no mailing address.

4. (4)   Only a licensed real estate broker may operate a real estate brokerage firm in Maryland.

5. (1)   All ads must contain the trade (now called the *designated*) name of the broker.

6. (2)   The licensed broker of a firm is the person primarily responsible for actions of the firm and its affiliates.

7. (1)   If a salesperson's phone number appears in an ad, the designated name of the broker and the phone number of the firm must also appear.

8. (2)   Unless there are instructions to the contrary, earnest money deposits held by a broker must be placed—and kept until properly disbursed—in a non–interest bearing account in an insured, approved Maryland depository institution.

9. (4)   The broker's signature is sufficient by itself, although other combinations of licensees and nonlicensees in the firm may also serve as signers.

10. (3)   Personal assistants (meaning *unlicensed personal assistants*) may assist in the holding of an open house but may not conduct one.

CHAPTER 4

Listing Agreements and Buyer Representation Agreements

1. (1)   A net listing is forbidden in Maryland real estate brokerage.

2. (3)   The Residential Property Condition Disclosure and Disclaimer Statement is to be completed before a listing is accepted by a firm. The proper time is during the listing process.

3. (2)   The buyer may rescind the contract before application for a loan is made. If no loan is needed, right of rescission could last until settlement.

4. (2)   Before the firm may offer a property for sale, a completed copy of the listing must be given to the seller.

5. (1)   A Maryland affiliate must hold a Virginia license and be working for a Maryland broker who is also licensed as a broker in Virginia.

6. (3)   Forms published by a multiple-listing service are copyrighted and may be used only by subscribers to that service (members).

7. (3)   To be valid and to conform to the Brokers Act, listing agreements for Maryland real estate must be in writing and signed by all owners and by an authorized representative of the brokerage firm.

8. (4)   Buyers who receive the form prior to submitting their offer may not rescind a contract based on that offer because of something revealed in that form.

9. (1)   The rate or amount of commission, as established by negotiation between broker and client, must be clearly stated in the listing contract.

10. (3)   The General Regulations of the Commission, supported by the Brokers Act, require listings on Maryland residential property to be written.

CHAPTER 5

Interests in Real Estate

1. (3)   These easements are to keep the land on which they are purchased in agricultural use.

2. (3)   A minimum of 20 years' *continuous* use is required by Maryland statute; "25 years" meets that requirement, but 20 years of *intermittent* use does not.

3. (4)   Prescriptive easement is recognized. The other three choices, examples of legal life estates, do not exist in Maryland.

4. (1)   An owner whose land is bordered by a navigable river owns to the average high water mark but may construct a pier that reaches farther out. This riparian owner owns the pier but not the water or land beneath it.

5. (4)   State real estate transfer taxes help fund the purchase of agricultural easements.

CHAPTER 6
How Ownership Is Held

1. (2)   Maryland is not a community property state.

2. (3)   It will be treated as a tenancy by the entirety.

3. (2)   When one dies, the survivor becomes owner in severalty. Concurrent ownership requires more than one owner.

4. (1)   Time-share developers must register with the Commission.

5. (2)   Unless specified to the contrary by its controlling documents, condo bylaws require a two-thirds vote of the council of unit owners. Notice and quorum restrictions may apply.

6. (3)   Rental conversion to condominium requires registration with the Maryland Secretary of State.

7. (2)   Those who purchase a new condominium from the developer may void their contracts until settlement if they have not received the Public Offering Statement.

8. (2)   They have a ten-day right of cancellation for any (or no) reason.

9. (4)   All these documents must be delivered to the purchaser 15 days before closing. When they have been delivered, purchaser has seven days to cancel without any announced reason.

10. (3)   The Maryland Attorney General's office mediates most forms of condominium disputes among these parties.

CHAPTER 7
Legal Descriptions

1. (1)   References to the recorded plat of subdivision are sufficient to describe lots within that subdivision.

2. (2)   A location drawing shows that the improvement is actually on the lot and other basic facts. Placing fences, however, requires a boundary survey.

3. (3)   This description makes permitted reference to the recorded plat of subdivision for its details.

4. (4)   This description makes use of distances, compass directions, and monuments to describe a parcel in outline—all characteristic of metes-and-bounds surveys.

5. (3)   Maryland descriptions use either the metes-and-bounds or the recorded plat of subdivision method.

CHAPTER 8
Real Estate Taxes and Other Liens

1. (4) Some jurisdictions at each of those levels have been enabled to levy taxes on Maryland real estate.

2. (2) Each parcel of residential Maryland real estate is reassessed once every three years at full market value.

3. (3) Contractors have six months from the completion of their work to record a notice of lien.

4. (4) The other statements are accurate.

5. (3) The Statute allows a first-time homebuyer to pay no state transfer tax and requires that the seller pay one-half of the usually required tax, levied at the rate of one-half of 1 percent. Therefore, the seller pays 0.25%. ($0.0025 \times \$100,000 = \$250$).

CHAPTER 9
Real Estate Contracts

1. (1) The Maryland Statute of Frauds requires that all contracts for transfer of interests in property for more than one year be in writing and signed.

2. (2) *Parol* clearly means *oral*. The other choices are debatable.

3. (3) Licensees dealing on their own behalf must disclose their licensee status to the other party. Typically such disclosure is written into the contract used.

4. (4) The others are all required.

5. (3) Inclusion of the notice is required in all counties.

CHAPTER 10
Transfer of Title

1. (3) Requirements for adverse possession include open, hostile, continuous possession for 20 years under claim of right or color of title.

2. (4) All three are true. Even when a valid will is left, a widow(er) who receives less than her or his intestate share can contest the will under the Law of Descent and Distribution.

3. (4) Deeds are valid *between the parties* even without recordation. Recording deeds protects grantees against third parties.

4. (3) To be recorded, a deed to Maryland real estate must have been prepared by either the grantor, grantee, or an attorney.

5. (4) Although often witnessed by three, a will with only two witnesses satisfies Maryland law.

CHAPTER **11**
Title Records

1. (4)   Instruments that affect land partially in each of two counties are recorded in both counties.

2. (2)   Customarily, title search is ordered by the settlement company on behalf of the buyer and at the buyer's expense.

3. (1)   Deeds and mortgages affecting Maryland land are recorded in the office of the county clerk of circuit court.

4. (3)   The selling broker's name is not a basis for recordation.

5. (2)   Witnessing will not take the place of the required acknowledgment before a notary.

CHAPTER **12**
Real Estate Financing

1. (2)   Federal Equal Credit Opportunity Law forbids refusal of credit to an applicant based on the applicant's religion.

2. (1)   Only ground rent properties in certain areas of the State are eligible for DVA loan guarantees.

3. (2)   Courts will not foreclose on an unrecorded mortgage.

4. (1)   Mortgages and deeds of trust are the two ways that lenders secure almost all residential loans.

5. (3)   Savings associations are required by federal law to credit the borrower with passbook-rate interest on such escrow accounts annually.

CHAPTER **13**
Leases

1. (2)   Absent an agreement to the contrary, common law provides that a tenant's right of possession is uninterrupted by transfer of ownership of the leased fee.

2. (1)   Maryland statutes require that landlords credit tenants' security deposit accounts with 1.5 percent interest for each six-month interval it is held. This is 3 percent per annum. Therefore, a deposit of $500 would earn $15.

3. (1)   A lease for seven years or less need not be recorded.

4. (2)   An annual ground rent of $240, capitalized at the rate of 8 percent suggests that the value of the land alone is $3,000 (240 divided by 0.08). By not selling the land to the buyer, the builder can lower his price for the house by $3,000, to $65,000.

5. (2)   Arthur will own a house situated on a rented lot. He will hold a leasehold estate in the land.

6. (2)   One who pays rent for the land he or she possesses "owns" (holds) a leasehold estate.

7. (1)   One purpose for which ground rents are created is to make the purchase of a developer-built house more affordable. The buyer *buys* the house and *rents* the lot, rather than buying the land outright.

8. (2)   The annual ground rent divided by the capitalization rate gives the cost of redemption. Example B is the only one of the four that fits this formula. [$180 divided by 0.06 = $3,000.]

9. (4)   Court seizure and sale of a tenant's personal property for unpaid rent is called *distraint*.

10. (1)   Five percent of the month's rent is the penalty for late payment allowed by Maryland statute.

CHAPTER 14

Environmental Issues and Real Estate Transactions

1. (2)   Leakage from USTs (underground storage tanks) mostly pollutes the ground and groundwater, rather than the air.

2. (3)   The two objectives are interrelated because preservation of open space is an important method of preserving ecological balance.

3. (3)   Revitalization of older neighborhoods is intended to slow "sprawl" into the open countryside.

4. (2)   Maryland law allows local jurisdictions to impose environmental regulations that are even more strict than those of the State. To take effect, however, the local regulations may *not* be *less* strict.

5. (4)   Addressing environmental issues involves multiple levels of government as well as overlapping geographic jurisdictions.

6. (3)   State agencies seldom allow local governments to approve any disturbance of the land in a "buffer zone."

7. (2)   Where a critical area ends, a 100-foot buffer zone begins.

8. (2)   There must be no other way to accomplish a worthy objective before filling of wetlands is allowed.

9. (1)   Environmental regulatory actions tend to make *less* land available for real estate development.

10. (2)   Even though the notice itself excludes *certain counties* in its warnings, the notice must appear in residential sales contracts in *every county*.

CHAPTER 15

Fair Housing

1. (4)   Any warning about hostile attitudes in the residents of the neighborhood would tend to discourage the purchasers and therefore amounts to *steering*.

2. (1)   Persons involved in real estate transactions are bound by all antidiscrimination laws. They are held to have "constructive notice" because ignorance of the law does not excuse its violation.

3. (2)   To show the property to prospects based—either positively or negatively—on their race is a violation of fair housing laws. It is *steering*, regardless of its motivation.

4. (1)   *Blockbusting* is attempting to frighten present owners into selling (listing) their properties. Although it is typically done for financial gain, that is not a requirement for prosecution in Maryland.

5. (4)   The situation described in one of the "exceptions" built into the 1968 Fair Housing Act. Maryland has parallel exceptions in its fair housing laws.

CHAPTER 16
Closing the Real Estate Transaction

1. (4)   Closings in Maryland are performed under the supervision of an attorney. This does not mean the attorney has to be physically present.

2. (3)   The settlement officer is required to account to the seller for the payoff not more than 30 days after closing.

3. (1)   No matter whom an attorney performing settlement represents, he or she owes all parties due care in conducting the closing, disbursing funds, and so forth.

4. (2)   Title evidence is usually ordered on behalf of and paid for by the purchaser.

5. (3)   Seven percent of the out-of-state seller's net proceeds must be withheld by the closing officer.

APPENDIX B
Practice Exam

1. (2)   No commission can be claimed by a firm based on the activity of a person who should have been properly licensed but was not.

2. (1)   Licenses are issued for a period of two years from their date of issuance.

3. (2)   Based on "presumed buyer/lessee representation," they are owed client-level duties.

4. (3)   Salesperson licenses must be displayed in the branch office of the broker out of which they work.

5. (3)   The maximum loss that is covered is $25,000 per transaction.

6. (3)   Of several possible courses of action, the only one they *must* follow is to stop performing acts of brokerage.

7. (3)   Membership of the Maryland Real Estate Commission comprises five licensee members (either salespersons or brokers) and four consumer (nonlicensee) members.

8. (4)   Although passing the courses is required, not all who pass apply for a license and not all who apply are granted one by the Real Estate Commission.

9. (2)   The State Real Estate Commission has authority over all Maryland licensees, while the Association of REALTORS® has authority only over its members. Not all licensees are members.

10. (3)   A partnership wishing to provide brokerage services must find a broker and designate that person as *the* broker of their firm. The broker could be one of the partners, but need not be. No unlicensed partner, however, may participate in any act of brokerage.

11. (1)   Although many builders use licensed brokers to sell their homes, the builders don't need to employ licensees or to be licensees. State law exempts them from the requirement of being licensed in the initial sale of houses they have built and still own.

12. (2)   The Maryland Time-Share Act requires that a developer converting a residential rental building into a time-share holding must give the residents 120 days' advance notice and provide them with other assistance in certain circumstances.

13. (3)   In fact, it is the responsibility of licensees *not* to give legal interpretations. Although they often must explain common contract provisions, they may give no advice concerning them.

14. (1)   In a title-theory state the mortgagee (lender) agrees that his or her claim will be extinguished by the borrower's paying off the debt secured by the mortgage. Until that time, the lender has "bare legal title" to the property under Maryland law.

15. (2)   The Commission may impose a fine as much as $5,000 and/or suspend or revoke the license of the offender. However, because the Commission is not in the judicial branch of government, it may not impose imprisonment.

16. (3)   It is a cardinal principal, in accord with National and State Antitrust legislation, that providers of a service such as real estate brokerage are not to establish, try to establish, or even discuss with one another the fees they charge the public.

17. (4)   Salespersons should never have trust accounts for customers' or clients' money. Neither should earnest monies be kept in the office safe. Such deposits must promptly (in not more than seven business days) be deposited in the firm's trust account.

18. (3)   When one of two tenants by the entirety dies, the one left is alone and has no one to hold "in common" with. The survivor's ownership is *in severalty*.

19. (3)   The broker's duty is to benefit the clients (sellers) not herself. If the clients can see both offers they can choose the one that is better for them and not be led into accepting an "in house" offer that would benefit the brokerage firm.

20. (4)   Maryland's Statute of Frauds requires that transfers of any interest in real property for more than one year must be in writing.

21. (4)   There is no requirement involving the Commission.

22. (1) Representation agreements are not created by delivery of this form. Neither does presentation of the form end presumed buyer representation or give permission for dual agency.

23. (4) Neither death of a client nor the ending of an agency relationship ends the requirement for confidentiality. The Statute of Limitations does not address this matter. It ends by permission of the client or by the information's becoming common knowledge from other sources.

24. (4) The Brokers Act, Title 17, specifies that the form be presented "not later than the first scheduled face-to-face meeting with a prospect." The REALTOR® Code of Ethics requires that it be presented even sooner: "at first contact."

25. (2) Neither the payment or promise of payment of consideration nor the delivery of ministerial (servant) acts can be held to create an agency relationship. On the other hand, a customer who received expert guidance from a licensee could infer that an agency relationship exists.

26. (2) The interest is computed in six-month intervals but is *not* compounded. The other statements are accurate.

27. (1) Although heinous, drunken driving is not one of the offenses listed in Title 17 as basis for penalty. The other three offenses are bases for such disciplinary action.

28. (1) Licensee duties to nonclients include honesty, reasonable care, and disclosure of material facts. A seller's brokerage fee may properly be shared with the agent of the buyer, but that agent is not a subagent of the seller. Compensation for representing a buyer requires a written agreement with the buyer.

29. (4) The declaration takes precedence over both the bylaws and the rules and regulations of a condo. On the other hand, it is subject to the federal statutes, Maryland Condominium Act, other statutes, and certain local ordinances.

30. (1) A property is placed under a condominium regime (governance) by recording its declaration.

31. (1) Deficiency judgments are possible when foreclosure has been court-controlled (judicial foreclosure). Deficiency judgments are not available to lenders in cases of nonjudicial foreclosure and of foreclosure of FHA-insured loans.

32. (1) The good-faith duty of fairness to both parties prevents a broker from putting the interests of his or her client ahead of those of the adverse party in deciding to whom contested earnest money will be paid. Title 17 makes the other three alternatives available to the broker in such situations.

33. (4) Security deposits may be withheld for actual costs of repairs for damage more than normal wear and tear *and for unpaid rent.*

34. (1) The mere physical presence of a broker, no matter how many hours are invested, is not one of the evidences of reasonable and adequate supervision listed in Title 17. No credit for attendance! The other three choices are each spelled out in that Statute.

35. (4)   Maryland law requires that "listing" agreements contain a termination date that is effective without further action by either broker or client. There may be no "automatic" extension provisions.

36. (1)   There is no limit on the interest rate for first mortgages. Second mortgages and land contracts are limited to 24 percent. Deeds of trust, used in place of the traditional mortgage, are subject to the same limits as mortgages.

37. (1)   They receive "presumed representation" (just like buyers) for which no fee may be claimed. The law no longer regards "walk-ins" as customers. Although the statute says, ". . . not later than the first *scheduled* face-to-face meeting," it is prudent to give unscheduled walk-ins the Agency Disclosure form immediately.

38. (3)   Biennial renewal for a licensee with fewer than ten years' active licensure in Maryland requires 15 clock hours of approved courses. Among them are at least three hours of ethics, one and one-half hours of fair housing, and three hours of legislative update.

39. (1)   It must be the place where the firm regularly conducts *Real Estate*, not *Insurance*, transactions. The other three requirements are stated accurately.

40. (1)   The Maryland Real Estate Broker's Act requires that the designated name of the brokerage company be included in advertisements.

INDEX